MAINSTREAM SERIES

Editors: Lord Blake, Leon Brittan, Jo Grimond,
John Patten and Alan Peacock

Present Danger
Robert Conquest

Britain in Context
John D. Hey

Education: A Way Ahead
Mary Warnock

Power and Parliament
Timothy Raison

Higher Education for the Future
Charles Carter

THE RECOVERY OF FREEDOM

PAUL JOHNSON

The Recovery of
FREEDOM

BASIL BLACKWELL • PUBLISHER

First published in 1980 by
Basil Blackwell Publisher
5 Alfred Street
Oxford OX1 4HB
England

British Library Cataloguing in Publication Data

Johnson, Paul
    The recovery of freedom. — (Mainstream series).
    1. Great Britain — Politics and government
    — 1964—
    I. Title   II. Series
    320.9'41'0857   JN231

ISBN 0-631-12562-0

Printed and bound in Great Britain by
The Camelot Press Ltd., Southampton.

This book is dedicated to Anthony Howard
to whose magnanimity as an editor
I owe the original publication
of many of these political essays

CONTENTS

Much of the material in this collection first appeared in the *New Statesman* and the *Sunday Telegraph*. I am grateful to the editors of these two publications for permission to reprint it in book form.

INTRODUCTION

Man is the most insatiably active animal in creation. He is compelled not only to do things but to be constantly seeking to do new things. That means he is also freedom-loving, impatient of any restraint. None of this is to say that he favours anarchy: on the contrary, it is his nature to abhor chaos. He has a passion for order, an instinct for regularity and an inveterate habit of devising rules. His zeal for action and innovation is competitive; competition implies comparisons, and so judgments under authority. As Thomas Hobbes pointed out, life in society can be compared to a race, and a race must be regulated to retain its zest. But, he added, the race of humanity has no finish: the excitement and point of life is to be in it, and happiness consists in being in front: 'There is no such thing as perpetual tranquillity of mind while we live here, for life itself is but motion and can never be without desire, or without fear, no more than without sense. . . there can be no contentment but in proceeding'. To proceed, we must be free; and since the race is unending, the whole of human history is the pursuit of freedom.

No student of history can have any doubt that, in the long run, the direction of mankind is towards greater freedom. We have moved progressively from the collectivist and tribal communities of antiquity to societies in which the uniqueness of the individual is conceded, theoretically at least, and the universality of human rights is given formal recognition. No one now denies, explicitly and publicly, the rights of man; all agree, as self-evident truth, that freedom is a public good. Just as hypocrisy is the tribute vice pays to virtue, so constitutions, endorsing human rights, are the homage which the most obdurate and enduring tyranny feels obliged to lay at freedom's feet. Even the most depraved African despot, who belabours his helpless subjects with every refinement of cruelty and savagery, sports some Utopian certificate to give his regime a spurious legitimacy; while the Soviet Union, the most authoritarian and restrictive system of government ever devised, flaunts a constitution of exemplary benevolence.

1

Such documents, of course, are fraudulent. Who can honestly claim that the total of human freedom has been enlarged in our century? Few today share the optimistic illusions of the age of Lincoln and Gladstone. Two horrifying world wars, in which the high liberal civilisation of Europe and the Western world came close to committing suicide - as ancient Greece did in the Peloponnesian War - have dulled our sensibilities and debauched our instinct for justice.

These wars also gave birth to the modern Frankenstein state. Governments have developed not only unprecedented new means to destroy, but new instruments of oppression and new ways to lie. All over the world the state has gorged itself on the evil novelties human ingenuity constantly makes available. The state has been the principal beneficiary of our twentieth century horrors. It is true that all but one of the old empires have been dismantled. But the states that replaced them have eagerly embraced and zealously fostered all the imperialist vices, especially militarism and bureaucracy, while abandoning such virtues, above all respect for the rule of law, which imperialism sometimes possessed. In all these states, government has become ubiquitous and menacing, mendacious and corrupt, and in consequence arbitrary and destructive of private happiness and wealth. As for the last and least liberal of the empires, the Russian monolith, it is in rude and brutal health, has enormously enlarged its boundaries, constantly extends its sphere of influence, arms ceaselessly and, within its totalitarian entrails, furtively breeds the ever-expanding organism of police terror.

What is more surprising, and still more disturbing, is that even in the liberal democracies of the Western tradition the Frankenstein state has contrived to establish itself. It is alive, well, living amongst us and flexing its muscles; looking forward with boundless confidence and insatiable appetite to an indefinite career of growth and consumption. The monster is at large all over Western Europe. In the United States it is the last, boldest and most insolent of all the immigrants to clamber onto her shores. But it is above all in Britian, the 'very pearl of the West', as Solzhenitsyn has called us, once the citadel of privacy and the acropolis of individual freedom, that the spectre of giant government overshadows our lives and threatens the total destruction of liberal values.

I once regarded the state as a means whereby the less fortunate among us could be enabled to achieve the self-expression and moral fulfilment which is their right as creatures made in God's image. While continuing to desire the end, I no longer have any confidence whatever in the state as the means towards this end. On the contrary, I have come to see it as the biggest obstacle to the individual self-expression and moral maturity of every single one of us, and most of all the poor, the weak, the humble and the passive.

I make no apology for this change of attitude. It has been brought about by age and experience, notably the grim experience of the last decade in Britain, where the cumulative evils fed by the growth of collective power and state expansion have become overwhelmingly manifest. But it has also been brought about by a wide range of historical study, covering not merely the whole of English and European history, but many of the remote societies of antiquity. The study of history is a powerful antidote to contemporary arrogance. It is humbling to discover how many of our glib assumptions, which seem to us novel and plausible, have been tested before, not once but many times and in innumerable guises; and discovered to be, at great human cost, wholly false. It is sobering, too, to find huge and frightening errors constantly repeated; lessons painfully learnt forgotten in the space of a generation; and the accumulated wisdom of the past heedlessly ignored in every society, and at all times.

Of all those lessons, the one which history most earnestly presses upon us, and which we most persistently brush aside is: 'Beware the state!' Man, as history shows only too clearly, has that element of the divine in him, the element which causes him ceaselessly to strive for the ideal. It is his glory and his ruin. For in his Utopian quest he embraces the political process as the road to perfection. But this political process itself is a delusion, more likely to lead to hell than to heaven. If a society is unlucky, the political road, pursued relentlessly enough, will carry it straight into Auschwitz or the Gulag Archipelago. But even the most fortunate society will find nothing at the end of that dusty track but the same man-made monster − the state − as greedy and unfeeling as it was when man invented it in the third millennium BC, with its cavernous mouth, its lungs of brass, its implacable appetite and unappeasable stomach, but with no heart, no brain and no soul.

I have learnt this for myself, and changed political direction accordingly, as I was bound in honesty to do. Thus I have conformed to what, to my mind, is the central political tradition in England: the

politics of persuasion and change. Tribal loyalties and static postures
are alien to our public life. Its intellectual vigour and growth have
depended very largely on the movement of public personalities, in
response to experience, reflection and external change. On all the
central religious and constitutional issues of our national life, there
have always been outstanding men with the open-mindedness and
fortitude to modify and follow their convictions. Some, like Becket
and Thomas More, paid with their lives; others, like Wycliffe and
Newman, endured obloquy and sectarian revenge. Such changes of
view have followed no set pattern. Sir Francis Bacon moved from
parliamentarianism to prerogative; Sir Edward Coke in precisely the
reverse direction. Clarendon and Strafford were Commons men who
became royalists; Cromwell a radical turned autocrat; Shaftesbury
moved from court to country. Fox was a Tory turned Whig, Pitt a
Whig turned Tory; Canning and Peel, Palmerston and Gladstone, all
moved from Toryism to various brands of liberalism; Disraeli and
Lord Randolph Churchill switched from the aristocratic principle to
the democratic one; Bright and Chamberlain went the other way.
Lloyd George was a little Englander who turned imperialist; Harold
Macmillan an imperialist who turned decoloniser. Winston Churchill
went from Tory to Liberal to Coalitionist to Tory again – and told a
friend of mine, right at the end of his life: 'I'm a Liberal – always
have been!' Even Aneurin Bevan switched from collectivism to individualism, before death halted further progression. Honest and
conscientious change is the best evidence not merely of growth itself,
but of moral purpose and intellectual power. Did not Locke, by practical enquiry, change his view on the central issue of his day, religious
toleration? Was not Bertrand Russell constantly revolving the fundamental concepts of his philosophical system, as he not merely ad-
mitted but boasted? Is not the second half of Wittgenstein's
philosophical development a hostile commentary on the first? But
the point is not worth labouring. Show me a man who has not
changed his public views in a quarter of a century, and you will show
me an unobservant fool or a place-seeker.

There is further argument in favour of change: the need to redress
an unequal balance. One of the commonest lessons of history is that
an opinion and a tendency which is healthy, desirable, even essential
in one epoch, becomes noxious and dangerous a few years or decades
later. The essence of statesmanship is the fine adjustment of rival

forces by political contrivance. The essence of public philosophy is the identification and measurement of those forces. Naturally the balance of forces is constantly changing, not least as a result of adjustments which statesmen make. The overwhelming imbalance in our age has been caused by the huge increase in collectivism. The power of the state has increased, is increasing and ought to be diminished: there, in a sentence, is the great redressment problem of our times.

Let us examine six distinct reasons why we must again tilt the balance against the state. The first is a purely intellectual one, but is in some ways the most important. The notion that government is not only the prime but ought to be the sole instrument for the improvement of human welfare — the notion embedded, for instance, in the idea of health and education services provided exclusively by the state — is based upon the single-answer theory of politics. Throughout history, there have always been elevated individuals who have believed they have discovered, in their own minds, the key to the universe, and consequently have evolved gigantic and unified systems for the transformation of mankind. These are the men Isaiah Berlin calls the 'terrible simplifiers. . .the great despotic organisers. . .single-minded monists, ruthless fanatics, men possessed by an all-embracing coherent vision'. They may live and die as harmless eccentrics; or they, or their followers, may become through the instrumentation of the state a danger to humanity. For there is no single answer, there is no unified theory, there is no comprehensive solution to the ills of humanity. Man is a creature of infinite variety who seeks and finds felicity — in so far as he finds it at all — through a boundless plurality of forms. Where the state is limited by law and custom, these forms flourish and proliferate. Where the state is ubiquitous and unconfined it presents an irresistible temptation to the monist simplifiers and their fanatical adherents, a huge machine for the imposition of their solutions, if necessary — and in the end, of course, they always judge it necessary — through aeons of misery and oceans of blood.

Which brings me to the second reason: the state necessarily, and always, exalts the compulsory principle. As the state expands, so compulsion, *pari passu*, invades and occupies the lives of individuals. I agree with Adam Smith, who argues, in *The Theory of Moral Sentiments*, that civilised politics are not designed to bring about the virtuous, perfect and comprehensive state, as Plato and some other Greeks argued, but to achieve consensus. Smith thought that the object of a constitution should be to permit the coexistence of large numbers of heterogeneous people. He was the first to note a very important distinction: that love of humanity in general (which he termed 'public spirit') was often accompanied by indifference to human beings in particular. Up to a point, 'public spirit' was necessary and desirable in society. But it was always liable to degenerate into what he terms the 'spirit of system', that is, the fanatical commitment to ideology and dogmatism. Smith thought that love of systems and gadgets was one of man's deepest instincts. It was the chief dynamic which created wealth; but, when reflected in the political love of systems, could also destroy wealth, and human happiness too. The 'spirit of system' was the insatiable desire of the gadget-lover to construct society like a machine:

The man of system is wise in his own conceit. He seems to imagine that he can arrange the different members of a great society with as much ease as the hand arranges the different pieces upon the chessboard; he does not consider that the pieces on the chessboard have no other principles of motion besides that which the hand impresses upon them, but that in the great chessboard of human society, every single piece has a principle of motion of its own, altogether different from that which the legislator might choose to impress upon it.

Two hundred years, and hecatombs of victims later, men of system are still trying to play chess with humanity. In his warnings against the spirit of system, Smith adumbrated all the horrors of modern totalitarianism, human chess played according to the rules of the Concentration Camp. In his plea for consensus politics, he indicated the only means by which such horrors can be avoided. The size and power of the state must be determined not by the supposed needs of humanity-in-general, but by the plainly expressed desires of humanity-in-particular. That means consensus; consensus means acceptance of the voluntary principle in government; and that, in turn, means a limited state.

The third reason is an economic one: the state is, of necessity and by its nature, an inefficient instrument for the allocation of resources and the taking of mercantile decisions. The notion of an efficient state is based upon an illusion, that there is a living abstraction called 'society', omniscient in its collective judgments, free from human frailty and weakness, and therefore morally justified in its claims to omnipotence, expressed through the state, which is its active agent. 'Society needs', 'society demands' – so the state must act. But there is no such creature as 'society'. 'Society' is merely the sum of loud voices, the orchestrated chorus of certain fallible individuals. Society is not a being; still less is its agent the state. Society is a thing. It does not have the capacity to think. It lacks the powers of human reasoning. It cannot make calculations of profit and loss and returns on capital. These, indeed, are built into the market: the market is the only kind of collective which conforms to nature and actually works after a fashion, because it is based upon the voluntary principle and remains a free combination of individuals. But the market is not the state: it is the exact opposite to the state. The state has no brain, collective or otherwise; all it has is an appetite.

Hence the fourth reason: the state is bound to be not merely inefficient, but prodigal; and it therefore, of necessity, breeds parasites. Here we have one of the oldest lessons of history. There were bitter complaints about the size and waste of the bureaucracy in Egypt of the second millennium BC, while government scribes, for their part, gloried in the fact that their clerical skills exempted them from manual labour. A study of villages in the Egypt of the Hellenistic period indicates the alarming ratio of bureaucrats to wealth-creating workers. Now that the deciphering of the Linear B script allows us to examine the economies of the Mycenaean city-states, we wonder how such a slender agricultural and trading base could support such prodigies of bureaucratic construction – Agamemnon and Nestor were evidently 'men of system'. But the answer, of course, is that they eventually failed to do so. The societies of antiquity were frequently destroyed by the growth of the state and its parasites. The process continues to our own day, changing only its outward form. It is one of the central themes of Smith's *The Wealth of Nations* that private individuals create wealth, and governments consume it. The more the government consumes, the less the private sector has to invest; so wealth accumulates more slowly, or not at all, or even declines.

Of course, Smith was thinking in terms of Versailles, the largest, most ostentatious and prodigal of the governments of his day. But in economic terms there is no difference between an eighteenth century court government and modern welfare bureaucracies, except that there are many more of the latter, and they are much more expensive. In the 1960s and early 1970s, the new borough of Hillingdon built itself a municipal palace which is bigger than Versailles; it does not have a Hall of Mirrors, but it has air-conditioning and an ultra-modern 'communications' system. As Versailles was a monument to monarchical autocracy, so Hillingdon Palace (its official name, a euphemism, is the Hillingdon Community Centre), which cost £20 million, is a symbol to the honour, glory and power of local government bureaucracy. These bureaucrats do not see themselves as parasites; nor did the Versailles courtiers, who hotly maintained that they performed important, nay indispensable, functions. When they were scattered by the Revolution, nobody missed them; just as, when the London social workers − far more numerous than the Versailles courtiers − went on strike in 1978-9, nobody missed them either. But the courtiers at least did not have unions, to protect and swell their numbers, and increase their stipends and privileges. The old-style court, as a vested interest, was a fairly fragile corporation. The modern welfare bureaucracy, by contrast, has powerful institutional defences and a noisy moral ideology.

This brings me to the fifth reason. There is no economic difference between the courtier and the welfare bureaucrat, since both are parasites who consume and destroy wealth. But there is a supposed moral difference between them; and that, paradoxically, makes the welfare bureaucrat a far more dangerous creature than the courtier. The courtier was a prop of hierarchy and degree; he could not claim to be anything else. The welfare bureaucrat justifies his existence by arguing forcefully that his work promotes social justice and equality. He is not a passive administrator, but an active propagandist. The larger the bureaucracy, and the more therefore it is criticised for its expense, the more loudly and insistently its members (and their unions) will proclaim the virtues of the Utopia they are employed to promote. Of course the Utopia itself is an illusion; and as the bureaucracy increases in size and cost, and the wealth available to promote social justice diminishes accordingly, so discontent will grow, fanned by the propaganda of the bureaucrats themselves. The old courtiers were parasites; but at least they had an interest in maintaining the social structure. The welfare bureaucrats, by contrast, have an interest in exciting public demands, real or imaginary, so that more bureaucrats will be employed in satisfying them. In particular, the welfare bureaucracy promotes the notion of equality, for nothing is more conducive to bureaucratic expansion than the pursuit, futile though it may be, of equality by Act of Parliament. But the urge to distribute wealth equally, and still more the belief that it can be brought about by political action, is the most dangerous of all popular emotions. It is the legitimation of envy, of all the deadly sins the one which a stable society based on consensus should fear the most. The monster state is a source of many evils; but it is, above all, an engine of envy.

The sixth and final reason why we must tilt the balance against the state is the spectre which state-promoted envy brings in its train. For gigantism in the state does and must set in motion a chain of events which ends in violence or its violent suppression. As the welfare state expands its activities, and increases its cost, so the wealth-creating sector contracts. But the state sector does not contract accordingly: it defends itself by inciting envy, and as envy remains unsatisfied — must, indeed, become even more dissatisfied, as wealth-production falters and falls — so the urge to seek violent solutions, fostered by the moralistic propaganda of the welfare bureaucracy, increases. It is no accident that the public service unions in Britain are now the most militant, the most vociferous advocates of the political strike, and form the core of mass demonstrations. They confront the public with a choice between the tolerance of anarchy, or the massive deployment of state force; and whichever is chosen, the freedom of the individual is the victim.

There is, then, a whole series of powerful reasons — philosophical, ethical, economic, political, moral and practical — why the further expansion of the state must be resisted, and its contraction progressively brought about. I call this process the recovery of freedom, and I believe it has already been set in motion by the movement of opinion, as the claims of the Utopian state are, one by one, exposed as fraudulent, and the evil consequences of its expansion are more fully examined and publicised. The virtues of individual freedom are so enormous and various, their role in the creation of wealth so central and irreplaceable, that in those parts of the world where debate is still free and public, the advocates of collectivism are already on the defensive. By the end of this century, if Western civilisation exists at all, it will have resumed its slow but sure progress towards the liberation of the human spirit and genius − that progress which was such a marked feature of the nineteenth century, and which was so tragically halted and reversed by the European civil wars of the twentieth. When we look back from the year AD 2000, I think we shall see the 1970s as the decade when the civilised world, not without pain and grief, returned to its senses, and began to roll back the collectivist advance.

PART ONE

The Failure of Collectivism

CHAPTER 1

A Brotherhood of National Misery

This article, published in the New Statesman *in May 1975, was my first broadside against the British trade union movement, which at the time was held to be virtually above criticism. It provoked uproar and fury but it broke the spell of immunity and brought the unions, kicking and screaming, back into the arena of open debate.*

People often assume that trade unionism and socialism are roughly the same thing; that a trade unionist is a socialist, and vice versa; and that trade union and socialist activities are designed to secure the same objects. I would like to show that these assumptions have always been dubious and are now demonstrably and flagrantly false. Indeed it is possible to argue that, in Britain today, the trade union movement is not only self-defeating, in terms of its own aims, but is a positive and growing obstacle to the accomplishment of socialist ones. Trade unionism is killing socialism in Britain, and it is time socialists did something about it.

First, then, let us ask ourselves: what is the object of socialism? The essence of socialism is not its method but its universality. It is based on the principle of general and equal benefit. It teaches that the wealth of a society should be administered in the interest of all; that every one of us, men, women and children, has an equal stake in our community, an equal duty to it − to do our best − and an equal right to share in its fruits. Socialism is not a programme for the in- dustrial workers, or the manual workers, or any particular group of

workers. It is not a programme for the working class. It is not a
programme for any class. Socialism does not believe in classes. It is
against particularism, group or sectional interest, and above all it is
against sectional interests which organise themselves to exploit the
rest of the community. Socialism expresses the essential unity and
common humanity of society – our sisterhood, our brotherhood.
That is why it is inseparable from democracy and why, to be true to
itself, it must work through a government responsible to a universally
elected assembly. *There* is where all the essential decisions which
affect the life of the community must be taken, and nowhere else.
Any institution in a society which challenges this principle cannot be
a socialist institution; indeed, it must be an antisocialist one.

Now let us look at the trade unions. A trade union does not
necessarily have anything to do with political morality. It is simply a
pragmatic arrangement. It grew up within the capitalist system as a
defence mechanism. In feudal societies, peasants protected
themselves from the grosser forms of exploitation, or from new im-
positions they found intolerable, by rioting. Unable to change
society, or to reorganise it on a more rational or equitable basis, they
seized what weapons they could, killed, burned and looted.
Sometimes they were mercilessly repressed. Sometimes they were
appeased. No one has ever suggested that rioting for the peasants was
a good way of rectifying social injustice. It was simply the only way
open to them. In the emerging capitalist societies, labourers also used
the riot. But they found it more effective to unionise themselves and
develop the strike weapon.

The union was not a socialist instrument. It was not a political instrument at all. It was an economic function of the capitalist system,
a defensive leaguing together of desperate and exploited men to
enable them to meet the owners of capital on something like equal
terms. Its great weapon, the strike, was essentially negative,
destructive and despairing, like the riot. It might fail at appalling
cost, or, even if it succeeded, might damage those who wielded it
almost as much as its opponents. It was used because there seemed no
other way.

Riots and strikes were the inevitable response of classes excluded
from any political part in the direction of their society. The enlarge-
ment of the suffrage introduced an altogether different perspective,
and for the first time a socialist one. It now became possible to con-

struct a political alternative to the existing society which, in turn, could exact legislation creating an economic alternative − one in which universality of benefit would be the paramount principle. Once the vote was secured, and the road to socialism lay open, the riot and the strike ceased to be the only weapons, and could be seen for what they were; methods socially destructive by their very nature, and therefore anti-socialist.

Of course the union still had a part to play. It was the best means through which hitherto unrepresented sections of society could organise themselves for political purposes and make full use of the new opportunities. The unions were empirical devices by which a socialist party could be brought into being and begin to establish its socialist objectives. This, indeed, was in a sense what the British trade union movement did in 1900 when it founded the Labour Party to secure increased representatives in Parliament. From that moment on, the emphasis should have shifted progressively from the out-moded sectionalist methods of unionism to the universalist methods of political socialism. Step by step, the socialists, elected by the community and serving the community as a whole, should have taken over from the unionists, serving sectional interests. Above all, the economic organisation of society, the way in which wealth is invested, and rewards distributed, to all of us who are its members, should have become the function of democratic governments.

But this is not what has happened. The unions have refused to recognise the limits of their historical role. They have not only rejected the idea of a progressive abdication, and the shift of their social and economic function to the political process, but they have flatly declined to allow the smallest diminution of their power to press the sectional interests they represent. Indeed they have steadily, ruthlessly and indiscriminately sought to increase that power. And in recent years, and in particular in the last five years, they have exhausted or beaten down any opposition and have finally succeeded in making themselves the arbiters of the British economy.

This has not come about as part of some deeply laid and carefully considered plan. It is not part of a plan at all. It has been, essentially, a series of accidents. Huge unions, each pursuing wage claims at any cost, have successively smashed other elements in the state − governments, political parties, private industry, nationalised boards − and now find themselves amid the wreckage of a deserted battlefield, the undoubted victors. They did not plan the victory. They do not know what to do with it now they have got it. Dazed and bewildered, they are like medieval peasants who have burnt down the lord's manor. What next? They have no idea, since they did not think ahead to this sort of situation, and indeed are not equipped by function or experience to embark on positive and constructive thinking. That is not their job.

Here we come to the heart of the matter. The trade union is a product of nineteenth-century capitalism. It is part of that system. Against powerful, highly organised and ruthless capitalist forces, it had an essential, even noble part to play. But when those forces are disarmed; when they are in headlong retreat – indeed howling for mercy – the union has no function to perform. The trade union movement may be dressed up with economic committees and so forth; but its only real purpose is to bargain for better wages within an all-powerful capitalist system. The British trade union movement has now been taken out of that context and placed in an entirely new one. Yet it is still carrying on doing the only thing it knows how to do – ask for higher wages. As it has beaten all its opponents, as it is for all practical purposes the state, it naturally gets them. A subject government prints the money, and the result is inflation on an unprecedented scale.

British trade unionism has thus become a formula for national misery. For, mark you, trade unionists have no means of enjoying the spoils they secure. The trade union movement is not a unity. It has no common interest. It is merely an amalgamation of sectional interests. And in an inflationary situation, where real wealth is static or, in our case, actually declining fast, unions demanding higher wages are simply competing against each other. Any union which does succeed, albeit temporarily as a rule, in raising its real living standards is and must be doing so at the expense of the community. How are we to describe a band of determined men occupying key positions in society and using their collective power to raise their incomes, regardless of the needs and interests of the rest? Powerful men who conspire together to squeeze the community are gangsters. Let us identify them as such.

Unfortunately, we now have not just one strong-arm trade union, but dozens – scores. We are approaching the condition which Hobbes describes as 'this war of every man against every man'. In such a state of anarchy, as Hobbes points out, men tend to treat all their fellows as enemies, and gradually the whole of morality collapses as more powerful and vicious weapons are brought into use. In its natural state, the trade union movement is disunited, since it is a collection of separatist interests. Under hyperinflation generated by wage demands, each union becomes the opponent of all the others. It asks for higher wages not because the money is there in real terms, nor even to keep up with rising prices, but because other unions have demanded rises of comparable size, and succeeded in getting them.

We call the process 'free collective bargaining' but it is really nothing of the sort. It is groups of people using their strength to force other groups, or society as a whole, into compliance with their will. And here, if anywhere, some people are 'freer' than others. It is notorious that certain groups, such as the electrical power workers, have a greater leverage over the community than others. Is it therefore suggested that they should automatically be paid more because of this fact? No one actually says so, but such is the moral logic − if you can call it that − of unrestricted wage bargaining. The logic, indeed, is that the most powerful must get the most money all along the line. This is not socialism. It has much more in common with capitalism. It has more in common still with a society in a state of pure savagery, where brute strength is the only criterion of worth.

One reply of the doctrinaire trade unionist is that some groups fare badly in wage bargaining because they are inadequately organised, or not organised at all. This is doubtless true. Hence we have seen, in recent years, whole new categories of workers joining in the competition for wage increases, demonstrating their militancy and smashing their fists in the community's face. Some have done so in pure desperation, as they found themselves impoverished by rising prices, and watched the greedy, the determined and the well-organised improve their position. Others have entered into the spirit of the thing. Thus the airline pilots, already paid £14,000 a year, are demanding that this be raised to £28,000, or they will not operate Concorde. They produce no justification for this claim, other than the fact − if it is a fact − that French pilots will be so paid.

Some middle-class groups, specialist doctors being one example, have shown that when it comes to sheer greed, and the unscrupulous exploitation of their position in the life of the public, they can beat 'the workers' every time. Other groups have been less ready to abandon their customary morality, and have suffered accordingly. One of the hateful things about wage inflation is that it punishes those with a social conscience and plays straight into the hands of the selfish and unscrupulous. In the eyes of the contemporary trade unionist, anyone who does not exploit his or her bargaining power to the absolute maximum is a fool. This is good trade unionism. It is certainly not socialism. Indeed, in a society completely dominated by the trade union principle of might is right, the true socialist cannot exist; he must go under.

For 'free collective bargaining' necessarily excludes huge sections of society. They are not organised. They cannot be organised. Rapid inflation inflicts the greatest possible suffering on the very poor, the old, the very young, the sick, the helpless, the physically and mentally handicapped, all the outcasts and misfits and casualties of society. Collectively, they number millions. Collectively – from a trade union point of view – they are powerless. They cannot, like miners, power workers, railwaymen, busmen and so forth, make the life of society miserable, damage its wealth and so force authority to surrender. They cannot batter the public with their fists. Old people open their newspapers with dread, knowing they will read of 30-, 40-, even 60-per-cent wage increases, leading inevitably to monstrous rises in the cost of essentials, like electricity and gas, transport and food, and to compulsory charges like rates.

They are utterly helpless and terrified of the future. How can they react? What can they do, except die? It is a lie for trade union leaders to claim that their vast wage demands have nothing to do with the poor and unfortunate. They know perfectly well that combating inflation means a special effort has to be made to divert resources to the public welfare sector; that such resources can only come from the private sector via wage restraint, and that their current demands not only make it impossible to cushion the poor against want but will inevitably lead to actual cuts in the welfare services. Those extra notes in their wage packets come, almost literally, from the less privileged sectors of society. Again, this may be good trade unionism, but it is not socialism as I understand it.

Just as the underprivileged suffer from wage inflation, so they are nearly always the most exposed victims of the strikes inflicted on the community to enforce inflationary settlements. The rich always have ways of escaping the worst consequences of strike action. They have alternative means of transport, or fuel; they can pay over the odds, and bribe or bully their way out of strike situations. They do not have to struggle to work, or suffer in angry, impotent silence. If they choose, they can just take a holiday. It is the poorer groups who are utterly dependent on public transport and public services, who have no store-cupboards or reserves, and who are the first to feel the deprivation which strikes are deliberately intended to inflict.

There are some trade union analysts who argue that, while very rapid wage inflation has undoubtedly inflicted injustice on some sections of the community, it has also brought real and permanent benefits to huge groups of industrial and manual workers. Such benefits, if they exist, can only be relative. Certain groups of workers have improved their position *vis-à-vis* others. A number of 'middle class' groups have gone hurtling down the scale, meeting well-organised unskilled and semi-skilled workers on their way up. But some working-class groups have gone down the scale too, as have millions of ill-organised and poorly paid workers, especially women. The adjustments which have taken place follow no rational pattern, and certainly no pattern based on any principle of social morality or worth. Indeed, why should they, since they are the result of economic force used in a random and arbitrary manner?

In any case, this is not really the important point. Since 1945, the British working class has been desperately badly served by the trade union movement. Its standard of living has gone up with agonising slowness. Britain's growth rate has been the worst of any major industrial power, indeed of any industrial power. Real wages have climbed *pari passu*. It is an unfortunate fact, which no amount of trade union militancy and rhetoric can alter, that unionism can increase nominal wages – paper money – but not real wages, at any rate over a period. What it can do, however, and what it has done most effectively in post-war Britain, is to slow down the rate of economic growth.

Britain's slow growth rate has been blamed on poor management, low investment and ill-judged Treasury management of the economy. Of course all three played their part; but behind all three factors there is the trade union factor too. The best management in the world cannot survive a sustained campaign of trade union militancy. For one thing, it has not the time. British Leyland was badly run because management had to spend far too much of its energy and resources on labour relations, and on mitigating the consequences of strike action. It will be badly run in the future for exactly the same reason. Fleet Street is another case. Good managers do not want to spend their lives arguing petty points with union officials, and on conducting emergency repair jobs to make good the damage of stoppages. So good managers do not, on the whole, go to Fleet Street. Indeed, they do not on the whole go to British industry. Since the war management talent has tended to drift increasingly to the financial sector, where there are no industrial unions and where the able can devote themselves to more creative and purposeful work. Hence the relative strength of Britain's financial sector. In industry, where the unions are strong and active there is bad management. Where good management is to be found, and that is increasingly rare, it usually coincides with inactive or acquiescent (or highly intelligent) trade unions.

The management problem is directly linked to investment. Able men will not join firms where investment is low, and where the future is accordingly unpromising. And British industrial investment is low almost entirely because the trade unions are either opposed to it, or make it unprofitable. There is no point in putting in new machinery unless it cuts costs, including labour costs. And these cannot be cut if the union insists on the original manning levels, as it almost invariably does in British industry. Where it negotiates lower manning levels, it does so in such a fashion as to reduce the economic benefit − and thus discourage further investment.

Indeed it is a common practice in British industry for the union to renege on its agreement once the machinery is installed, and insist that the original manning be maintained. These union attitudes are characteristic of both the public sector and the private sector, so there is no question of the unions being motivated against capitalism as such. Their motives, indeed, are difficult to analyse on any rational basis, being a mixture of hatred of management, dislike of change of any kind, fear of unemployment, unwillingness to adapt to technological improvement, and an almost childlike faith that the system will somehow continue to provide for them.

The idea of a vast left-wing conspiracy within the trade union movement is a figment of right-wing imaginations. British trade unionism does not have sinister ideas. The trouble is that it has no ideas at all. Most of its leaders are perfectly well-meaning. Some are very intelligent. But the movement as a whole is dominated at all levels by the complacent, the conservative, the unimaginative, the lazy-minded, men soaked in old prejudices and habits of mind, Bourbons to the core, forgetting nothing, learning nothing, negative, obstructive, slow, dull, long-winded, unadventurous, immensely pleased with themselves and quite determined to resist planned change of any kind.

But of course what they cannot resist, and what they have not resisted, are the unplanned, unwelcome changes forced on Britain by the economic facts of a harsh and competitive world. In the British Labour movement it is absolutely forbidden, especially for socialists, to criticise the trade union movement in any respect whatever, and in particular to cast doubt on the intellectual brilliance of its officers. Infractions of this rule are severely and permanently punished. But the tragic truth is that British socialism has a devastating case to make out against the post-war union leadership. Men ought to be judged by their record, and their record is contemptible. Smug and self-assured, oblivious of any criticism, they have encouraged British industrial workers in habits and attitudes, in rules and procedures, in illusions and fantasies, which have turned the British working class into the coolies of the Western world, and Britain into a stinking, bankrupt industrial slum.

For the third factor in Britain's slow growth rate, Treasury management, can no longer be held responsible for what is happening to our country. Even in the past, the stop-go system used by the mandarins was not uninfluenced by trade union attitudes. If the unions had not always and immediately insisted on putting shortterm wage increases before any other consideration, the Treasury would have been less chronically inclined to use deflation and unemployment as a control mechanism. And if the unions had shown more willingness to accept realistic manning levels, sufficient investment would have been made during the downturns in the cycles to ensure real and permanent expansion during the buoyant periods. But in both respects the unions were never ready to think except for the moment. Thus the Treasury conservatives could always reject longterm planning because they could argue, truthfully, that long-term planning was hopeless without planned wages and planned productivity increases, and that the unions would accept neither, at any price. Time and time again, British Labour governments have seen their programmes for growth smashed to bits on these obstacles.

As for the situation today, there are very few people in the Treasury who claim to have anything to do with it. So far as they are concerned, it is out of control. With union leaders asking for wage increases, immediately, of up to 70 per cent, and deaf to threats or entreaties, the magnitude of the inflation involved is outside the experience of anyone in Britain, or indeed anyone in a modern industrial economy. Union leaders have told their members confidently that they will get such increases, and that they will do so in real terms and without any further risk of catastrophic unemployment. They know they can subdue the Government. They beat and humiliated, Harold Wilson and Barbara Castle in 1969. They humbled Edward Heath and his Tory majority in 1974. They rightly regard the Prime Minister as a man who will not risk the same punishment twice. So they are exercising no restraint on their followers but are simply pushing forward to the front of the scurrying Gadarene herd.

There are rich men in the City and the world of international finance who have publicly pointed to the dangers that face Britain. At a time when other industrial powers are pulling out of the inflation, we are plunging more deeply into it, and at an accelerating pace. They regard the situation as so serious as to be almost hopeless. But their warnings, in view of the gravity of our affairs, are curiously muted; and many financial pundits who might be expected to be bellowing with terror and rage have remained silent. Why? I regard this silence as ominous for British socialism. The rich, I fear, are happy to see the pantomime last a little longer because they know it must shortly be concluded by a total collapse of government and the imposition of a 'sound' and authoritarian economic regime. They are banking on it. They see it as inevitable if the wage inflation continues. They argue: 'Give the unions a little more rope so they can hang themselves and their socialist friends with them.'

This is one reason why I think it right and important to make an indignant protest against the present behaviour of the British trade union movement. Only they can halt wage inflation without a constitutional struggle. In theory of course it would be possible for Denis Healey to impose immediately an Excess Wages Tax, retrospectively dated to, say, 1 January, which would claw back through PAYE any increases over a minimum norm. But there is no prospect, as I understand it, of the present Government being able to do such a thing. It will continue to surrender until it finally disintegrates, leaving any dirty work to its successor. But much more is at stake than the future of a Labour government. We are talking about the whole future of our country, of the very fabric and texture of its social life. The sort of wage inflation on which we are now embarking inflicts the kind of damage which it takes a generation or more to repair. It makes social planning impossible. It means yet more overcrowded schools, underpaid teachers, under-equipped hospitals, rebellious nurses, bankrupt universities, lecturers who cannot afford to study or buy books, students without text-books, slum council houses, despairing social workers, dismal hells for the mentally sick and miserably inadequate pensions, supplementary benefits and welfare payments of every kind.

It means the poor will have to argue more to get help and traipse around from office to office as the rules are tightened. It means more 'problem families' and so more crime. It means even more grievous distortions and injustices in the rewards each of us receive for our efforts. It means more old people dying secretly in extreme privation. It means libraries virtually without money to buy books; and so fewer books; and fewer writers. It spells disaster for the theatre, music and the arts generally. It is no accident that one of the first victims of the new 'grab everything' union tactics was a ballet season at the Coliseum. Indeed, hyper-inflation is a mortal enemy of civilised living in any shape or form. It means drab buildings and poor craftsmanship, ill-kept public parks, fewer and poorer radio and TV programmes, less public or private sponsorship of talent, less risk-taking on genius, and much, much more rounding down to the lowest commercialised level.

And, in addition to all these evils — some distressingly evident already — uncontrolled wage inflation means a voracious moral corruption eating out the heart of society. It is the very antithesis of the socialist ideal. Where socialism teaches us to see ourselves as part of a whole, members of a human society based on comradeship, mutual help, friendliness, trust, magnanimity and hope in the future, wage inflation is the very worst kind of rat-race. It sets group against group and makes self-interest the guiding principle of life. It makes money seem the only social nexus, and the sole criterion of well-being. It forces on us all the aggressive posture of comparative envy. It turns money and its ever-changing value into the chief preoccupation not just of the miser and banker but of every human being, the dominant topic of conversation, the source of all anecdote, the ever-present, ever-nagging word behind every plan and move. It makes the young predatory, the middle-aged apprehensive, the old fearful. It penalises not just the poor, the old, the sick and the weak, but the decent, the diffident, the unselfish, the reasonable, the temperate, the fair-minded, the loyal and the generous. And, by contrast, it allows the social mood to be set by the rapacious, the unscrupulous, the anti-social and the bully. Hyper-inflation forces us to accept a world of blind materialism where ideals cannot be realised, where force, power and selfishness are the only dynamics, and where charity is dead.

This plea from a socialist to the trade unionists of the Labour movement may well be a cry from the wilderness. Amid the Babel of pay claims and the rattle of price increases, it is hard to hear the voice of elementary common sense, let alone socialist idealism. But I shall have achieved my object if I persuade even one responsible trade union leader to think again about where he and his colleagues are leading society. I am not just debating this issue in terms of future prosperity. That, clearly, will depend greatly on our ability to emerge from this crisis still in possession of a working industrial economy — the only other, appalling alternative is mass emigration, and who today will have us? Obviously, one must think in such economic terms. But the problem is not just economic. It is also social, human and moral — indeed, it is supremely all these things. In short, it is a socialist problem, and it is high time we abandoned gangsterism and started looking for a socialist solution.

CHAPTER 2

The Rise of the Know-Nothing Left

In this article, published in the New Statesman *in September 1975, I expressed my alarm at the manner in which the slogans and violence of Rentamob were replacing Labour's distinguished intellectual tradition.*

The biggest change that has overcome the British socialist movement in my time has been the disintegration of Labour's intellectual Left. The outstanding personalities who epitomised, galvanised and led it are dead and have never been replaced. I am thinking, for instance, of G. D. H. Cole, whose activities covered the whole spectrum of working-class activism and whose voluminous writings constituted a *summa theologica* of left-wing theory and practice; of R. H. Tawney, who placed the modern Left firmly in a long historical context and who endowed its philosophising with enormous intellectual and literary distinction; of R. H. S. Crossman, who brought the bracing austerities of reason into the grosser skulduggeries of practical politics; and, above all, of Aneurin Bevan. The majesty of Bevan's contribution lay in the fact that he transcended classes and categories – a working man with the instincts and capacities of a philosopher-king, a man of action with a passion for reflection, a romantic devoted to the pursuit of pure reason, and an egalitarian obsessed by excellence. Around these, and other, great planets swam many scores of satellites, collectively constituting a huge left-wing galaxy of talent and intelligence.

And where do we find the left wing of the party today? Without a

struggle, with complacency, almost with eagerness, it has delivered
itself, body, mind and soul, into the arms of the trade union movement. There is a savage irony in this unprecedented betrayal, this
unthinking *trahison des clercs*. For Labour's intellectual Left had
always, and with justice, feared the arrogant bosses of the TUC, with
their faith in the big battalions and the zombie-weight of collective
numbers, their contempt for the individual conscience, their invin-
cible materialism, their blind and exclusive class-consciousness, their
rejection of theory for pragmatism, their intolerance and their
envious loathing of outstanding intellects. The whole of Cole's life
was devoted to demonstrating, among other propositions, that trade
union organisation was not enough, that there was a salient place for
the middle-class intelligentsia in the socialist movement, and an
essential role for didacticism. What Labour lacked, argued Tawney,
was what he termed 'the hegemonic way of thinking': it concentrated
on the base trade union aim of sectional gains for its own members
instead of trying to create a new moral world.

Bevan, though a trade unionist, never regarded trade unionism as a
substitute for socialism — in some ways he thought it an enemy, indeed a part of the capitalist system. He fought bitterly against the attempts by the TUC to determine Labour policy in conference and to
usurp the political role in government. He believed passionately that
Parliament was the instrument of strategic change, and its control the
political object of social democracy — he would have resisted at all
costs the brutal threat of a syndicalist takeover. Crossman put the
anti-union case a little more crudely: what invalidated the TUC claim
to control Labour was its sheer lack of brains and talent. Hence his
notorious article pointing out that only five trade union MPs were fit
to participate in a Labour ministry. For this heinous heresy he was
dragged before the inquisition and, just as Galileo was forced to re-
cant his heliocentric theory, Dick was made to pay public homage to
the dazzling genius of his trade union 'friends'. Afterwards, he said
to me: 'There was only one thing wrong with my article — I should
have written three, not five.'

In those days, it was a dismally common event to see a left-winger
stretched on the rack of trade union power. Intellectuals from
Stafford Cripps to Bertrand Russell were the victims of drumhead
courtsmartial conducted by the union satraps. Yet today the leaders
of what is hilariously termed the Left look to the unions as the foun-

tainhead of all wisdom and socialist virtue. Mr Michael Foot, a Minister of the Crown, will not stir an inch unless he has the previous approval of the TUC General Council. Mr Eric Heffer, Foot's *doppelgänger* and cheer-leader on the back benches, regards any criticism of British trade unionism as a compound of high treason and the Sin Against the Holy Syndicalist Ghost. Did this gigantic U-turn come about because the trade union bosses have undergone a cataclysmic change of heart and transformed their whole philosophy of life and politics? Not a bit of it. It is true that the general secretaries of the biggest unions no longer, as in Deakin's day, pull the strings from behind a curtain, but prefer to strut upon the stage of power themselves. It is true, also, that they inspire more genuine fear than they did 20 years ago, as their crazy juggernaut lurches over the crushed bodies of political opponents. In other respects, however, their metaphysic has not altered: it is still a relentless drive to power by the use of force and threats.

The union leaders still regard money as the sole criterion of success and (to them) social progress. They are prime victims of what Tawney, in *Equality*, called 'the reverence for riches, the *lues Anglicana*, the hereditary disease of the English nation'. Blind to the long-term, to the complexities of the economic process, to the well-being and rights of other human beings − blind, in fact, to what Tawney called 'fellowship', to him the very core of the socialist ethic − they see the whole of the political struggle in immediate cash terms. The other day one of them said he would not hesitate to bring the entire publicly owned steel industry to a halt, and throw perhaps hundreds of thousands of his 'comrades' out of work, unless he was offered 'more money on the table', as he put it. Asked if he would heed the activities of the government conciliation service, he said he was not going to take advice from those he contemptuously referred to as 'college boys'.

Indeed, one of the startling characteristics of modern British trade union activists is their systematic dislike for intellectual and cultural eminence and their hostility towards higher education. Here a great and deplorable shift in attitudes has taken place since the nineteenth century. To me, the saddest newspaper report of recent years was a survey of the miners' clubs of South Wales, which revealed that their large, and often rare and valuable, libraries of political books and pamphlets had been sold off to dealers in order to clear space for jukeboxes, pin-tables and strip shows. Part of the price the left wing of the Labour Party has paid for its alliance with the trade union bosses has been the enforced adoption of a resolutely anti-intellectual stance. If miners prefer strip-shows to self-education, the argument runs, then so be it: the fact that the collective working masses express such a preference *in itself* invests the choice with moral worth. Anyone who argues the contrary is 'an elitist'.

'Elitist', in fact, has become the prime term of abuse of the syndicalist Left; it heads the list of convenient clichés which are brought on parade whenever the Eric Heffers put pen to paper, or give tongue. It is a useful bit of verbiage to be hurled at those who, by any stretch of the imagination, can be accused of criticising wage inflation, strikes, aggressive picketing, the Shrewsbury jailbirds, the divinity of Hugh Scanlon, 'free collective bargaining', differentials, overmanning and other central articles of syndicalist theology. And equally, anyone who pays attention to quality, who insists on the paramountcy of reason, who does not believe the masses are always right or that the lowest common denominator is the best, and who considers there are more things in heaven and earth than are dreamt of in the philosophy of a Mick McGahey or an Arthur Scargill — well, he or she can be dismissed as an elitist too. Crossman, Tawney, Cole, above all Bevan, would have been given short shrift today — elitists, the lot of them.

It says a great deal for the power of the syndicalist Left in the councils of the Government, and even in the immediate entourage of Harold Wilson (who, secretly, is one of the outstanding elitists of our time), that anti-elitism has, to some extent, become official government policy, at any rate in the sphere of higher education. Our universities used to be autonomous, and for all practical purposes exempt from state control or guidance — a very elitist and reprehensible state of affairs! But all this is now being changed as the financial cuts begin to bite and the University Grants Committee progressively takes up its role as the Government's instrument of supervision.

The new anti-elitist spirit in the realms of higher education both complements and echoes the alliance between the trade unions and Labour's know-nothing Left. Away with the ivory towers! To hell with expensive research which ordinary people can't understand, and will probably come to nothing anyway. The job of a university is to turn out field-grey regiments of 'socially relevant' people, with the right egalitarian ideas, the capacity to learn by heart the latest fashionable slogans, and to march, shout, scream, howl and picket as and when required. Degradation of the universities, of course, would fit in neatly with the syndicalisation of the Labour Party, since the ideal student – according to the anti-elitists – is one who conforms as closely as possible, mentally, emotionally and culturally, to a trade union militant. The operation is part of an uncoordinated but nevertheless impressive effort to proletarianise the educated classes, and to smash to bits what are venomously referred to as 'middle-class values' (such as honesty, truthfulness, respect for reason, dislike of lawbreaking, hatred of violence, and so forth).

It is by no means confined to students. At a recent conference of local authority education officials, a former headmaster and university vice-chancellor had the temerity to attempt a half-hearted defence of elitism and was promptly denounced, by a yobbo from Glamorgan, as 'an educational fascist'. But students are the prime targets of the anti-elitists because they can be so easily organised into Rentamobs by Labour's syndicalists and their allies (and future masters) even further to the Left. As all totalitarian rulers have discovered, once you have hacked away the logical and rational foundations on which the edifice of civilisation rests, it is comparatively easy to invert the process of ratiocination, dress up the results in verbiage, and sell them to thousands of apparently well-educated people.

A typical example of anti-elitist Newspeak is a dissenting minority report of a Yale Committee on Freedom of Expression, appointed after left-wing students smashed up a meeting addressed by William Shockley in 1974. The overwhelming majority of the Yale academics concluded that disruption of a speech should be regarded as an offence against the university, and one which could lead to expulsion. The dissentient, speaking for the Left, argued that free speech was both undesirable and impossible until there had been 'liberation from, and increased self-consciousness of, the social and irrational factors that condition knowledge and preform the means and structures of language'. Hidden in this ugly gobbet of verbiage is the thoroughly totalitarian idea that the meanings not merely of words but of moral concepts must be recast to conform to political expediency – the very essence of Newspeak. The example is American; but there are plenty of parallels over here, not always expressed quite so naively as by the Essex student leaders who refused even to discuss an 'independent report' on their activities, for which they had clamoured, on the grounds that 'reason is an ideological weapon with which bourgeois academics are especially well armed'!

When reason ceases to be the objective means by which civilised men settle their differences and becomes a mere class 'weapon', then clearly the anti-elitists are making considerable progress. How long will it be before the books are burning again, and the triumph of the 'Common Man', that figment of violent and irrational imaginations, is celebrated by another *kristallnacht*? Already, at the extreme fringe of the syndicalist Left, the aggrosocialists are taking over public meetings, with their ideological flick knives and their doctrinaire coshes. Not long ago, hearing and seeing a group of students and trade unionists giving the Nazi salute, and shouting 'Sieg heil!' at some very stolid-looking policemen, I shut my eyes for a few seconds, and tried to detect the redeeming note of irony in their rhythmical chanting. For the life of me, I could not find it. What differentiated these mindless and violent youths from Hitler's well-drilled thugs? Merely, I fear, the chance of time and place, a turn of the fickle wheel of fortune. Unreason and thuggery are always the enemies, whatever labels they carry; for labels are so easily removed and changed. I remember Adlai Stevenson – an elitist if ever there was one – saying wearily: 'Eggheads of the world unite, you have nothing to lose but your yokes.' Perhaps it it is time for the elitists to stand up for themselves – there may not be so few of us, either – and start the long business of rescuing the Labour Left from the know-nothings and the half-wits.

CHAPTER 3

The Plight of the Left

This article, published in the New Statesman *in March 1976, comments on the spread of Yah-boo politics within the Labour Party and the Left's intellectual bankruptcy.*

It says a lot for the intellectual disintegration of Labour's Left that the abrupt departure of Harold Wilson has not only taken them totally by surprise but finds them without any strategy whatsoever. Here they are in striking contrast to their Bevanite predecessors. In the 1950s, their criticism of Labour's leadership was based upon a coherent economic philosophy and a carefully worked-out alternative programme. Though no one could match the oratory with which Bevan expressed it, behind him there were a dozen first-class political brains and a real measure of administrative talent. Hence, the Left was able to survive the sudden death of Nye; and when in turn, Hugh Gaitskell was struck down – an event almost as sudden and unpredictable as Wilson's resignation – the Left was ready to present its challenge to the party establishment, with a designated leader, an agreed programme and a first-class organisation.

Today, the Left is in panic. It is not so much an organised, articulate and calculating ideological faction as a kind of parliamentary football mob, braying slogans and shouting abuse, and anticipating – one feels – the day when all rational discussion will be scrapped and punch-up politics will take over. 'I hope there is a row at next week's party meeting,' says one *Tribune* pugilist, 'I shall certainly be in there swiping myself.' It is characteristic of the more mindless

Marxists first to destroy serious discussion, and then brazenly to lay the blame on their opponents. It does not seem to me that Messrs Wilson and Healey were particularly offensive in their treatment of the Left last week.

Harold Wilson knew it was his swan-song, and he wanted the occasion to be a demonstration of his political mastery rather than his command of invective. Anyway, prime ministers and chancellors who have been defeated by their followers on the floor of the House are surely entitled to show displeasure. Yet the two ministers have been subjected to a volume of orchestrated Billingsgate rarely heard on this side of the Iron Curtain, reminiscent, in fact, of the mechanised verbal ferocity which marks the culmination of power-struggles in Moscow, Peking, Tirana and other points East. Wilson and Healey are filled with 'hysterical fear', they are behaving 'hysterically'; they are 'sterile'; indulging in 'the rottenness of parliamentary patronage', concealing their betrayals by 'undignified verbal attacks' and 'a very special brand of parliamentary thuggery'; they are 'political thugs', or alternatively 'blustering and bullying . . . frightened men'; respectable *Tribune*ite ladies did not 'come into Parliament to be obscenely abused by bullyboys'; Mr Healey in particular 'just disintegrated', and his language was 'unprintable and obscene in the extreme', he behaved like 'a completely irresponsible man', a 'drunken oaf' and a 'taproom brawler'. The choice of phrase has the weird Dickensian archaism beloved of *Pravda* hacks, for it must be years since even the oldest *Tribune*ite got the chance to visit a taproom to watch the brawling.

Of course this hyper-inflation of language springs from a very understandable cause. The know-nothing Left have been stripped, exposed, degraded and humbled. They have been revealed as ranting impostors, screaming their deathless devotion to 'socialist' principles, and then scurrying to conform at the first sniff of the whips' leather. Maybe a canine metaphor is not so amiss after all: last Thursday night, some of the Left did present the image of a pack of curs, snarling and whining their impotent rage as they were flogged back into obedience. One made an obscene gesture at ministers, and chanted 'Bastard, bastard!' — as he trotted off to be the first to vote for them. Another shouted out 'Stalinists, Stalinists!' — all the way into the government lobby. What is the message of the *Tribune*ites to the toiling millions? It is that the Labour Party is run by frightened and hysterical bullyboys, drunken oafs, taproom brawlers, bastards and Stalinists, and that, taking all in all, and bearing in mind this and that, and in all the circumstances and at the end of the day, the only thing to do is to vote for them.

One may well ask: why are the *Tribune*ites so afraid to turn out the Government if, as they claim, they — and not ministers — speak for the millions of ordinary working-class voters? But it is precisely at this point that the bluff of the Left can be called. In their secret minds and hearts they recognise that they are a small group of unconvincing extremists whose only hope of exerting influence is by operating cunningly within the great amorphous body of the Labour movement, and whose sole chance of power is to prey upon the parliamentary insecurity of a Labour government.

That is why they will put up with any humiliation rather than submit their claims to the test of a democratic vote. They know that if they beat the Government and so precipitated a general election, Labour would almost certainly be defeated, and that more than half of their own number would lose their seats. They also know, and this is even more crucial to their tactics, that if, following such an act of treachery, they were deprived of the Labour Party's countenance, and forced to appear before the electors under their own political colours, not a single one of them could hope to get himself, or herself, elected to Parliament.

The events of last week have served a real purpose in bringing this critical fact right into the open. The know-nothing Left has no alternative to behaving in a cowardly fashion because it has a great deal to be cowardly about: it has no mass popular support, and survives purely by virtue of its nominal Labour label; once it loses that, it is finished. True, in recent years, the Left appeared to possess a real power basis by its alliance with certain trade union leaders. But those days are over. Messrs Wilson and Foot, by dint of extraordinary concessions and a vast and painful amount of bootlicking, have managed to detach the key trade union leaders from the Left. Harold Wilson would claim this was his last service to the party. The price paid is a heavy one in terms of human liberty, but Mr Wilson would argue that the reward has been worth it: he has begun to recreate the party leadership-trade union alliance which was the mainstay and ballast of the Attlee epoch, and which had ceased to exist since the death of Hugh Gaitskell. Mr Jack Jones may not behave with quite the slam-bang crudity of Arthur Deakin, but he and others are now dutifully performing the same role; and the bonds which unite them to the Government are likely to be tightened by the atmosphere of venomous personal abuse and open enmity which the abortive *Tribune* revolt has created. This is an important development in British politics. The trade union movement is once more part of the Labour Establishment and severed from the Marxists by a deep and widening chasm.

Does this mean that the new party leader will be able to dismiss the claims of the *Tribune* Left to have a share in shaping policy? It looks like it. Mr Wilson believes most of the mistakes he has made in the past two years arose from an over-estimation of Left-wing strength, and a corresponding willingness to concede them points in reaching decisions. His successor's best hope of steering Labour to an election victory in, say, autumn 1977 or spring 1978 is to push the Government more firmly into a centre posture. This means not only ignoring *Tribune*ite clamour but reversing many of the assumptions on which the present Government has been conducted. Of course there is a risk that, in exasperated fury, some of the *Tribune*ites will smash up the Government. But this is probably the least of the many dangers which Mr Wilson now faces. For the choice of the *Tribune* group is a pitiful one; between abject servility on the one hand, or political extinction on the other. In view of their long record of pusillanimous hedging, there can be little doubt they will prefer to remain in the safe Labour pastures than jeopardise their careers in the cold world outside. No one can quite match Harold Wilson in straddling the divisions in the Labour Party. But the new leader will enter office knowing that the Left, if not exactly dead, has been successfully emasculated.

CHAPTER 4

Towards the Parasite State

In this article, published in the New Statesman *in September 1976, I broadened and deepened my attack on the unions, presenting them as part of the new 'Corporate State'.*

Exactly 200 years ago, Adam Smith, in *The Wealth of Nations*, celebrated the liberation of the working man. Since the earliest times, he had rarely been fully free in an economic sense. He had been classified and bound, not by his ability and his willingness to work, but by his status. In the declining Roman Empire, he had been herded into state-defined corporations, which compelled him to exercise a certain trade, and no other, during his lifetime; and later, the idea of the corporation was extended, to cover his children and grandchildren, so that status and trade became not merely compulsory, but hereditary. It was on this basis that the serfdom and rigid categories of the feudal society evolved; and when, after centuries, the feudal ties were loosened, they were replaced by the guild system, which again rigidly defined and controlled occupational status, prevented freedom of movement, especially upward progression, and was backed up by government legislation — known in England as the Laws of Settlement — whose object was to petrify the existing mould of society.

In his own lifetime, Smith saw the system finally break down, the guilds crumble, the Laws of Settlement repealed or ignored. He rejoiced at these events. He saw mankind, for the first time in history, move from a society dominated by status to one based on contract, a freely signed document by which one man pledged to work for another; a pledge revocable under law. This, to Smith, was real freedom; true justice. Above all, the change benefited most of the lowliest elements in society, those who had hitherto been the invariable victims of all political and social systems. To Smith, the right of a man to work where, when and how he wanted was the most important of all freedoms − far more vital to his well-being than a mere parliamentary vote. He wrote: 'The property which every man has in his own labour, as it is the original foundation of all other property, so it is the most sacred and inviolable . . . to hinder [a poor man] from employing his strength and dexterity in what manner he thinks proper without injury to his neighbour is a plain violation of this most sacred property.'

Now, 200 years later, the burgeoning freedom which Adam Smith recognised and applauded is in imminent danger of extinction. The freedom of labour contracts is being removed by law, the worker is again judged not by his power and abilities but by his status − as a trade union member − and the jaws of the corporate state once more close around us.

In Britain today, a man can no longer freely sell his labour, since the union stands between him and his potential employer. An employer cannot make a contract either, since the union tells him which categories of men are employable, and which are not − the union often, indeed, acting as a compulsory labour exchange. And what are these categories of the non-employable? Those who do not belong to a union, or *the* union, or who belong to the wrong union. The most important fact in an economic sense about a worker in Britain today is not his skill or his training or his character but his union membership − in short, his status.

The terms of classification, of course, have changed. Men are no longer divided into peasants, bourgeois, gentry, but into members of the NUM, the TGWU, the AUEW, and so on. Since unions, like the old classes, are increasingly difficult to get into, or out of, union membership stamps a man for life − like a penal brand on his forehead − inhibiting his movements, or his wish to change his trade, or his will to remain an individual instead of a unit in an anonymous mass. A union card already confers a greater degree of real political power than a parliamentary vote. Increasingly, it is the title deed to full citizenship, more important than a birth certificate or a passport − an identity card, in fact, the only document which proves a man exists and has rights. Michael Foot and his gruesome trade union cronies have made it plain that a man without a union card will soon be a second-class citizen, a kind of non-person, a concept very familiar to the citizen-slaves of the Soviet Union.

The compulsory enforcement of the closed shop by parliamentary statute is the greatest disaster which has befallen liberty in my lifetime, a defeat for freedom comparable to those the Stuart kings attempted to inflict − and failed. What is more, there was a time, not so long ago, when even the most enthusiastic supporters of trade unionism would have recognised it as such. George Howell, a union witness to the first Royal Commission on Trades Unions, wrote in 1878: 'The common sense of the majority of unionists will soon consign a policy of this kind [closed shop] to the limbo of the past, as it has done in the case of opposition to machinery and many other matters . . . the practice cannot be defended on either social or political grounds.' Until recently, virtually all exponents of trade union theory and practice deplored the concept. Dr N. Barous (*British Trades Unions*, Gollancz 1947) called it 'a child of the most violent period of industrial conflict'. He thought it self-evident that 'in a democratic state, where the freedom of the individual and his association are protected by law, where the use of brute force in industrial conflicts is a punishable offence, and where a highly developed practice of conciliation and arbitration exists, there is not much need, and little justification, for the unions employing a closed-shop policy'. V. L. Allen (*Power in the Trade Unions*, Longmans 1954) argued that a union 'can regulate but it must not coerce, and if it is unable to retain its members by inducements, by satisfying their wants, then it is not entitled to have members'.

Moreover, until recently, even militant trade unionists felt ashamed of the term 'closed shop', and sought to disguise it by euphemisms − 'all-ticket job', 'all-union house', '100-per-cent trade unionism'. The most thorough investigator of the closed shop in Britain, W. E. J. McCarthy, noted: 'In the writer's experience, [trade union leaders] invariably use the phrase [closed shop] to describe *any* situation where union membership is a condition of employment so long as they are talking among themselves, or in front of an observer they have more or less accepted.' Officially, though, it was TUC policy to use the term '100-per-cent shop', which, the General Council noted in 1946, did not 'imply a claim on the part of any particular union to exclusive rights of organisation where *bona fide* unions are concerned'. Indeed, in the same year, the TUC, in its annual report, stated flatly: 'The "Closed Shop", in the sense of an establishment in which only members of a particular union can be employed, to the exclusion of members of other unions, is alien to British trade union practice and theory.'

How times change! Now that the unions have Michael Foot on their side, now that they command a servile parliamentary majority to pass statutes at their orders, there is no longer any attempt to disguise the closed shop behind euphemisms. On the contrary, it is enforced openly, ruthlessly and with complete disregard to the injustice it inflicts on individuals. No one glories more in sheer brute power than a trade union bureaucrat who has got the opposition on the run. The number of victims who have lost their livelihood grows daily. There is, for instance, Mrs Iris Batchelor, who lost her job as a checkout operator because she refused to join USDAW − despite the fact that union membership was not stipulated in her contract. The management, under pressure from the union, simply changed her contract and she was sacked. No redress, of course. And, as it happens, her husband had just been made redundant. A fat lot the union cares about that! Or there is George Lilley, aged 61, sacked by British Rail after 24 years' service, who refused to attend the inquisitorial court at Peterborough to 'state his reasons' for not joining the 'stipulated union'. British Rail said he had 'frustrated his contract' − and promptly replaced him by two men.

Britain, it should be noted, is the only country in the EEC where legislation is in force which specifically enables the closed shop to be introduced. Implicitly, or explicitly, the closed shop is illegal in France, West Germany, Italy, Ireland, Denmark and Belgium. Indeed, it is very likely illegal under the European Rights Convention, of which Britain is a signatory, and which upholds the right to 'freedom of thought, conscience and religion'. Some of the victims are to appeal to the Strasbourg Court under this convention. They are getting no support, needless to say, from that 'progressive' pressure group laughably calling itself the National Council for Civil Liberties. Asked why the NCCL were not taking up the cause of the closed-shop victims, Howard Levenson, legal officer to the NCCL, replied, in a choice example of Stalinist prose: 'So far as the sphere of employment is concerned, we take the view that most of the civil liberties that the citizen enjoys at work derive from the opportunity to combine and to negotiate collectively, and we resist limitations on this opportunity to redress the balance of power between employer and employed.' Get it? Whatever the unions do is right so far as the NCCL is concerned.

That the closed shop is a threat to civil liberties is self-evident. But it is perhaps a greater threat than most people yet realise. Once the closed shop is legal, as it now is, the principle is capable of almost in-definite extension. Thus one 'closed' plant, firm or corporation can enforce a closed shop on another − even if all its employees are against it. This is already happening. In June, for instance, Chrysler, a union-dominated firm just saved from bankruptcy by the British taxpayer, decided to entertain tenders submitted for contract only from firms with a 100-per-cent closed shop. Chrysler contract specifications read: 'The contractor should note that all labour which he intends to utilise on this project must be a current member of the appropriate trade union as applicable to his trade.'

Indeed, once a closed shop is established, and enforceable at law, there is literally no limit to the power of the trade union bureaucrats. They are not only above the law; they can openly laugh at it. At Vauxhall motors, Luton, Stephen Rosengrove had caught more than 100 pilferers in six years, saving the firm £100,000. Leaders of the three biggest Vauxhall unions, the TGWU, the Engineers and the Electricians, formed up and forced the management to shift Rosengrove from gate-duty to a harmless test-track four miles away. As an official of the Joint Union Works Committee said: 'This man has been a problem for a long time.' Of course he had: he had caught, red-handed, union members 'in good standing' stealing property! Certainly ordinary people who see militants break the law, or who are themselves the victims of their increasingly violent activities, are most reluctant to apply for legal redress: they know they are unlikely to get it − and there may be unpleasant consequences too. Thus the union bureaucracy tightens its grip.

Originally, of course, the wholly exceptional, indeed unique, legal privileges granted to unions − privileges which go against the spirit of English jurisprudence and the Common Law − were justified by the fact that workpeople were weak in the face of capital, and that ordinary union members were the victims of poverty, hardship and discrimination. Who would maintain such a fantasy now? The union bureaucracies who enjoy these privileges, like all other bureaucracies, operate not so much in the interests of their members, as in their own interests, which may be quite different. And the union structures themselves pay only lip-service to democracy: they are created and reinforced to further the objectives of the militant minority.

Anyone who takes the trouble to examine union rule books will find a bewildering jungle of ancient shibboleths and anomalous practices. Seven of the 20 biggest unions now have their elections supervised by the Electoral Reform Society. But the rules thus supervised may, or may not, have anything to do with democracy as ordinary people understand it. One of the principles of democracy, for instance, is periodic election. But Jack Jones, general secretary of the TGWU, got the job for life when he was elected, by individual ballot at branch or place of work. Out of 1,418,140 members, only 529,546, or 37 per cent, voted; of these, Jones got 334,125 votes. So Jones secured a lifetime job, with the votes of less than a quarter of his members. David Basnett, elected general secretary of the GMWU, also has the job for life. But in his union the 'block' branch ballot system applies: that is, whoever gets the majority of votes of those who bother to attend the branch meeting, is automatically assumed to have the votes of all that branch's members. Officially, then, nearly 90 per cent of the branches voted; in fact the number of individuals who actually did vote was probably less than 10 per cent.

You may well say: some democracy. As it happens, there have been improvements recently, thanks to postal balloting. When Hugh Scanlon, who has strutted importantly about the national stage for some years, was elected the president of the Engineers in 1968, only 11 per cent of members voted. Introduction of postal balloting raised the total to 38 per cent. Bob Wright, candidate of the 'Broad Left' (i.e., left-wing Labour plus Communists), regarded as Hugh Scanlon's 'natural' successor, has accordingly been defeated in three successive postal ballots. The inescapable inference is that if a postal ballot had been used in 1968, Scanlon would not have been elected, and none of us would ever have heard of him.

The ways in which 'democracy' is supposed to operate among this privileged section of society are almost infinite. In NALGO, for instance, the general secretary is appointed by the 70-strong national executive, itself elected annually; once in, however, he is mighty difficult to shift.

In ASTMS, national executive members are elected by a show of hands – always a bad principle – though branches have the option of organising a secret or postal ballot. These executive members are elected every two years; but the general secretary, Clive Jenkins, no less, got his job for life: he may be in it for another 20 years! The Building Workers have no option but to vote by show of hands, and not even at their place of work but at the branch; no wonder participation is very low – not much democracy there. And where participation is tiny, as in UCATT and USDAW, once a group of men get their hands on the machines, they are almost impossible to shift. Such strangleholds have little to do with politics.

Trade unionism, indeed, is not basically about political principles and humanitarian ideals. It is about jobs, money and power. The top trade union bureaucrats, irrespective of their political views, are the new elite, a privileged aristocracy enjoying perks and immunities virtually unknown in Britain since the eighteenth century. They are what Disraeli termed, in *Sybil*, a 'Venetian oligarchy', like the old Whig grandees, raised above the common herd and enjoying full access to all the sweets and savouries of a juicy and inequitable political system. They toil not, neither do they spin. Some, an increasing number, have never done manual work of any kind; they have been happily fulfilled bureaucrats all their adult lives. The rest have long since forgotten what the shop floor is like. Much of their time is spent travelling abroad, at 'international conferences'. And abroad, these days, British embassies are expected to jump to attention when the general secretaries heave in sight, howling for free meals, accommodation and the usual flunkeyism. They demand that big lunch and dinner parties be given for them to meet their 'opposite numbers' – who are, as it happens, increasingly highly educated and intelligent men (and women), who find the average British trade union general secretary an object of ribald amusement.

Few of these privileged bureaucrats make any secret, at least in practice, of their determination to use their growing power to the full. Occasionally they mouth platitudes about the need for national effort – the phrase 'the Dunkirk spirit' is always on the lips of Brother Jones – but in reality they are irrevocably wedded to restrictive practices of every kind. What is holding back investment in

Britain, what is principally responsible for the low standards of living of the British working class, and what is now causing high unemployment — which seems almost certain to become again a permanent feature of our economic life — is the insistence, by the union bureaucrats over a period of a quarter of a century, on overmanning. In 1966, *The Sunday Times* published (6 November) a study by William A. Allen, 'A Question of Manpower', which showed that British manufacturing industries are overmanned, on average, by a factor of two, and that the humane redeployment of labour could double Britain's GNP over ten years. No union leader has ever been able to produce a satisfactory answer to these and similar studies. There is no answer.

But the top trade union bureaucrats are not interested in such arguments, which they dismiss as 'biased'. They are interested in power. And they would rather have power in a bankrupt nation than impotence in a prosperous one. They have no feeling for Britain. To the trade union barons patriotism is an empty word, an expression coined by 'them' for 'class purposes'. The fall in the pound is caused by 'them'. In their hearts, they do not really believe that Britain is becoming poorer. That is just 'their' story. The truth, so they tell themselves is that buried somewhere, perhaps under the Stock Exchange or the Bank of England, is an enormous deposit of money, filched from 'the workers' over the past 150 years, and just awaiting discovery and disinterment by sharp-eyed trade unionists. They simply cannot bring themselves to believe that the British capitalist cupboard is bare.

Indeed, the trade union bureaucrats have joined forces with their colleagues in the town halls and Whitehall to conduct a highly successful smash-and-grab raid on the public till. The biggest beneficiaries are in local government, where spending, in real terms, has risen 25 per cent since 1970. Does this mean more and better houses, schools, hospitals? Not a bit of it. It means bigger salaries, and more jobs, for the members of the public sector trade unions.

The unions of bureaucrats are, furthermore, beginning to use their increased muscle power, based of course on their multiplying numbers, to force the Government to adopt policies which suit the interests of their members. A good example is the Inland Revenue Staff Federation, whose pressure this year persuaded the Chancellor to include in his Finance Bill provisions which give income-tax inspectors rights of entry and search already enjoyed by the Customs men who administer VAT. Here we see one way in which unions dictate policies which are erosions of ordinary freedom − for, to the average union bureaucrat, a knock on the door in the early hours is 'building socialism'. The man behind the clause which will allow 60,000 tax men to enter private homes is Cyril Plant, for the last 16 years general secretary of the IRSF, and this year's chairman of the TUC, no less. 'The Finance Bill will give our boys the chance to do something they have wanted for a long time,' he gloats. 'Why are people squealing when they have nothing to hide?'

Of course the idea that people might actually be devoted to individual freedom in the abstract is totally alien to the mind of the trade union bureaucrat. Plant says only six premises will be searched every year. But the Customs admit they have already been granted 352 search warrants since April 1973. Any magistrate can issue a warrant, though some warrants, under complicated regulations, can only be issued by permission of a General Commissioner of Inland Revenue. Does that make you feel safer? It ought to, according to Plant. 'They are responsible men,' he says, adding fatuously: 'They won't give the green light until they are sure there is no smoke without fire.' Then − a sinister point this: 'The PAYE worker has nothing to worry about.' The implication is that tax evasion is confined to the self-employed who, being the hardest-working group of people in the country, are the object of peculiar hatred among the union bureaucrats. But, as every household knows, the most widespread form of tax-evasion occurs among PAYE workers who do jobs in their spare time and insist on being paid in cash.

Clobbering the self-employed and what are anachronistically termed the 'middle classes' is, of course, a primary objective of TUC policy, and it has been carried out with ruthless thoroughness, especially since spring 1974. Professor Newbould, who runs the department of managerial economics at Bradford Management Centre, has calculated that in the decade 1965-75, while the Gross National Product rose by 26 per cent, only two tiny 'middle-class' categories registered gains in incomes (senior hospital administrators were up 1 per cent; senior managers in clearing banks and senior accountants were up 2 per cent). Incomes of the rest actually fell, from 11 per cent to 19 per cent, in the case of senior university staff.

But did the 'ordinary' workers do all that well? Comparatively, yes. But in absolute terms they did very badly, since the average gain for manual workers, 13 per cent, is only half the increase in the GNP. Where did the rest of the money go? Why, in 'building socialism' of course – that is, in the expense of maintaining bureaucracies.

Indeed, any idea that trade union policy materially assists the members it claims to serve, any idea that it helps anyone except the union bureaucrats, vanishes as soon as one begins to probe details of the unions' own finances. In a few years' time, as the closed shop completes its stranglehold on the nation, every British working man and woman will be forced to pay out to the union bureaucracies, just like income tax. Where does this money go? That is not an easy question to answer. Mr Christopher Storey, who has investigated the returns made by eight major unions for 1974, filed at the Certification Office for Trade Unions and Employers' Associations in Vincent Square, found that seven out of the eight spend much more on 'administrative expenses and other outgoings' than on unemployment pay or any other benefits to members. Jack Jones's union paid out £2.6 million in benefits to members, but it spent £8.6 million on 'administrative expenditures'. The GMWU spent only £900,000 on benefits, but a lordly £4.6 million on administration. NALGO seems to have spent £2 million on administration. The AUEW spent £4,396,692 on administration, which included £2,216,681 on staff remuneration, and (interesting, this) £148,339 on 'commission for collection of subscriptions'. In 1974, Jack Jones's union spent £381,660 on 'fares and motor expenses'. Clive Jenkins's lot spent £103,043 on travel. The GMWU paid out £158,691 on new motors, taking account of the value given for vehicles in part exchange.

Whether or not such details are obtainable is entirely fortuitous. The form entitled Annual Return for a Trade Union (form AR21) which must be completed under Labour's Trade Union and Labour Relations Act, 1974, has a space for the salaries and wages component of 'administrative expenses', but for 1974 six out of the eight unions examined failed to give this information. Separate figures ought to be provided for the expenditures of head office, where the fat cats operate; but here the Certification Office has failed to get the unions to give details. Indeed, it does not have the statutory authority to enforce the provision of such information: in general, statutory requirements governing these returns are extremely lax – Michael Foot, or whoever was responsible, has done his work well.

But woe betide any humble trade unionist who questions the doings of the mighty above him! The union bureaucrats have ample power to deal with their recalcitrant subjects, including the right to expel. It is this which makes the closed shop such a terrifying weapon in their hands, because today expulsion means automatic loss of job too; indeed, if some Labour MPs get their way, men and women thus expelled, and so unemployable, will also lose all entitlement to social security, and so will be driven to beg in the streets.

How easy is it for the bureaucrats to expel a member? The simple answer is: the easiest thing in the world. Most union rule books contain what Cyril Grunfeld (*Trade Unions and the Individual*, Fabian Society, 1957) calls 'rules which confer on the appropriate union body a general or blanket power of expulsion' — that is, for example, power to expel a member guilty of what one rule book calls 'conduct whether in connection with [the union], the trade, or otherwise, which is, in the opinion of the committee, directly or indirectly detrimental to the interests, welfare or reputation of the union'. This is the exact equivalent of the old Section Nine of Queen's Regulations, 'conduct prejudicial to good order and military discipline', which allowed the army to 'get' a soldier otherwise guiltless of any specific charge.

What it means, in practice, is that the union bureaucrats can expel anyone they want. It is a perfect example of absolute power, such as that enjoyed by the Dominican Inquisition in sixteenth-century Spain. The research-worker F. P. Graham examined the rule books of 80 unions, representing 94 per cent of the TUC's general membership, and found that 66 books contained a clause of this type. (F. P. Graham: *A Legal Analysis of Trade Union Discipline in the United Kingdom*, DL Thesis, Oxford 1960.) In some rule books, quite deliberate attempts are made to avoid the necessity of spelling out the offence in even the most general terms. In the case of the NUJ rule book, the key clause could be operated to impose a complete censorship of the press. How fiercely are these clauses actually enforced? Professor Dennis Lloyd, in *The Law Relating to Unincorporated Associations* (London 1938), argues that unions ought at least to observe the principles of natural justice, that is, to serve a notice setting out the charge, and making it specific, to hold a proper hearing and give the accused the chance to defend himself, and to confine the hearing to the charge specified; he also argues that decisions must be reached in good faith and without bias. But how can such rules of natural justice, in practice, be enforced, especially now loss of union membership deprives a man of his livelihood — something which was *ultra vires* even for the Court of Star Chamber in its heyday? In fact some rule books specifically repudiate the rules of natural justice. In the case of one big union, the rule book allows the executive to refuse to give the victim any reasons for expelling him; and it does not provide either for a notice of the charges, or the right to a hearing.

Presiding over this ramshackle system of injustice are the top union bureaucrats. They may not cut much of a figure abroad, where Britain — largely thanks to their efforts — is now regarded as a joke country, but here they inspire fear or respect among high and low. They regularly collect 'the peerages that are their due'. They recall to me James I's words to Parliament: 'Kings are justly called Gods, for that they exercise a manner of resemblance of divine power on earth . . . they make and unmake their subjects, they have power of raising and casting down . . . judges over all their subjects and in all causes, and yet accountable to none but God only' — the Great General Secretary in the Sky. MPs are at their beck and call. Recently, in a peculiarly humiliating exercise, Labour MPs hoping for sponsorship by NUPE had to write a 1,000-word essay, set by NUPE's general secretary, Alan Fisher, disproving the view that trade unions have too much power. The object was to discover which MPs, out of 16 applicants, had the requisite 'political fitness'.

Of course, we must accustom ourselves to the spectacle of MPs, who are after all elected only by the people, grovelling before union bureaucrats. Union muscle-flexing has only just begun. We noted the peerages that are their due. Would that a peerage was all! In fact, the trade union bureaucrats are now demanding, and getting, more and more of the top jobs. Here the master spirit is Jack Jones — who else? A few weeks ago he told a rally of transport workers at Alexandra Palace: '[At British Leyland] we have evolved a system of joint union-management committees based on the shop stewards . . . We hope that soon we will be able to cap this scheme with 50 per cent of the seats on the top board of British Leyland . . . This reform will be the most radical, the most far-reaching of any of the reforms of the present Government.' Of course, once he has secured 50 per cent of the top jobs at Leyland for union bureaucrats, Jones can move to his wider objective, which is to secure 50 per cent of board-room jobs-for-the-boys in all companies controlled by the National Enterprise Board, and eventually on all large companies throughout the private sector. These directors will, naturally, be selected from a list drawn up by the TUC barons. What a victory that will be for the brothers!

In the meantime, there are 3,000 professional trade union officials in Britain, and 500 national officers – all clamouring for government Quango jobs. This is about the same number of political hangers-on who, in the good old eighteenth-century days of Whig corruption, could expect, or at any rate hope, to get sinecure offices. The union bureaucrats are, in fact, luckier than their Whig precursors, since the numbers of government jobs available to them are constantly increasing, as more and more boards and paid committees are set up, and the proportion of salaried jobs going to the union men is increasing too.

Keeping union bureaucrats happy with Quangos is only one small aspect of the corporate state which is now enveloping us. As Professor Pahl and J. T. Winkler, who have described the new corporatism in the most striking manner in *The Times*, put it, the system has nothing to do with justice, or equity or law. It is 'a comprehensive economic system in which the state directs and controls predominantly privately owned business according to four principles: unity, order, nationalism and success.' They add: 'In order to guard against latent anarchy, submission of the particular interest to the general will is a corporatist principle, collaboration at work a duty . . The corporatist value is discipline, not liberty: the corporatist vice is licence, not compulsion.' Hence corporatism is 'a collectivist system, not an individualistic one. National economic performance has moral primacy over personal affluence or mobility. "Individualism" is a label for stigmatising recalcitrance, not eulogising freedom . . . it puts greater value on achieving targets than on the maintenance of legal rights and processes.' Therefore it involves 'the rejection of the rule of law'.

We have certainly been warned where we are heading. But Labour MPs, even those who ought to know better, disregard or affect to disbelieve such admonitions. Of course, most of them, in one way or another, are dependent on union approval for their seats. Take, for instance, David Marquand, a middle-class intellectual, heavily beholden to the miners' vote in his safe seat of Ashfield. Writing in the *Guardian* − of all papers − he accepts the loss of freedom and the erosion of parliamentary democracy with complacency rather than resignation:

. . . corporate power is now a fact whether we like it or not. Governments can propose as much as they like but in the end it is the great producer groups that dispose . . . Governments that try to force their policies down the throats of the producer groups will fail, and deserve to fail. And the only alternative to force is negotiation . . . To try to dismantle the Corporate State and return to the imaginary golden age of parliamentary supremacy, in the way that some Liberals and Conservatives want to do, would be a foolish and destructive waste of energy.

Just so, in their time, did pusillanimous men justify Munich.

And what of the people? It is, of course, the thesis of the bureaucratic brothers that they represent the people; that what they are doing, in erecting their private empires, in extending their bureaucratic control and grabbing jobs for their boys, in remorselessly driving their juggernaut over the prostrate bodies of individual men and women, that all this is done by, with, for and in the name of the people. Jack Jones, who might well be described as the Louis XIV of the trade union takeover, has seemingly convinced himself that '*Le peuple, c'est moi!*' − or, as General Amin put it, 'De people am me!' But all the available evidence suggests that, at a time when so many members of the Establishment − ministers and MPs, dons and civil servants, experts and publicists − are hurrying to pay their respects to the new totalitarianism, and sell their shares in individual liberty, the ordinary decent people of Britain are strongly opposed to rule by trade union bureaucrats.

I defy the Emperor Jones, or any other trade union tycoon, to produce a single scientific opinion poll or survey, taken during the last ten years, which lends any support for the assertion that their corporatist views represent the majority of the British people. And if they will not accept the authority of polls, let us, for instance, have a national referendum on the subject of the closed shop. After all, the union bosses are not opposed to referenda; they strongly advocated one, and they got their way, on the subject of British membership of the EEC. Is not the closed shop, in terms of everyday life, just as important? Is there any reason why ordinary British men and women should not pronounce on the subject? Of course the union brothers will refuse. *They know they would lose.* And not only lose; they would lose heavily, overwhelmingly. Gone, once and for all, would be their arrogant claim to speak for the people. But, however hopeless, I think it is right that this challenge to a referendum should be put to them. At least it would help to expose them for what they are. Not a group of idealists. Not men who devote their lives to the welfare of all. Not even ideologues. But, rather, an ugly factional interest, like any other which has stained the pages of history, operating at the expense of the community, and motivated by an insatiable lust for personal power, and by enormous greed.

CHAPTER 5

Why Labour betrays Socialism

By November 1976, though still a socialist, I began to see the Labour Government not merely as a failure, but as a fraud, and the Labour Party as the enemy of the principles it professed. This, too, appeared in the New Statesman.

What is the object of a Labour Government? To promote socialism. How is this done? By transferring the ownership of production from private to public hands, in order to increase the generation of wealth, and ensure it is distributed fairly; by rewarding the industrious and helping the needy; and by applying intelligence and reason to the organisation of society. Next question: has the present Labour Government advanced towards these objectives in the last two-and-a-half years? No. Has it in fact made them harder to attain? Yes.

Now, I don't suppose Jim Callaghan asks himself these questions, let alone answers them so frankly. He is not given to self-scrutiny or any other disquieting mental activity. By taste, temperament, instinct and experience, he is closer to the state of mind of, say, the average Tory backbencher, than of a socialist; and it is merely an accident of social origin that he is a Labour prime minister. Asked what his policy is, he is more likely to reply with a 'Steady as she goes', or some such meaningless nautical placebo, than to formulate a rational response which makes sense to a socialist. Nevertheless, there are plenty of people in the Labour Party who should be interrogating themselves along such lines, and who ought to be profoundly disturbed that the answers are so unsatisfactory.

For in the first place, a socialist government must *produce.*

Without increasing the total of goods and services, which means not only raising productivity but making the maximum use of existing plant and manpower, a socialist government is nothing but a mockery, since it cannot do any of the things which it claims are its reasons for existence. What is Labour's record? It appears to have settled for an unemployment rate of 1 to 1½ million as a permanent fact of life. Chancellor Healey told Labour's NEC recently that there could be no question of spending public money directly to create jobs, since there was no money to be had. He went on to say that the government's objective was for a growth rate of 8 per cent for three years in a row. Such optimism is not merely hilarious but downright insulting. When Labour took office in 1974, the manufacturing index stood at 109.3 for the second quarter (on a 1970 base of 100). By the beginning of 1975 it had fallen to 105.9. By early 1976, it had dropped still further to 101.6. In some months during Labour's term of office it has actually been below the 1970 base, and at present it is less than two points above it. In short, under the present Government we have had not so much nil growth as minus growth. Why should we suddenly switch to a growth rate never before attained in our history?

Well, then: what about rewarding the industrious and helping the needy? The present government is engaged in a deliberate policy (in the sense that it is the inexorable consequence of its decisions) of reducing real incomes. And, by its failure to control the money supply, and so the inflation rate, this assault on living standards has necessarily fallen most heavily on the poorest. As everyone knows, the poorest spend the largest proportion of their income on food. In the last year alone, food prices, despite subsidies, rose by 20 per cent. By next April, the Government plans to scrap the subsidy on flour, halve it on bread, and severely reduce it on butter and cheese. At the same time, even if ministers do not give way to growing pressure to devalue the 'green pound' – and they will – prices of basic home-produced food will rise sharply next year, and imported supplies will reflect the much-reduced value of the pound. The poor will go hungry in 1977. What does the government propose to do about it? Nothing.

The anti-socialist cast of government policy, its flagrantly contrasting attitudes towards different wealth-groups in society, is illustrated even more strikingly in its handling of savings. For the poor and the ordinary wage-earner, it has a National Savings scheme

which involves 60 monthly contributions of a minimum of £4 over
five years. The borrowed money is then returned, increased pro-
portionately by the amount of the rise in the Retail Price Index. The
small saver thus gets his money back in real terms, but is paid no interest at all. The Government borrows his or her money for nothing,
and dubs it a privilege that it doesn't also confiscate part of the
capital. What about the rich; the big savers? By contrast they, thanks
to Mr Healey, now get 15-per-cent-plus on their money; in many
cases they will be getting rates of 19 or 20 per cent. This is not the
haphazard working of wicked market forces but the direct consequence of Healey's decision to raise minimum lending rates. The rate
was 8 per cent in 1970. In 1971-72 it was as low as 5 per cent (under a
Conservative government, be it noted).

The truth is that we have in office a usurer's government.
Moreover, the fact that the Chancellor has made it impossible to borrow money at much less than 20 per cent is in flagrant conflict with
the activities of his colleague, the Secretary for Prices and Consumer
Protection, who is hounding TV rental companies because their profits are 'too high'. How high? Oh, between 15 and 20 per cent. We
have here, in short, an almighty muddle; but it is certainly not a
socialist muddle.

Super-dear money is, of course, fatal to investment. As Francis
Bacon noted at a time when money was cheaper than it is now:
'Usury doth dull and damp all industries, improvements and new inventions, wherein money would be stirring, if it were not for this
slug.' At present it is virtually impossible to borrow money for
manufacturing investment in Britain. Is it a socialist object to
discourage investment? No; obviously not. How, then, does the present Government propose to resolve this problem? By investing
public money. Where is this money to come from? No answer. The
Government has lumbered itself with such an enormous burden of
debt (£12,000 million for nationalised industries alone) that interest
payments are now the biggest single item in its recurrent expenditure.
And it has further lumbered itself with grossly inflated, notoriously
underworked and munificently overpaid civil and local government
services. These locust-like armies eat the seed-corn and make it increasingly difficult for investment cash to be provided from public
funds – index-linked pensions of the central government alone now
cost over £1,000 million a year. How has this been allowed to hap-

pen? Is it a socialist object to accumulate vast foreign debts? No. Is it a socialist virtue to roam the world like a seedy Micawber, perpetually cadging money from prosperous capitalist powers? No. Should socialists create a huge bureaucracy, and endow it with privileges denied to the rest? Is it socialism to place all the financial burdens on the wealth-creating sector of society? No, no, no. Why, then, is the Labour Government doing these things? No answer.

One reason, of course, why the Government cannot reduce the size, salaries and perks of the central and local bureaucracies is that they are now protected by powerful and militant unions, who are taking more MPs onto their payrolls for additional security. And this is merely one way in which unions inhibit the Labour Government from creating a situation in which socialist policies might conceivably be pursued. Why should Labour ministers have to govern under the shadow of a union veto? Is it socialist to have rival centres of power to the democratically elected Government? Emphatically not. On this point socialists have always agreed with Thomas Hobbes: 'For all uniting of strength by private men is, if for evil intent, unjust; if for intent unknown, dangerous to the public.' He compared the legitimate power-centre, Parliament, to the muscles of the body; all others are 'wens, biles and apostems, engendered by the unnatural conflux of evil humours'. Yet it seems a kind of law of nature that a British Labour government must always carry the unions, like the Old Man of the Sea, clamped round its neck. In the new, just published volume of Crossman's *Diaries* there is a touching picture of a frustrated Harold Wilson, in March 1967, musing on 'the idea of forming a Labour Party independent of the unions, like the American Democratic Party'. Nothing came of it. Like the poor (and the unemployed) the 'wens, biles and apostems' are always with us.

The increasing unwillingness of members of the Labour movement to seek the truth about themselves and where they are going, and to recognise it when it is thrust under their noses, accounts for what can only be described as the party's intellectual collapse in recent years. Of course the Government, being now the helpless victim of events, has no time for strategy. As Dr Johnson put it: 'A man doubtful of his dinner, or trembling at a creditor, is not much disposed to abstract meditation or remote inquiries.' In any case serious thinking can only be based on truth, and because the truth about Labour is too awful to face, everyone − from cabinet ministers to ordinary party workers — falls back on vacuous slogans, the lowest-common-denominator clichés, and dregs from the ancient vats of the thirties and forties, once filled with the heady wine of socialism. Labour is in imminent danger of usurping the Tory title of 'the stupid party'. I followed the antics at Blackpool from the United States, where I noted down a few jewels of conference wisdom, not from the rank and file but from those occupying high places in the movement. 'I would be in favour of Britain adopting a siege economy, cutting ourselves off from the rest of the world.' 'We should tell the IMF that if they will not grant us an unconditional loan, we will not take it.' 'Once the speech by the Prime Minister has been digested, the pound will strengthen.' 'We should tell the IMF that they have to bail us out or we go down, and if we go down we pull half the developed world with us.' 'The world cannot afford to let the British economy collapse.'

One hears similar ravings on the radio. Thus, one union leader recently blamed the whole thing on what he termed 'multinational conglomerates'. His copious expatiation on this theory was difficult to follow, but I was much struck by his loving repetition, over and over again, of these two words, to him beautiful and all-potent; just so, in 1452, did the Orthodox clergy of Byzantium howl their litanies at the advancing Turkish hordes, in a vain attempt to save their city. I heard yet another Labour satrap tell listeners that those who were selling sterling were 'totally irrational'. It is, of course, a common illusion among the mentally disturbed that the world outside is mad; and the Labour movement, in its retreat from the truth, similarly takes refuge in rodomontade, on the lines of 'Fog in the Channel: Continent Isolated', and in hallucinations, seeing monstrous plots everywhere. The fall in the pound, one major union leader told the conference, is 'an international effort to defeat the growth of socialism'.

Really? What socialism? Where exactly is it growing? True, you can still hear vague socialist noises. Earlier this year it was explained that the growth of public spending was, in itself, a form of socialism. We owe this dazzling insight to Michael Foot, the symbol (we are told) of the party's integrity, etc. Is it, however, socialist to spend above your income? Well, no — not exactly. And in any case, is not the question of what you spend it on, and how you spend it, relevant to socialist objectives?

Again, there is a constant hubbub of noise about nationalisation. But what happens *after* nationalisation? Silence. Inside the government, little or no attempt is made to make nationalisation work. The frivolity with which Labour governments approach the topic is well illustrated by Crossman's account of how the Cabinet treated the 1967 White Paper on the nationalised industries, which involved vital issues of policy and which he described as 'enormous'. It turned out that he was the only member of the Cabinet who had read it. He goes on: 'We had exactly twenty minutes to consider it . . . As I got up from the table I said to Callaghan: "This is a very poor paper." "What does it matter?" he said, "it's only read by a few dons and experts. Personally as Chancellor I couldn't care less. I take no responsibility and I took no part in composing it." Here was a key issue of socialist strategy and the Chancellor of the Exchequer washes his hands of it.' Yet the Cabinet over which Callaghan now presides has a massive programme of nationalisation, which it insists on equating with socialism. What is so tremendously socialist about the behaviour of the Gas and Electricity boards, the Post Office or British Rail? Do not these unloved organisations resemble, not so much public services as blind and gigantic conspiracies against the ordinary consumer? Yes; they do, actually. Then why is it socialist to add to their number? These questions are no longer asked in Labour circles. No one dares to ask them. Instead, the ritual, liturgical clamour for more public spending and more nationalisation goes on, the object of the exercise being lost to sight. So, Konrad Lorenz noted, does the male stickleback carry out its elaborate mating dance, a performance so obscured by ritual that its original object has been totally forgotten.

But if the Labour Government does not, and seemingly cannot, advance the elementary and obvious purposes of socialism, what is it *for*? Mr Callaghan would react angrily to this question, rather like a chief petty officer invited to explain why one salutes the quarter-deck. Because it's there, you fool. No doubt Callaghan feels like the king in the cartoon, who was asked by an impudent child what he did all day. 'What do I do all day? I *reign*, that's what I do.' Socialism, said Aneurin Bevan, is about priorities. Yes; and a Labour government is about Quangos, life peerages, and other delicious things. It is no accident that the chief relic, indeed the only important relic, of those interminable Wilson years was a vast increase in government patronage. No accident, either, that Mr Callaghan has already crisply indicated that, in this respect at least, he fully intends to follow his old leader's example. Socialism may be a dream, but jobs-for-the-boys are an ever-present reality, the real nitty-gritty of politics. What is a public-owned corporation for? Why, to provide well-paid and undemanding sinecures for former cabinet ministers, senior Labour Party hacks, and other unemployables in good standing with Downing Street. Is that why Labour wants more of them? Obviously, brother. But enough of these endless questions. Sticklebacks of the world unite! Don't you see that everything is part of the gigantic strategic plan to make Labour 'the natural party of government'? And socialism has nothing to do with *that*, thank God.

CHAPTER 6

Labour and the New Leviathan

In this article, published in the New Statesman *in February 1977, I began to recognise that the real enemy was not so much the British trade unions or the British Labour Party, but the very principle of collectivism itself.*

It is now fashionable to express concern about the anti-democratic threat to the Labour Party constituted by the totalitarian Left. Shirley Williams has made a much-publicised speech about it, and even Jim Callaghan has weighed in, though his concern is characteristically practical rather than philosophical – 'trouble makers in my constituency'. In fact the threat to democracy within the Labour movement, and indeed in Britain, is both wider and deeper than such pundits suppose.

Most of us, nowadays, are social democrats, whether we vote Labour, Liberal or Tory; that is, we believe in a society in which the state acts in the interests of everyone, regardless of group or class, or sex or colour, and in which the individual is accorded equal rights and given the chance to realise his capacities. The object of the social democratic state is to strike, and to hold, the correct balance between the requirements of social justice and the rights of every individual. But alas! That is not the kind of society we are actually creating. Very largely by accident, and certainly without any conscious grand design, we are slipping towards a Leviathan state, in which organised force, violence or compulsion is the prime determinant of politics, and in which, increasingly, the brute power of the group, buttressed by statutory privileges which place it above Common Law, overrides the public and the individual in the pursuit of its sectional interests: a society in which the ordinary person is nothing, and the corporation everything.

Left and Right are now increasingly meaningless terms; the true dividing line runs between those who put their trust in the individual and those who insist on the moral righteousness of the collective. It is no accident that the collectivists, from whatever end of the spectrum they claim to come, always tend, in the end, to hate parliamentary institutions, because such free assemblies at their best exalt and ennoble individuals, and at the worst accord them some degree of protection.

There can be no doubt that the extremist groups who have successfully penetrated Labour constituency parties are committed to the destruction of the parliamentary system in Britain. Some of them admit it quite openly. *Socialist Worker*, the organ of one such group, states flatly in a recent issue: 'There is no parliamentary road.' The workers must 'collectively seize control'. It insists that 'The present system cannot be patched up, or reformed . . . It has to be overthrown.' What must replace Parliament is 'a workers' state based upon councils of workers' delegates and a workers' militia'. Parliament should be used only 'to make propaganda against the system', the ultimate aim being to destroy it utterly.

Reading such journals, one is at a loss to understand how the Labour Party's attempts to protect itself, and its MPs, from such authoritarians can reasonably be described as 'witch-hunting'. The essence of the witch-hunt, I take it, was that it was aimed at people who were, almost by definition, innocent, for the most part bewildered old women; even in its modern incarnation, under Senator McCarthy, the victims were guiltless, or at the worst dupes. You cannot witch-hunt the aggressor. Those who are trying to take over the Labour Party are, quite consciously, committed to destroy its political philosophy and its institutions, and see it simply as a convenient vehicle from which 'to make propaganda against the system'. Indeed, in their contempt for the individual – particularly the individual voter or MP – and their habit of working in tightly organised groups or packs, they are not so much hunted as hunters. With their fanatical dogmatism and intolerance, their ideological ancestors are the heresy-hunters and militant theologians of the Dark

Age church, the bloodthirsty friars of the Dominican Inquisition, the men who lit the fires at Smithfield and at the *auto-da-fé*, and the Puritan bigots of Geneva, Scotland and New England. Such Pharisaical creatures, born to believe and minded to ram their nostrums down the throats of the rest of us, have stained the pages of history in every age. In the name of humanism and reason, we have not only a right but (I would claim) a positive duty to stand up to them and kick them off the stage – not least in self-defence, since behind their *odium theologicum*, their sanctimonious canting and stiff-necked religiosity, is a lip-smacking taste for violence.

For it is a fact that collectivism and violence always go together. Human beings do not need much urging to kill and terrorise, at the best of times; supply them with the moral authority of the collective, and they will do so with enthusiasm and pride. St Augustine felt he was speaking for the collective church and the entire Apostolic Succession when he first abused the biblical text 'Compel them to come in' to justify official persecution of heretics. Moses, speaking for God and history as well as the Chosen People, made no bones about massacring the Midianites: 'Now therefore kill every male among the little ones, and kill every woman that hath known man by lying with him' (*Numbers*, 31:17). The Old Testament prophets were never slow to bid their followers to smite hard. Karl Marx, the last of them, had no doubt that the moral authority invested in the collectivist forces by his determinist theory of history justified any resort to violence which was necessary to realise his vision.

There is not much evidence that Marx enjoyed violence for its own sake. But many of his followers did and do. A taste for violence was of the very essence of Trotsky's character, of his methodology and his philosophy of action. Without violence, the man's whole life is meaningless and empty. Indeed, I would argue that it was inevitable that Marx's collectivist determination (or historicism) should breed violence on an unprecedented scale once his teachings spread; as was equally true of Hitler's rather different version of historical necessity. It is always a temptation to the *exalté* to hurry along whatever apocalypse he believes in. That is one of the many reasons why communist and fascist revolutionaries have so much in common; and why their differences are, by comparison, of little importance. Hence there have been many important bridge-figures between the communist and fascist ideologies.

Thus Georges Sorel, the French communist and the most influential of Marx's deviant followers, effectively transplanted Marxist violence to the fascist ideological *corpus*. In his *Réflections sur la violence*, he argued that the necessary use of force tested the virility of a people, a class or a nation. The class war was historically inevitable and indeed desirable in itself. 'Proletarian violence', he said, should be 'carried on as a pure and simple manifestation of the sentiment of the class war'; this 'fine and heroic thing' might not bring 'immediate material advantages' but it would 'save the world from barbarism'. He was disgusted by the fact that 'ever since social democracy has become the centre of government policy it has inculcated the adoption of pacific tendencies in worker-management relations'. That was treason, since 'The class struggle is the Alpha and Omega of Socialism' (*Matériaux d'une théorie du proletariat*). Sorel's form of Marxism was a potent influence on French and Italian fascism. His heirs, such as Jean Luchaire and Marcel Déat, later formed the radical wing of the Vichy movement and Gallic National Socialism. Sorel was one of Mussolini's favourites, along with the equally violent Blanqui and Kropotkin. In fact the young Mussolini used to refer to himself as *un apostolo di violenza*, and the first paper he founded was called *La Lotta di Classe* (The Class Struggle). When Italian fascism took over Sorel's ideology, it devoted particular emphasis to his condemnation of parliamentary democracy as essentially a middle-class phenomenon that corrupted and distorted the correct moral instincts of *il popolo*.

It is impossible to read the newspapers associated with the groups now taking over the Left of the Labour Party without catching the fascist overtones, the obsession not only with violence but with such concepts as virility and energy, and the need for 'action', preferably 'direct action', as opposed to 'words'. There is a constant reiteration of the words 'vital' and 'energy' in every conceivable context. One paper, organ of the Young Communist League, has a strip-cartoon, showing a handsome, virile and muscular hero, 'Super Red', hitting opponents on the jaw 'Sock!', with the snarl: 'How does it feel to be on the receiving-end, fascist?' There is much discussion about 'harnessing the energy' of pop fans, particularly those addicted to the more violent, activist musical forms. Thus one writer argues: 'Punk Rock, particularly the Sex Pistols, is *not* on our side . . . The Clash bands are different, but that is precisely the reason *not* to identify them with deviation-mongers like the Sex Pistols.' But some dispute that Punk Rock is fascist, seeing its fans as putative Marxists: 'I think it is an important part of our work to try and win the energy of Punk Rock fans to socialist politics, as an alternative to barbarism.' Several papers praise an organisation called 'Rock against Racism', designed to ensure 'we use all the energy available'.

In choice both of language and content these anti-parliamentary groups and their papers stress the importance of 'action' and the centrality of violence in politics. The papers abound with stories of murder and massacre of workers abroad, of police violence at home; they are, as it were, political horror comics. The key words, endlessly repeated, are struggle, hounded, upsurge, harassment, vandalised, campaign − hallmarks of what you might call the 'Out! Out! Out!' school of thought. The good are characterised by activist vigour, furious emotion and boiling determination; the class enemies are dismissed with such words as senile, gibbering, futile, supine, hack and puppet (unless they are police, in which case they are vicious). Attention is constantly drawn to papers published by other related causes, such as homosexuality, women's lib, black power; one such, called *Flame*, is said to be 'burning now'. Another is *Fight*, with its slogan 'Smash the Social Contract!' The headlines reflect a crude marriage between the class-warfare obsessions of Sorel and sub-editorial Flash Gordonism: 'Kill the Cuts!', 'Firemen Hit Out over Whisky Blast!', 'Fury Over Early Retirement Deal!', 'Vicious Frame-up by Police!', 'Remember Bloody Sunday!', 'Secret Plan Threat to Students!', 'Jobs Battle Looms!', 'Prisoner of Terror!' and 'Fight the Mish-Mash Menace!'. The tone is summed up by a reader's letter beginning: 'Sadie Blood's article last week on how our kids are being sacrificed was great.'

The concern with activist violence is, of course, directly related to the belief in collectivist historical forces, whose triumph is pre-ordained and inevitable. With it goes a profound indifference to the individual except as a class symbol; only thus can the hideous sufferings inflicted by the 'necessary' violence be comfortably brushed aside. The ordinary human being is of no importance compared with the organism, whether it be class, party or state. Here we can trace the influence of Hegel, father of both Marxism and fascism. To Hegel the individual only fulfilled himself when he was subsumed in the higher collectivity of the group. To Marx, he bequeathed the intellectual machinery of communism, the weird system of non-logical argument known as the dialectic, which Marx brought down from the empyrean of ideas to the brutal plane of material forces. To Hitler Hegel donated the practical machinery of German race-discipline, for it was Hegel, well described by Kierkegaard as a 'horrid little academic', who supplied the ideology of Prussian authoritarianism. To both Marxists and fascists he gave the idea of the allencompassing state, as opposed to the parliamentary individualism of the democratic West. It was in the state, he argued, that the individual lost his demeaning uniqueness and was merged in a higher corporatist form. As Mussolini put it: 'Everything for the state, nothing outside the state, nothing against the state.'

Until recently, it has been difficult to see the Labour Party as a corporatist movement. True, it had always paid verbal tribute to collectivism; but the individualist tradition of Locke, embodied in the parliamentary system, had been strong and all-pervasive enough to capture and civilise Labour's political wing. And, in addition the Labour movement contained a powerful element of Nonconformist Christian individualism, animated not by a corporatist church but by a tradition of direct communion between the individual and the Deity via the Bible. It was this conjunction which made Labour the social democratic party par excellence. But things have changed greatly over the last generation, and the process is accelerating fast. Since the war, no force in Britain has declined more swiftly than Nonconformity. As a recent survey of the reading habits of Labour MPs suggests, the Christian presence has virtually disappeared from the party.

The Marxist element, by contrast, has grown with astonishing speed, especially with the huge expansion of working-class university education in the 1960s and the consequent explosion of the sociology industry. With its doctrine of class-warfare, and its anti-individualist cult of violence, the new Labour Left is, as we have noted, strongly corporatist and directly related to the main body of Marxist-fascist ideology. Hence the tramp, tramp of totalitarian feet marching into the constituency parties has been accompanied by the pitter-patter of middle-class liberals scuttling out. That, of course, is one important reason why the Marxists find it so easy to take over − in many local parties they are largely filling a vacuum. But the Marxist invasion is not the only, or even the chief, reason why the middle class is deserting Labour. The explanation lies in the rapid shift of the balance of power within the movement to its corporatist element – the unions.

It is not my intention here to analyse the process whereby the union bosses hijacked the Labour Party. The man who made it possible was, of course, Ted Heath. In one of his essays, Karl Popper suggests that the real task of theoretical social scientists ought to be to trace the unintended social consequences of intended human actions. A case in point is Heath's Industrial Relations Act. It not only wrecked his government but led to a huge and rapid increase in union bureaucratic power. Of course Heath's error was to test his theories to destruction against the mineworkers, the one union (apart from the electrical power men) not easily scared by a whiff of judicial grapeshot. As a result, not only the Labour leadership but the entire nation is in danger of being frightened to death by paper tigers. In its terror, it is embracing the corporate state.

The Bullock Report here marks a milestone. Indeed, it may well go down in history as Britain's first corporatist state paper. As the terms of reference were deliberately framed (on the lines of 'Have you stopped beating your wife?') to make a union victory inevitable, the result was bound to be intellectually beneath contempt. How it could receive the signature of the head of an Oxford college surprises me; but we have learnt from bitter experience that academics, once separated from their pupils and studies, are capable of anything. Some of its statements seem to verge, at first glance, on the satirical; as, for instance, the observation that it has been the policy of all British twentieth century governments, 'particularly over the last ten years', to strengthen trade unionism; or a glutinous passage praising the moderation, good-sense etc. of shop stewards. Their system, we are assured, is more democratic than 'other bodies which are organised on democratic lines'; and, since their hatred of extremism is so well known, 'We think that companies in this country will find it useful to have such people on their boards.' No: this is meant to be a serious report; and reading it is like spending several hours in a stifling room, being hit over the head with a wet copy of last year's *TUC Report*.

Two points in particular strike me as indicative of its strongly corporatist philosophy. One is its deep-rooted distrust of ordinary counting-heads democracy, which it sees, rightly in my view, as absolutely fatal to the objects, methods and claims of the present trade union movement. Indeed, it seems to regard any form of activity among industrial workers outside the trade union framework to be dangerous and illegitimate, if not actually illegal. This philosophy crops up throughout the proposals: in the framing of the ballot-question, in the selection of worker-directors, in their removal or reappointment, and in machinery for any changes in the system. The entire majority report can be summed up in one sentence; 'Everything for the union, nothing outside the union, nothing against the union.' Now, where have we heard *that* before?

The second observation concerns what the majority report, with a significant genuflection to violent phraseology, calls 'the trigger-off system'. This sets the process of industrial democracy in motion, or fires a pistol through its heart, depending on your point of view. Such a ballot, the only occasion on which all work people are allowed to vote, is regarded by the authors of the report as an immense concession. They write: 'We noted in Chapter 5 the widespread belief that most employees do not want to be represented on the board and that trade unions are not democratic enough to speak on behalf of their members. The ballot we propose will allow both these propositions to be tested.' In fact this is exactly what it will not do, since the ordinary workers are not to be asked whether they want industrial democracy but whether they want 'employee representation through trade union machinery'. Hence, even assuming that all workers are in practice allowed to vote, the question, being loaded, deliberately frustrates the process of democratic choice.

Now, this is something that both Marx and Hegel would have applauded. Indeed, being themselves both, to some degree, disciples of the metaphysical belief in the General Will, they would have liked the idea of a once-and-for-all and final vote to launch the totalitarian system. All mountebank dictators, from Napoleon III to Mussolini and Hitler, liked to be able to claim, with some plausibility, that they had been put in power by a 'free vote', and that the people had, as it were, walked willingly into the dungeon before the portcullis slammed down for the last time. It is a scenario all communist regimes try to arrange if possible. But it is notable that Bullock, while granting a general-will vote to set up the system, makes no such concession to democracy when it comes to dismantling it; that, of course, can only be arranged through the 'single channel of trade unionism', a phrase which crops up in the report with sinister reiteration.

What separates the 'single channel' in the factory from the 'single party' in Parliament? Not much, I suspect. For, by its very nature, the corporate state cannot remain static; it must advance to new captures, or risk retreat; it cannot rest content until its absorbs everything. If trade union membership is essential to participate in 'industrial democracy', how long will it be before it becomes mandatory to 'political democracy', that is, the right to vote? You ask: can it really happen here? Or: is it not absurd to present an average British union general secretary as a Hegelian or corporatist? But a union boss can be an idealogue without knowing it, rather as M. Jourdain spoke prose. As Keynes pointed out, the world is ruled by little else but the ideas of economists and philosophers, whether right or wrong: 'Practical men, who believe themselves to be quite exempt from any intellectual influences, are usually the slaves of some defunct economist. Madmen in authority, who hear voices in the air, are distilling their frenzy from some academic scribbler of a few years back.'

And, whatever may be thought or intended by those trade union bosses whose commitment to freedom is still comparatively genuine, the introduction of corporatist ideas under the guise of 'industrial democracy' — let alone their logical extension into the parliamentary field — will be eagerly seized upon and exploited by the totalitarian elements whose devotion to violent class war we have already noted; indeed, their chief, and growing, strength lies not so much in the constituency parties but precisely in the shop steward movement. As this process gathers momentum, where will the Shirley Williamses or even, for that matter, the Jim Callaghans, find themselves? Between class-war extremists on the one hand, and union corporatists on the other, they will discover that they are a very thin slice of democratic meat in a very thick totalitarian sandwich.

CHAPTER 7

Farewell to the Labour Party

This article, published in the New Statesman *in September 1977, summed up and clarified my reasons for leaving the Labour. Party I had joined a quarter of a century before.*

'We are all socialists now.' Sir William Harcourt, generally credited with these words, said in his 1893 Budget speech that he could not remember uttering them. He did not know what 'socialism' meant, other than the vague aim to act in the interests of the people as a whole. Who can do better than Sir William? What *is* socialism? Can Callaghan define it satisfactorily? Can Foot? Not to my knowledge. If it is simply the public ownership of the means of production, distribution and exchange, then we have it in Soviet Russia and a score of other state-capitalist tyrannies; and who wants that? In part of Africa there is a new kind of black socialism almost indistinguishable from barbarism; as Shaw used to say, taunting Kingsley Martin, 'What is so socialist about cutting off people's genitals?' Or, if socialism is about equality, as Gaitskell in his muddled way used to think, how do we answer Karl Popper's point that the pursuit of equality, if ruthless enough, is certain to extinguish democracy? One's reason, intuition and the facts of recent history support Popper. And one has only to read the papers to discover that, with democracy gone, new hierarchies and inequalities rapidly emerge.

The name socialist, then, can mean anything – or nothing. It is what a party does in power which matters. How does one act in the general interest? This is where most people who call themselves socialists go astray, for they assume that the furtherance of the general interest implies collectivism. I believe the exact opposite. Not only, in a negative sense, does socialism − properly understood − insist that the individual must be politically and economically free, but it should also, in a positive sense, give meaning and richness to that freedom. In the 1920s the Viennese socialists, by most accounts a singularly gifted group of idealists, later scattered or murdered, used to proclaim quite simply that they believed in 'the liberation of mankind'. And by this they meant not only the end of tyrannies and colonialism but the inner liberation of each individual spirit. The point was noted by Trotsky before the Stalinist darkness closed in: 'The working class has suffered not from an excess but an atrophy of individualism.' I remember discussing this subject with Aneurin Bevan, who never made the mistake, except sometimes in anger on a public platform, of seeing socialism in terms of class-warfare and vast categories. People, he said, were not given equality of brains or physique, but each had a unique personality and the object of a socialist society was to enable each to unleash or realise it. So the political process was not about equality and collectivism, but about individuals and freedom. The enemy was the advocate of compulsion and its mainspring, dogma. Socialism was an aspect of civilisation, as he saw it, and he defined the essence of civilisation as 'imaginative tolerance', to him the true mark of a civilised mind.

It was Bevan's lot to be committed throughout his political life to the Labour movement. It was not a matter of choice or intellectual conviction. He did not join it. He was born into it. It was like belonging to a race or a tribe. But then in Bevan's day, and in part through his efforts, Labour could accommodate a gigantic individualism such as his. It is true that Labour began, in 1900, as the mere parliamentary voice of trade unionism. Its origins were thus collectivist. But after the catastrophe of 1931 a new party was born. Labour emerged from its trades union carapace and in the thirties and forties exercised an increasing national appeal to an infinite variety of individuals who, in one form or another, saw it as the custodian of individual freedom and self-expression. Unemployed, oppressed workers, militant women, pacifists, teachers and educationalists, prison reformers, homosexuals, writers, artists, opponents of censorship, cranks and religious weirdies, puritans and free-lovers, Quakers and atheists, ordinary working men who dreamed dreams and, together with them, the bulk of the educated middle class — the richness of human idiosyncracy and the whole spectrum of civilised mankind belonged. In 1951 Labour scored over 13 million votes, the highest total in British history, and this after six painful and difficult years in office — proof that its bounds were wide enough to accommodate the whole nation and an infinity of individuals. This was the party I joined. The authoritarian elements were also there, true enough, as Bevan frequently reminded us, in the disciplinary procedures of the parliamentary party and, still more, in the union block votes and the men who wielded them. But such restraints were balanced by the movement's capacity to tolerate awkward members and (so it seemed) by its genuine commitment to liberty. In those days it was the Conservatives who stood for conformity.

When did it all begin to go wrong? I caught the first whiff of disaster in the spring of 1969, when the Wilson Government and (as later events showed) Wilson himself, were broken on the wheel of trade union power. The legislation foreshadowed by *In Place of Strife* was unsatisfactory in a number of ways but it was plainly motivated by the laudable desire to curb the political and economic power of huge collective forces manipulated by small groups of men. As such its aim was libertarian and individualistic. The projected Bill was destroyed by a conspiracy of cynics, defeatists and trade union authoritarians, inside and outside the Cabinet — a Cabinet which, as Wilson himself told me at the time, 'turned yellow' at the crucial point. It was no accident that the conspiracy was led by Jim Callaghan: his first, decisive step on the road to Number Ten. I say Wilson himself was broken by this episode because, it seems to me, he was never quite the same man after he experienced, as he put it, 'Hughie Scanlon's tanks on my front lawn'. Few people are prepared to meet a Waterloo twice. When, to his surprise, the Tories' own entanglement with the unions flung him back into office in 1974, he was no longer prepared to fight the TUC barons. He allowed Foot to negotiate the surrender terms and, thereafter, watched with growing lassitude the collectivist element take over the party. No one to this day knows quite why Wilson resigned. But I suspect that disgust at the way things were going played a part in it. Wilson, with all his faults, once had liberal roots, a perky individualistic spirit of his own, and a genuine reluctance to see people pushed around. Lacking the will and the power to reverse the trend, he may have concluded that a collectivist party should be led by those who believe in authoritarianism, and so made way for Callaghan – whose type Francis Bacon had in mind when he wrote: 'Nothing doth more hurt in a state than that cunning men pass for wise.'

In the meantime the unions had been given the 'closed shop' as part of the surrender. For me this way was the turning-point in my loyalty to the party. For whatever the private reservations of certain cabinet minister and backbenchers — and some of them, I know, hate it as much as I do myself — they united without public dissent to legalise the closed shop. It became the Mark of Cain, blazed on the party's forehead. It was what the party now stood for: the right of union bureaucrats and bully-boys to coerce individuals into collective conformity, as a prelude to further erosions of human freedom. There might be grounds for argument over *In Place of Strife*. The events of winter 1973-4, when the triumphant miners trampled over the prostrate body of Ted Heath, are open to a variety of legitimate interpretations. But there can be no doubt about the closed shop. I know it in my intellect, I feel it in my bones. It is, in all circumstances, and whatever the specious justifications of time, place and convenience, morally wrong. It is wrong in the sense that imprisonment without trial is wrong, and conviction without due process. It hands over the individual to the mercy of the kangaroo court and the menace of the militant shop-floor mob.

One reason why I joined the Labour Party was that I believed it stood by the helpless and persecuted, and by the angular nonconformist who – wrongheadedly perhaps – reserved the right to think for himself. Labour's closed shop legislation represented a historic shift in its doctrinal loyalties, from the beleaguered individual to the grinning triumph of the field-grey regiment. I, and others, found ourselves deceived. Where now was Bevan's 'imaginative tolerance'?

Moreover, the closed shop opened the road to the corporate state, in a peculiarly British version which proceeds by imperceptible gradations rather than a sudden *coup d'état*. With the handover from Wilson to Callaghan, the tone, attitudes and language of the party began to change. For Callaghan had never made any secret of where he thought the party's emphasis should rest: 'The Labour movement,' he said in 1955, in an attack on Bevan, 'would never have reached the peaks and heights of power unless we had been prepared to subordinate our individualism to our socialism.' Of course in this respect he merely echoed the voice of the union bosses, few of whom have ever believed in liberty and democracy as they are commonly understood in free societies. Recently, debating with Hugh Scanlon on TV, I was saddened but not surprised to hear him assert, as his bedrock article of faith: 'Liberty, in my view, is conforming to majority opinion.' And we all know how, in our rotting union structures, such 'majorities' are created and maintained. Scanlon conceded that a religious crank might be permitted to escape the closed shop but, asked about other objections of principle, replied: 'I do not know what others there can be.' Here is a man, speaking on behalf of the trade union movement, who cannot conceive of a secular political conscience, for whom nonconformity and individualism are illegitimate. A man after the heart of Callaghan, Foot and the new Labour Party.

For the party has taken over the collectivist philosophy of the union bosses. In one of his TV broadcasts, Callaghan let slip the phrase (if my memory serves) 'each one of you in your unions'. This is the corporatist vernacular. A man has political existence, and the right to indicate his views, not as an individual voter but as a trade unionist, and solely through the mechanism of his collective. Business is tidier that way, when the state simply arbitrates between huge, anonymous categories of men and women. Those who do not fit in, who, for one reason or another, do not have a union card, or the right union card, become non-persons and, if awkward, enemies of the state. This was what Mussolini believed, taking his example from the compulsory corporations of imperial Rome in its decadence; and, in turn, Hitler and Franco and the score or more communist despots who, today, hold down a third of the world in corporatist societies.

We see the corporatist drift in the manifest preference of Callaghan, Healey and their colleagues for determining policy not in the arena of Parliament which with all its limitations still reflects the political individualism of the ballot box, but in secret and unrecorded talks with union leaders, and sometimes with the capitalist bosses. We see the drift again in the 'findings' of the pro-Government majority in the Bullock Report, whose terms of reference were rigged in advance and whose corporatist conclusions – that 'industrial democracy' should be operated solely through and by the trade union bureaucrats – were therefore predictable. Anyone in the Labour Party who does not like the corporate state has one of two choices. They can seek fresh pastures outside British politics – and there has been a steady drift of MPs that way, to the EEC, to television, to academia. Or he or she can conform. But mere conformity is not enough. To get on, positive enthusiasm must be demonstrated, rather as, in the sixteenth century, recusants were obliged to take the Anglican sacrament in public, and heretics driven to confess their errors in the streets, wearing white paper caps. So we find Shirley Williams and others trooping to the Grunwick demo, like broken butterflies, to express their sincere support for trade union extremism. The surrender is clinched by Labour's manipulation of the legal process, whereby Common Law or statutory barriers against union tyranny are progressively dismantled or, when necessary, legal safeguards which protect the individual are simply not enforced.

Corporatism is carrying Labour into strange and chilly waters. The party's emotional origins lie, in great part, in the outraged protest against the mass anonymity of industrialism, the intrinsic inhumanity of drumming thousands of individuals into vast factories. Socialist pioneers, whether Chartists, or disciples of William Morris, or angry Clydesiders, loathed the colossal scale of the capitalist world, which dwarfed the workers. But it is of the essence of corporatism that the units must be large. And it is of the essence of modern union bureaucracy that workers are easier to control in big factories, where the organised, militant clique rules all. So Labour ministers and union bosses are united in their up-ending of Labour's old posture. Both loathe the small business and the little workshop, and penalise them viciously; both exhibit a positive hatred for the self-employed, who cannot be unionised or corporatised at all. The aim of some union bigots is to make it impossible for self-employment to exist. So the thrust of Labour policy is now to crowd everyone into the giant firm – whether publicly or privately owned is a detail – where they can be dealt with and disciplined more easily. This real but concealed approach by Labour creates precisely the inhuman bigness once so trenchantly attacked in Chaplin's *Modern Times* and Orwell's *1984*.

Of course you cannot crush individuals without destroying creativity too. Labour is now the anti-creative party. Its leaders, for instance, classify the self-employed as tax-dodgers; to the corporatists they are 'social enemies', to be stamped out of existence.

But the self-employed include scientists and inventors, writers and musicians, painters and sculptors, men and women who make films and TV programmes, design ballets and write songs — the essential creators who keep civilisation going. There is no room for them in the new Labour Party. On the contrary, it is increasingly composed at both the parliamentary and the constituency level of those who have never made anything in their lives, by hand *or* brain. Have you ever studied the kind of jobs advertised in, say, *New Society*? There they all are. Labour's mercenary army: the burgeoning bureaucrats of expanded local and central government; the new breed of 'administrators' who control schools, hospitals and even the arts; sociology lecturers and others on the fringe of the higher education afflatus; so-called social workers with their glib pseudo-solutions to non-problems. With this tribe aboard, Labour has lost its secure anchorage in the wealth-creating sector of the nation and is drifting to sea in a swell of sterility.

Even in the creative world, the pressure to conform is on. It is no secret that the closed shop in journalism has been particularly welcomed by the envious and incapable. No writer or editor of real talent wants to impose the NUJ on the unwilling or supports the ruinous strikes mounted to coerce them. The pattern is repeated in films, TV, the theatre. It is fear of the free play of brains, the consciousness of inferiority, the hatred of the energetic and the successful which inspires extremism in these professions. We should modify Shaw; he who can, does; he who cannot becomes a trade union militant. There is, for instance, a grisly little plot to form a closed shop of writers for the state theatres. Successful playwrights whose work is not exclusively determined by the sectarian politics of the extreme Left are vigorously opposed to it. One of our leading playwrights told me: 'If the scheme goes through I will never write another word. I would rather earn my living as an unskilled labourer than submit to those bastards.'

How has Labour thus succeeded in alienating the creative and constructive, the talented and wealth-producers? Why has it become a repository of destructive envy and militant failure, a party of green-eyed monsters? The answer is that Labour has starved itself of intellectual nourishment and the stimulus of debate. The Wilson years shrouded it in a false ecumenicism; the quest for compromise at any cost, just for the sake of a spurious unity, brought emasculation and the peace of the grave. Once, the great debates of the 1950s between Bevan and Gaitskell revealed differences and posed alternatives. As Bevan said, the party was not a corpse to be dissected but a living, breathing body. It would die if theoretical thinking were neglected. Labour must use its brains to pursue what he called 'the grand design'. We needed 'lamps for our feet or we shall stumble'. The internal debate, however erosive, was a necessary function of growth, what Darwin, in the final chapter of *The Origin of Species*, calls the 'struggle for existence leading to the preservation of each profitable deviation'. No such struggle is now articulated. Reading *The First Fabians*, recently published by Norman and Jeanne MacKenzie, I am reminded of the astonishing breadth of the intellectual debate amidst which Labour was born, the rich variety of the contending views, and the atmosphere of high moral seriousness in which they were put forth. But Labour was then a nonconformist party wedded to individualism. Today the takeover by the trade union bosses has brought theoretical argument to a full stop and replaced it by mere raucous assertion – and by the Scanlonesque doctrine of 'conforming to majority opinion'. Callaghan was the natural choice to preside over such an empty sepulchre.

It was inevitable that the Marxists should fill Labour's intellectual vacuum. For in the sixties and early seventies, thanks to the reckless and unbalanced way in which higher education was expanded, Marxism enjoyed a meretricious revival in the guise of social science. To frail-minded inquirers, and to those born to believe but lacking religious faith, it offers glib answers. It was the last thing Labour needed, for it is not only a non-science but an anti-science. Marxism closes, rather than opens, debate; its constant osmosis – the sure sign of invalid theory – means that it cannot be falsified within its own terms of reference; and, as Einstein showed when replacing Newtonian cosmology with a new hypothesis, falsifiability is the decisive characteristic of any theory about the real world. Jacques Monod, the Nobel prizewinner and biochemist, whose book *Chance and Necessity* seeks to relate political theory to our expanding knowledge of life processes, is right to insist that Marxism is a caricature of science; it lacks the ethics of scientific discovery no less than a true theory of knowledge – to Monod the essential basis of socialism. In fact Marxism is a form of animism, for it invests 'forces', real or imaginary, with life. Hence it cannot be satisfactorily 'revised' or adopted in part for its 'insights', as many social democrats foolishly suppose; it must be rejected *in toto* as a paralysing disease of the intellect and of our moral sensibilities.

Alas, Labour has never been able or willing to throw out Marxism bodily; it has always held there must be *something* in it. Such feeble resistance as it once offered has been overwhelmed, and the crudest kind of Marxists now roam through the party at all levels. Battered by Marxists from below and the trade union bosses from above, the slender structure of reason which Labour once possessed has collapsed in ruins. Or, to vary the metaphor, Labour's intellectual development has slowed to a halt like an exhausted glacier, leaving pools of melted ice and terminal moraines − slag-heaps of abusive clichés still feebly voiced amid the silent desolation: 'Elitist!, Middle-Class Values!' and so forth. Needless to say, when reason flies violence takes over: and Labour's new masters, the Marxists and the union satraps, form a unique combination for promoting it. Marxism is a form of secular prophecy equipped with a methodology of violence if it fails; and British unionism has repeatedly demonstrated in recent years that it will use brute force if the simple strike weapon falters.

Where, then, does a Labour government, representing this captured movement, stand? Of course it does not stand anywhere at all. It compromises. It meets violence half way. It tries to rationalise and legitimise force. It lets it be known that to invoke the law against the unions would be more trouble than it is worth. Some members of the Cabinet are wealthy men who expect the police to protect their extensive properties in the salubrious areas where they choose to live. But the government attitude to law enforcement becomes much more ambivalent when the police are obliged to operate, in a political context, in slum areas like Lewisham and Ladywood. The growth of a fascist Left, led by increasingly professional street-fighters, fills ministers with fear and indecision. The Marxist-fascists find friends, admirers and supporters not only in Labour constituency parties, some of which they control, not only in the National Executive and the Parliamentary Party, but in the Government itself. Ministers cannot advocate the stringent measures necessary to subdue left-wing violence without making powerful enemies and risking their constituency nominations. So they are silent. Moreover, there is a belief in the Labour Party that where, as in the Grunwick dispute, management appears in a particularly objectionable and unreasonable light, violence on the picket line is thereby justified. So it is an axiom of government policy that if trades unionists use violence ministers simply avert their gaze; or, indeed, give it moral support by ostentatiously joining the pickets, to curry favour with the extremists.

One of the clearest lessons of history is that compromise with violence is fatal. Once some degree of violence is accepted there is absolutely no point at which the line can be drawn and the slide to savagery arrested. The whole emphasis of British political theory, from Hobbes and Locke onwards, is that politics is a substitute for violence, a higher and more sophisticated answer to the problems of resolving conflicts of view. It is astonishing that the British Labour movement, whose original aim was to civilise industrial society, should repudiate this tradition, turn again to the dark past and harbour the thugs. Nor will the men of violence be content with the mere patronage of Labour. They are on the march. Violence feeds on its triumphs over the law. Labour's leaders may think that beastliness on a picket line is acceptable. But violence is an evil continuum which begins with the inflammatory verbal pursuit of class war, continues with Grunwick and the lawless use of union power, progresses to the knives, clubs and acid-bombs of Lewisham and Ladywood, and then − as we may well fear − rapidly accelerates into full-blooded terrorism, with firearms, explosives and an utter contempt for human life. This is where the Labour party is heading. It has already embraced corporatism, which ultimately must mean the end of parliamentary democracy. But corporatism *plus* violence is infinitely worse. It is fascism; left-wing fascism maybe, Marxist-fascism if you like, but fascism all the same.

Naturally this progressive abandonment by Labour of its fundamental political ethics has led to demoralisation. Having no rational ideology, bereft of a sense of purpose, terrified of the electors, Labour in Parliament is ceasing to be a party, honourably organised to secure clearly defined public objects, and has become a mere faction, with office as its sole aim. Cynicism and corruption have taken over. The Government has bought the Liberals' votes, and is now bargaining with the Ulster Unionists. In the Tammany world it inhabits, everything can be bought and sold. The ripples of cynicism spread outwards from Downing Street to embrace the departments and Parliament. Ordinary people see nationalised industries simply as legal conspiracies against the public. To ministers they are a never-ending source of patronage, part of an immense system of jobs-for-the-boys, operated with all the ruthlessness of a Walpole. There may be 1,600,000 unemployed in the sticks but in ministerial quarters there are plenty of plushy berths to be filled. Quangos, life peerages, honours and baubles of all kinds flow in steady profusion to Labour benefactors, businessmen with good connections on the Left, pliant academics, well-disposed newspaper executives, friends of friends of friends, relatives, hangers-on, fixers, little men who find it inconvenient to be photographed, all the bit-players and spear-carriers of that grubby and interminable farce, *Labour in Office*.

Where will it all end? For the decaying rump of the Labour Party it will end, I suspect, in electoral catastrophe, reflecting an unparalleled record of economic failure. I can see the voters echoing Cromwell's words to another demoralised faction: 'Ye are grown intolerably odious to the whole Nation. You were deputed here by the People to get Grievances redressed, and are yourselves become the greatest Grievance.' For me personally, the issue is not primarily political but moral. As Labour has drifted into collectivism, I have come to appreciate, perhaps for the first time in my life, the overwhelming strength of my own attachment to the individual spirit. The paramount need to keep it alive, I now see, is so great as to override any other public principle whatever. Studying the past has persuaded me that the emergence of the individual is the first, decisive step in any civilisation. Recently I have been working a good deal on the history of Ancient Egypt. There, in that overwhelmingly totalitarian society, a social miracle occurred when the pristine belief that the Pharaoh encompassed the collective soul of the nation gradually yielded to the conviction that all men and women possessed individual natures, and that each played a unique role in the moral order. A great archaeologist called this development 'the dawn of conscience'. The individual conscience is the most precious gift humanity possesses. A political creed which respects it − whatever evil it may otherwise do or stand for − is inherently healthy, for it contains within it a self-correcting mechanism. But in a system of belief where conscience is collectivised, there is no dependable barrier along the highway which ultimately may lead to Auschwitz and Gulag. I do not intend to travel even one miserable inch along that fearful road.

PART TWO

The Plight of Britain

CHAPTER 8

The Tyranny of Politics

In March 1978, I expressed in the New Statesman *a feeling that had been growing on me for some time - that an obsession with the political process, and an overestimation of the results that could be obtained by political action, produced not only disillusionment, but in the long run tyranny.*

When De Montfort was crusading in the South of France against the Albigensians, and about to take a heretic city, he turned to his spiritual adviser, a Cistercian abbot, and asked him how his soldiers, who had orders to slaughter the Albigensians and spare the orthodox citizens, would be able to tell them apart. 'Oh, kill them all,' replied the abbot, 'God will know his own.' I thought of this chilling response when I saw a TV film of an African village in Rhodesia, which had been burnt by the 'guerrillas'. Some of the children had been bayoneted, in the name of one man one vote. Which god would know his own there, amid the charred bones and tiny, twisted limbs? Is there some god of multi-racial justice to be appeased by this sacrifice of the innocent?

Throughout the ages, the zealots have trundled their juggernauts over humanity. Granted their premise, that it is possible not only to conceive of a detailed moral order but to enforce it, their nightmare logic flows, as the Marxists say, ineluctably. The end result may be atrocious, and absurd; but the links in the chain of reasoning hold firm. We saw another case last year on TV − the image remains deeply etched on my memory − of a black police constable being stoned by white youths. These young men were members not of the National Front but of some extreme left-wing sect. Doubtless well-educated and articulate, after the modern fashion, for all I know they may, each one of them, have had degrees in sociology. They were there to stop an NF march. Since the police would not let them stop the march, for which legal permission had been given, they were fighting the police. And since the black was a policeman, they were hurling bricks at him. He looked very frightened, as well he might; no pack of Pharisees stoning an adulterous woman to death could have been more single-minded than this mob. They were swelling with self-righteousness and moral indignation. 'Why are you stoning that black man?' 'Because we believe in racial harmony.'

The history of mankind can be seen as a series of attempts to impose a moral order on our somewhat chaotic natures. In a sense this is not only right but admirable; the search for moral order is of the very essence of civilisation, even more crucial to its emergence than the building of cities. The mistake we constantly make is to construct a moral order which is far too detailed – and so open up for ourselves the savage pit of ideological conflict, into which we repeatedly tumble. The strategic error in the organising of society is to invest regulations which are mere matters of temporary expediency with the force of moral compulsion. This is the origin of totalitarianism.

The difficulty which our earliest civilised forebears faced was that they found it impossible to frame a code of law without religious sanctions. The earliest law codes, of the Babylonian Hammurabi and the so-called Mid-Assyrian period, were deliberately put in a divine setting. They were sometimes very detailed, and the ferocity needed to enforce them was justified by the wrath of god aroused by infractions. On this Mesopotamian plinth the Hebrews built their great structure of theocratic jurisprudence. The ponderous law codes of Leviticus and Deuteronomy are attempts to construct a real and actual moral order on earth, down to the last multi-coloured tassel on a high-priest's garment. Morals, economic necessity, political and social convenience are all hopelessly confused in these efforts to legislate a Utopia into existence. Moreover, they were presented not as collective wisdom, the deliberations of an assembly, but as divine revelation, part of a historicist unfolding of events, valid for all time and place. It says something for the lasting impact of this Hebraic moral order on mankind that, in 1531, over 2,000 years after it had first reached written form, the tranquillity and concord of Renaissance Europe was broken by an argument between Henry VIII, based on Leviticus 19: 16-21, and Pope Clement VI, who defended Catherine of Aragon's marriage on the basis of Deuteronomy 15 : 5, in Henry's eyes a much inferior text. Heads rolled, stake-fires burned in consequence.

Our glory is that we have always produced people who have revolted against the constrictions of these compulsory moral orders, and who have used the critical principle to bring about a drastic simplification. The desire to create Utopia by statute has come up against a libertarian ethic based upon a simple moral framework, the gaps being filled by the internal moral order created by the individual's own conscience. The totalitarian straitjacket imposed on the Jewish people by the law was challenged, in the first century BC, by a liberal rabbinical tradition, which culminated in the teaching of Jesus. The essence of his work was not only the simplification of the law but the insistence that the law's desirable essentials be promoted by the imaginative morality of an informed conscience. He might have put it, as J. S. Mill later did: 'No great improvements in the lot of mankind are possible until a great change takes place in the fundamental constitution of their modes of thought.' Hence the 'new' man of whom St Paul wrote. His one major theological essay, the Epistle to the Romans, is determinist in one sense, but liberal in another. Paul was urging men to escape from the totalitarian theocracy of the law and find 'freedom in Christ'.

It is one of the tragedies of history that this new Christian liberalism, based on free will and conscience, was not married to the political and economic liberalism of the Roman Republic. The Romans were great empirical legislators, and they had the sense to impose only the essential framework of law on their complicated empire, throughout which goods, ideas, creeds and men of all races circulated freely. Alas, Christianity was married not to the liberal Rome of the first century AD but to the Byzantine oriental despotism of the fourth, an autocracy already committed to legalistic compulsion on an unprecedented scale, and a corporatist state in embryo. Christianity took on its colouration and ideological habits. From this developed the 'total Christianity' of the Dark and Middle Ages, a society in which every aspect of existence was provided for by authority in the most minute detail, and in which, in theory at least, God's Utopia was enforceable, by the evangelising church and its physical arm, the state. Thus the burden and straitjacket of the Jewish law was recreated in Christian form. The thirteenth century Bishop Grossteste of Lincoln, one of the finest and noblest diocesans of the Middle Ages, believed it his duty to visit every family in his diocese, if possible once a year, and ensure it was keeping Christ's law, infractors being dealt with in his courts. But even he could not carry out this plan; and Grosstestes were rare: the Middle Ages were saved from the worst totalitarian horrors by human weakness and the corruption of authority, just as Soviet Russia is humanised by the black market and the underground press.

Of course the danger of detailed Utopianism is that there can never be agreement on the details. The Albigensian crusade was essentially an argument over details. As the Middle Ages progressed, there were more details, and so more issues to be argued (and fought) about. One of the great merits of Erasmus is that, in the true tradition of Jesus, he sought to re-simplify Christianity. Christian peace and unity could be preserved, he argued, 'only if we define as little as possible'. 'All that is of faith should be condensed into a very few articles.' On many points 'everyone should be left to follow his own judgment'. Otherwise, 'the long war of words and writings will end in blows'. How right he was! The eirenic wisdom of Erasmus was brushed aside by the eager zealots. Theology expands to occupy the time of the theologians available to practise it; and there were a great many theologians in sixteenth century Europe. Luther did not oppose Rome with simplicity: he opposed it with a different set of details. Calvin did not want to overthrow the totalitarian theocracy of medieval Christendom, merely to replace it with another of his own. Like Grossteste, he thought it essential to visit and inspect every home annually in his Geneva fief, and castigate backsliders. The Reformation was not a conflict between freedom and authority, but between rival authorities. Thus the long war of words and writings *did* end in blows, which lasted for a hundred years.

We stand aghast in disgusted wonderment at the Wars of Religion: how could Renaissance Man do such things? Many people were aghast at the time, but powerless to prevent the slaughter and savagery as the zealots took over. *'Surtout, pas trop de zèle!'* The cry may be Talleyrand's, but it echoes through the ages. Sensible men recognised, like Erasmus, that religious warfare was the product of too much definition. In the exhaustion that followed the Peace of Westphalia in 1648, lessons were learnt and the idea that private judgment should hold sway in large areas took root — and took root not only in the religious but in the civil sphere. 'The freedom of the subject is the silence of the laws,' noted Hobbes sagely. The moral order was threatened by anarchy but could also be destroyed by legislative overkill. Locke reintroduced the Erasmian concept of 'minimum Christianity' and added to it his own vision of the night-watchman state, in which the law protected life, property and a reasonable order but did not indulge in positive Utopianism. The law, moral and civil, merely held the ring, and within Renaissance Man was free to seek fulfilment, guided solely by the dictates of an informed conscience. If Christianity was reduced to a minimum, so was political action. The notion of religious liberalism corresponded to the developing notion of a liberal economy. Thus in the advanced society of the eighteenth century — England — man was left fairly free to believe and act. The invisible hand of the market controlled the external world of commerce and manufacture, and the invisible brain of the conscience controlled the moral individual. This unleashing of human genius and energy produced the great creative leap forward of the Industrial Revolution, and its related political concept, democracy.

The notion that mankind progresses most swiftly, and that the essentials of a moral order are most secure, when Utopianism is held at bay, is not one which appeals much to present-day opinion, though I believe (and hope) it is due for a revival. The pattern of history suggests that creative forces operate best in a framework of scepticism and indifference, rather than in one of enthusiasm and zealotry. A collective assent that little can be known for sure opens the road for the individual pursuit of truth — the surest way of finding it. The century 1750-1850, when the Wars of Religion were already deep in the past, and the Wars of Politics far in the future, was one of great creative power. The received wisdom of that age seems to me to have corresponded more closely to a just and sensible assessment of the human condition than that of most times, before or since. For the construction of a moral order must start with a recognition of the limitations of political (and religious) action. Perfection cannot be organised. Happiness cannot be planned or engineered. Even justice is an aim and an ideal, rather than an actual condition to be brought about by legislation. A society under the rule of law is a plausible, and attainable, objective. But a Just Society is a Utopia. The piecemeal solution may lack divine symmetry but there is about it a huge humanity. Not only is the best the enemy of the good: a totalitarian moral order is bound to be an enemy of justice, and so in the end destructive of order itself.

But the kind of society which produced Mill's *Essay on Liberty* did not and perhaps could not last, for its stripped-down, simplified framework of moral order permitted injustices which drove men to clamour for more details. There was a revulsion of opinion, and in the new climate Marx reintroduced the notion of a total society, governed in all its details by moral necessity. Of course this new Utopian society was in theory secular; but in the organising of human societies the distinction between religious and secular is at bottom false. The theocracies of antiquity were political states. The totalitarian states of today are the realisations of quasi-religious theories. Politics is the pursuit of religion by other means. It was that shrewd observer Junius who noted as early as 1769 that the fanatics who made the Wars of Religion possible had merely changed their occupation: 'There is a holy mistaken zeal in politics as well as in religion.' Marx thought himself a materialist; but he was at heart a Jewish prophet and eschatologist, with a historicist vision of human development derived from the Old Testament, and with a determinist plan to control and perfect human behaviour which was positively Deuteronomic in scope.

It was in the 1880s that clever men in large numbers began once more to argue about the details of the moral order. The Age of Politics had begun. The brief, sceptical period, which supervened after the end of the age of faith and the Wars of Religion, was dismissed as cruel, uncaring and selfish, an abdication of moral responsibility. Men again began to plan the regeneration and improvement of society down to the last detail, and in due course to enforce their moral wisdom. Inevitably this new 'war of words and writings' ended in blows too. I do not know how exactly to date the beginnings of the Wars of Politics — the Nazi invasion of Russia in 1941, perhaps? — but they are plainly upon us, and there is no possible knowing when humanity will emerge from them. Will it be decades? Centuries? The desire to make men perfect by law and force is strong in mankind, and it is heedless of the lessons of history or even the dictates of common sense and experience. The human raw material of zealotry is always there, waiting to be conjured out of the mass by some religious or political charismatic. Where have all the monks gone? Why — they are with us yet, in political committee rooms all over the world. Where are all the theologians of yesteryear? Flourishing mightily, thank you very much, on *Pravda* and the *People's Daily*, on *L'Humanité* and *Paese Sera*, on *Le Monde* and the *Guardian*.

And the martyrs, too: they, most of all, are with us still, and in ever growing numbers. As the Cuban 'enforcers' spread over Africa, like the Counter-Reformation Jesuits, sleepy tropical cities leap into horrific life and enact their own, secular Massacres of St Bartholomew. *A la lanterne*! — the cry of the savage Utopian through history. The newspapers show us photographs of black men hanged at the street-corners of Addis Ababa. They are labelled counterrevolutionaries. They might, with as much sense or justice, have been branded Albigensians, or supporters of Consubstantiation. Were these murdered Ethiopians conscious martyrs, dying for a belief like More or Michael Servetus? Or mere innocent victims of zealotry on the rampage? Plenty in both categories, I should think. But it is notable that the political juggernaut, as it trundles across entire countries, even continents, is far more prodigal of human life, and less discriminating in exacting it, than its religious prototype. In central Europe, tens of thousands died in the wake of Wallenstein's Catholic army. In South-East Asia today the victims of Marxist Utopianism number millions, perhaps tens of millions. They will never figure in a Foxe's *Acts and Monuments*, any more than there can be a martyrology of Auschwitz; there are too many of them. And the vast majority simply have no idea why they are being killed. In a way, that is the most horrific thought of all.

It would, however, be a mistake to see the new Tyranny of Politics simply in terms of its murdered victims. A totalitarian moral order is not merely a way of death; it is a way of life too. In Grossteste's Lincoln or Calvin's Geneva the most notable feature was not the persecution of dissidents but the daily oppression of ordinary people. Even outside the totalitarian structures of our age, there is the same risk of enforced conformity in societies — albeit nominally free and democratic — where the state is theoretically striving to achieve perfection for its citizens. In the West, over the past half-century, the state has ceased to be a night-watchman and is turning itself into a nanny, who in turn threatens to become a mental hospital orderly. A very representative figure in this process was the late Professor Richard Titmuss. His latest editor, Davis Reisman, rightly notes that he possessed 'a pronounced authoritarian streak, as one would expect from an interventionist with a belief in monolithic bureaucratic government'. Titmuss believed that life was a vast number of problems to be solved. When the last problem was solved, the moral order would be complete. Problems were solved as and when the means to solve them became available to the state: 'We do not have policies about the weather because, as yet, we are powerless to do anything about the weather'. As technology advances, so the area of life in which the state, and politics, operate expands, and the moral order becomes progressively more detailed. Conscience contracts, or atrophies.

This central characteristic of the tyranny of politics — its all-pervasiveness — is defended on the grounds that, whereas individual freedom is of value only to the economically privileged, it is meaningless to the poor, who need and want increasing interventionism. Of course this is a fallacy. A year ago, the poorest group on earth, the Indian peasantry, decisively repudiated compulsory contraception, the form of problem-solving interventionism practised on them by Mrs Gandhi's Government. Loss of freedom hits the poorest hardest, for they do not have the consolations of property and their privacy is so vulnerable. So easily made the objects of Utopian experiments, they are the chief victims of the all-pervasive state. But of course in a society where politics are compulsory and ubiquitous, as in a legalistic theocracy, there can be no true privacy for anyone, and all are necessarily involved in the experiment. The principal hallmark of a total moral order is equality of subjection.

Another is the need for demonology. Once men begin to claim a monopoly of righteousness — and the blueprint for Utopia — they tend to treat those who hinder them, deliberately or not, as evil. The Old Testament is littered with the reviled corpses of men and women who, somehow, found themselves opposite Yahweh in the moral equation, and were accordingly 'smitten'. As Christianity ceased to be a simplifying religion, and moved inexorably towards the construction of a total moral order, it acquired *odium theologicum* and the terrifying aparatus of hell and eternal damnation. Indeed, once you seek to impose this moral order by force it is necessary to create the concept of men wholly possessed by evil. Then you can destroy opponents without compunction. It is hard to kill the obstinate or misguided, but who hesitates to slay a demon?

That is why the erection of a new demonology was one of the most crucial steps in the creation of totalitarian politics, and why it remains a distinguishing characteristic. Jews, capitalists, kulaks were types of evil collective forces. And archetypal individuals were also constructed to epitomise wickedness. The extreme left-wing weeklies are full of the monster-figures once beloved of Redemptorist or Dominican preachers. Sir Arnold Weinstock, for instance, is portrayed as a truly dedicated oppressor of working-class humanity, who scarcely sleeps at night so busy is he evolving spider-like schemes for the further impoverishment of his employees. 'Remember,' Dean Farrar used to say, '*the Devil is a very hard-working fellow*!' But did even he ever work as hard as the Gang of Four, sabotaging the steel-works, spreading lies on the radio and TV, importing pornographic films, making the trains late, lowering artistic standards, destroying the harvests? I am not even sure that they have escaped blame for a number of floods and earthquakes, these busy Shanghai demons. And the trouble with political demonology is that, like *odium theologicum*, it is very catching. Those hate-words come so easily to hand – do they not? – and so easily obliterate shades of political discussion in favour of absolute good and absolute evil. Thus a judge who says something which does not square with current race relations orthodoxy is not misguided or foolish: there are zealots outside his court next day screaming at him that he is a Nazi.

The creation of imaginary devils is used, in turn, to enhance the self-righteousness of those seeking to impose the new moral order. A characteristic of the tyranny of politics is that the political activists present themselves as more estimable than the rest of us. Militancy is a virtue *per se*. It is a new priesthood, whose ritual lustrations and phylacteries endow its members with peculiar claims on our approbation. It is then only a small step to claim privilege, as of course all priesthoods have done throughout history. With privileges necessarily goes the power to oppress. In Soviet Russia, where the moral order of totalitarian politics is firmly institutionalised, scarcely any attempt is made to hide the new privileged class of party members, the Levites of the Communist Utopia. Their power in the new order is justified by their theoretical purity and enthusiasm. Similar claims are being advanced even where the full tyranny of politics has not yet been established. 'We believe,' said one zealot at last year's Labour Party conference, 'in the Democracy of the Committed.' A nice little bit of doublespeak, that; of course he means he believes in oligarchy − that is, an elite of militant enthusiasts whose devotion to the cause of total politics, and whose mastery of its apparatus, entitles them to herd the rest of us along whichever path they wish to go. 'Commitment' is not only an intrinsic virtue but is itself an emblem of political sanctity; we have here something very close to the Calvinist doctrine of the elect.

Such totalitarian devices as the closed shop make a 'democracy of the committed' a practical proposition. Once we are all coerced into unions, we become institutionalised in the tyranny of politics. The 'committed' can then speak in our names. They attend all the union meetings, and keep them going until after midnight if necessary, so that the rest of us − if we go at all − will leave in disgust, and they can then pass any resolutions they please. In the spurious moral climate thereby created, participation is almost a duty, and non-participation a social crime. The non-participant cannot protest at what the elect minority do in his name, for he has forfeited his status in the moral order. By means of this 'democratic' manipulation it is possible to erect monstrous tyrannies, which destroy the notion of a private individual, and do so with a spurious moral authority.

The tyranny of religion was halted and reversed only when men, in weariness and desperation, joined together to limit the degree to which clericalism could penetrate their lives. They thus devised the private sphere and, as it were, erected a protective constitutional framework around the individual conscience. We now face the threat of an assault on our personalities and privacies by the collective moralism of politics − which is nothing more than a mask for the egotism and ambition of tiny bands of bigots. We must erect constitutional defences here also, and say: 'Thus far may politics enter, and no further. Within these frontiers let scepticism flourish and the private non-political being be left in peace!' In short, let us make a corner of the world safe for the Erasmian majority, who have the refreshing modesty to wish 'to define as little as possible'.

CHAPTER 9

The State of the Nation

In the summer of 1978, during the very darkest days of the Callaghan Government, I wrote three long articles for The Sunday Telegraph, *analysing the weakness of the British economy and social structure. I drew attention to two particular evils: the growth of parasitism, and the tendency of Labour policies to produce not democracy, but oligarchy.*

History teaches us that nations do commit suicide; they do destroy themselves by acts of folly and arrogance, collective madness – or communal cowardice. Travelling round our beloved country in recent weeks, and talking to people in great places and small, I found myself asking: 'Are we, the British, preparing a similar tragedy for ourselves?' Certainly, all the elements of self-destruction are there. We are using them on ourselves at this very moment, in scores of different ways.

If there is one particular line of thought, above all others, which is turning Britain into a poor and badly governed country, an industrial slum characterised by increasing violence, it is the notion that political action can promote happiness. The more political acts we perform, the more money we spend through the collective political process, the greater will be the sum total of human felicity.

This cardinal fallacy of the modern age has produced vain-glorious monuments to itself. The vast new Hillingdon Civic Centre, built at a cost of almost £20 million, is at last nearing completion. This pink

brick palace – the Blenheim of our day – now dominates the
ancient borough of Uxbridge, and displays to its ratepayers, who
willed it not, the full effrontery of the political process in all its ocular
triumphalism. It has, in fact, a distinctive military air, and certain
architectural features of it remind me strongly of the menacing brick
castles the Teutonic knights set up along the Baltic to hold down the
pagan Slavs; it is a Home Counties Marienburg.

Looking at these municipal Versailles, of which scores were built in
the sixties and seventies, the outward and visible sign of the vast expansion of local government, one has to ask: *cui bono*? Have they
and what they represent actually served the ratepayers who paid for
them, any more than Louis's château served the people of France?
Are the streets cleaner? Are the roads kept in better repair? Better
policed? Do the libraries offer a wider selection of books? Are there
more civic amenities of every, or indeed any, kind? Everyone knows
that the answer to all these questions is an emphatic No. In almost
every area of Britain, over the past 20 years, the quality of local
government has degenerated in inverse ratio to the expansion of its
income and the scale of its activities. The municipal palaces were
built to serve the egos of Sun-King councillors, and to create jobs for
a proliferating race of courtier-bureaucrats.

Behind the theory that political action promotes happiness is of
course the related notion that all areas of human activity are susceptible to public treatment and that, as and when the physical means
become available, 'policies' should be adopted. The late Professor
Richard Titmuss, one of the key figures in the huge expansion of
public spending in Britain, used to argue that, as soon as the
technology was developed, we would need to produce a policy for the
weather. Few now have the humility to say with Socrates: 'I know
that I do not know.' Perhaps the most characteristic institution of
our times is the Think Tank which, for the Government, serves as a
kind of convenient substitute for actual thought. It is an irony that
the Tank should have been instituted by a Conservative government,
albeit with a covert collectivist, Edward Heath, in charge, for it is
essentially the Labour Party which possesses most completely the
restless urge to develop pseudo-solutions to non-problems, dressed
up in sub-intellectual fluff and sociological jargon.

Perhaps Heath became a political hyperactivist because, to quote
Kenneth Minogue, he saw society as a great organ and could not

resist trying to play great tunes on it. But even if the hand is sure, no one can be certain what will emerge from the pipes. Political hyperactivism always produces results different from those intended, and often the very reverse. There is, however, one constant and reliable factor: more 'policies' mean more bureaucrats. The 1977 official employment statistics tell a horrifying tale of lost jobs: total unemployment rose from 541,500 when Labour had just taken over in June 1974, to 1,341,691 in May 1977 (it has since risen much further). There was a comparable decline in jobs in virtually every productive industry, great and small, old and new.

But the bureaucrats flourished. Customs and Excise, thanks to VAT, were up from 18,000 in 1968 to nearly 30,000 in 1977; Inland Revenue from 63,600 to 83,900; the Department of Employment from 29,700 to 52,500; Social Security from 70,300 to 98,300. While Defence had actually fallen − naturally! − by 50,000, the civil departments had risen by nearly 80,000 new jobs. Hence, during this period of productive decline, local government placemen had increased from 859,000 to 958,000, a net gain of nearly 100,000 jobs; those in national government had jumped from 529,000 to 623,000.

The dramatic expansion in local and central government which has taken place over the past 20 years has, of course, and especially recently, led to a very rapid unionisation of their employees. Bureaucratic unions now have terrific firepower within the TUC and with Labour ministers, they are among the most militant and ferocious in resisting any cuts in jobs, and they are extending the closed shop more quickly than any other sector of the trade union movement. They are in addition demanding an increasing share in making the policies of which they are nominally the servants, and particularly the job policies. We can thus be pretty confident that the expansion of local and central government will continue. The bureaucracy has become the Sacred Cow of Britain.

This expansion of the non-productive workforce is taking place during a period when the productive sector is declining. There are fewer and fewer workers producing the wealth needed to sustain the Sacred Cow.

This might not matter quite so much if the extra bureaucrats actually did nothing whatever. But they, in their own way, are also hyperactivists. Those extra men and women taken on by Customs and Excise, Inland Revenue and the Department of Employment are busy smothering productive management, small employers and the self-employed in new forms and regulations, and ensuring that they are filled in, and kept. The bureaucratic sector is not only parasitical upon the productive sector but enthusiastically harasses it. Such harassment obviously reflects the legislative hyperactivity of the House of Commons, which in the past ten years has passed more column-inches of statutes than in the whole of the nineteenth century. But the bureaucrats increasingly determine the manner and scale of the harassment as power within the ministries slips from the normal Civil Service hierarchy (and thus from the minister and Parliament, too) and into the hands of the bureaucrats' unions and staff associations — themselves slowly falling under the domination of the extreme Left.

The pursuit of political activism at all costs is bound, in the end, to damage the national economy simply because it costs so much money. This can be expressed in a number of ways. In the first place it takes away in direct tax so much money from the individual as to destroy the dynamic which makes us, as Milton put it, 'scorn delights and live laborious days'. St Paul said that love of money was the root of all evil. It is also the principal agent in any rise in productivity and the chief reason why the GNP increases at all.

It is well known that Britain has the highest top tax-rates in the world: 98 per cent, compared with 75 per cent in Japan, 70 per cent in the US, 60 per cent in France and only 56 per cent in West Germany. What is less well known is that it also has the highest starting rates, so that once a British worker begins to pay tax at all — and high inflation means that he pays tax the moment he passes into paid employment — he pays at the whopping rate of 25 per cent, as against 22 per cent in West Germany, 14 per cent in the US, 7.2 per cent in France and only 7 per cent in Japan. In Britain overtaxation is now a problem for the average worker, as well as for the middle classes and the rich. In 1955 a man on the average wage, with a wife and two children, paid less than 4 per cent of his wages in income tax and national insurance; by 1975 the proportion had risen to 25 per cent; it is now probably in the region of 30 per cent.

This monstrous tax burden is, interestingly enough, most resented by skilled workers — that is those who have served a proper apprenticeship, and not been simply churned out by the Government's pathetic 'Skill-centres'. They have had their differentials eroded anyway, as a result of the rigid pay policies engineered by Jack Jones and other representatives of the unskilled and semi-skilled. Now, on top of wage control, steep 'progressive' taxation, fired by inflation, has made the differentials practically meaningless. That is one reason why ICI, lacking enough skilled workers, is closing down a huge factory on Teeside, an area with one of the highest unemployment rates in Britain.

High taxation necessarily acts as a disincentive to acquiring skills; so the shortage of skilled labour has in no way diminished with the rapid rise in general unemployment. But high taxation among the lower-paid also generates unemployment since it not merely diminishes but actually (in many cases) reverses the differential between the take-home cash of the employed and the unemployed. As a result it is also producing tax-evasion on an unprecedented scale — an activity by no means confined (as the Inland Revenue appears to believe) to the self-employed but engaged in by large and increasing numbers of PAYE earners and the unemployed.

All three groups are conjointly creating a moonlighting or shadow sector, dealing entirely in cash, which is beginning to form an economy of its own, a sinister and illegal *doppelgänger* of the real one. This black market economy, produced not by shortages but by high taxation of the working class, is enormous. But no one knows its exact size. You may search through all 400 large pages of the magnificent new *CSO Guide to Official Statistics 1978* (price £8.25, no less!), which rightly won the Library Association's Besterman Medal for its outstanding contribution to bibliographical guidance, without finding any reference whatever to this ghost economy. But it is there, huge, hideous and malevolent; one index of the breakdown in national morale created by the reckless pursuit of political action.

But the effects of high taxation on national health can be seen in other ways, notably in the rate of inflation, which is a moral as well as an economic disease. In 1945 Colin Clark and Lord Keynes argued that inflation must follow when taxation exceeded 25 per cent of net national income. They have been proved abundantly right, as more and more nations have stepped over the 25 per cent mark, and provided the evidence. Taxation rates, themselves reflecting political hyperactivity, are almost certainly the biggest underlying cause of the inflationary stagnation which has made the present deep recession the most severe in nearly half a century.

Britain is the worst sufferer because she is the worst offender. Successive governments have greedily pushed up public expenditure as a percentage of GNP. Its post-war low, under Churchill and Butler, was in 1955, when it was 41.88 per cent of GNP – already well above the danger mark, and already therefore generating inflation. But since then it has risen steadily. The worst single period came in the two years between the spring of 1974, when Labour ministers rode back to power on the shoulders of the mineworkers, and autumn, 1976, when they were practically put under lock and key by the International Monetary Fund. In 1975 public spending rose to 59.06 per cent of the GNP. There was a budget deficit of £10,515 million, itself representing 11.4 per cent of GNP.

But once again, I must ask – *cui bono*? Who benefits? If this prodigal expenditure of public money were protecting the weak, succouring the poor, healing the sick, helping widows and orphans, generating employment – diminishing misery and creating happiness, in short – it might be defended. But it is doing no such thing; indeed, in many cases it is producing exactly the opposite to these admirable objectives.

For instance, during that prodigal year 1975, the Health Service employed 33,017 hospital medical staff – that is, those actually engaged in caring for the sick. Their number had increased very slowly over the previous decade, though the total of cases treated had risen substantially – indicating an improvement of their professional skills or (if you like to put it that way) productivity. In the same year, 1975, the number of administrative and clerical staff in NHS hospitals had risen to 105,781, a spectacular increase over the decade, so that they now outnumbered the medical workers by three to one.

Moreover, as we know from a growing number of cases, this grotesque imbalance produces antagonism between the medical and non-medical staff in hospitals, to the point where doctors, surgeons and nurses are actually impeded from saving the lives of patients by the barbarous trade unionism of the non-medical staff, much of it inspired by envy of the skilled workers. Here is a classic example of political activism producing the reverse of what it claims for itself.

We are learning from bitter experience that to pump more money into the public sector does not produce better services, but simply more bureaucrats. Throughout the sector, the wage and salary bill is by far the dominant element in all spending, and rises steadily as a proportion of the whole as public sector salaries outstrip all others, and public employees grab such perks as non-contributary index-linked pensions. There is less and less left for hospital equipment, school textbooks, road repairs and other physical manifestations of public welfare. More and more public sector employees are engaged in pure administration as such; indeed, more are actually called 'administrators' — a prodigiously philoprogenitive breed.

Pure 'administration' expresses itself in a growing number of circular money transactions, VAT being the perfect example. Employers in the north-east are paid money by the state to take on school-leavers, and then have it taken back again by the state because they have to pay older employees correspondingly more, and so break the state 'guidelines'. In 1975 the Mermaid Theatre got Arts Council grants of £76,575, and then paid £38,500 back in VAT. Almost anyone in business can provide his own examples. These activities exasperate the creative and productive people forced to engage in them by statutory regulations, but they keep Civil Service 'administrators' in happy, gainful and, above all, safe employment. That must be the rational object of the operation. There can be no other.

Political activism designed to produce Utopia does not of course produce Utopia; but, like medieval Christianity, another, more ancient form of ideological activism, it produces a variegated breed of what might be termed well-meaning parasites. Like the Benedictines and Cistercians, the Premonstratensians, Brigentines, Dominicans, Servites and Augustinians of old, these new public service 'orders' rejoice in colourful names. 'What is happening to society?' reads an advert; 'discover the answer in *New Society*.' In a sense the claim is valid. A recent issue of this journal carried 28 closely printed pages of job vacancies. Apart from a few teachers, and I think one doctor, all the jobs advertised came into the cateogory of what I would call the New Secular Religious.

Here is a very small selection: Intake Social Workers, Home Help Organisers, Juvenile Delinquency Project Co-ordinators, Senior Social Workers — lots of these, and junior ones, too — Residential Child Care Officers, Deputy Community Education and Recreation Officers, Social Workers for Alcoholics Recovery Project, Locum Development Workers, Youth Leaders, Day Care Advisers, Senior Playleaders, Houseparents, Group Controllers of Domiciliary

Services, Supervising Wardens for Travellers' Sites, Team Leaders, Adventure Playground Leaders, Area Co-ordinators for Self-help Projects, Long-term Play Leaders, Care Co-ordinators, Play Specialists. And so on.

A sharp-eyed visitor to Britain's big cities, especially the poorer parts, will notice that, as houses and shops become run down and vandalised, they are frequently taken over and 'refurbished', at considerable public expense, by various types of social worker — rather as the Franciscan friars used to move into the popular quarters of the new cities of the thirteenth century. Indeed, in many mean streets nowadays, the offices of these people are the only flourishing buildings to be seen.

I took a long walk round the East End recently — parts of Hackney and so forth — because I wanted to see the background to such outrages as the Brick Lane riot. Here are plenty of 'social centres' of all kinds; some businesses, too, a few of which appeared to be flourishing. But in many streets every tenth house or building had been systematically vandalised. Ground floor windows had been boarded up or enclosed in heavy steel netting. The reinforced plate-glass window of one deserted office I inspected had had two enormous boulders hurled through it, an operation requiring, I would think, great strength, dexterity and devotion to duty. A Play Specialist at work? Inside was a chalk message: 'Have another go — we're not here any more.' Social workers, vandalism and the flight of capital go together.

What seemed to me manifest about this area was that there was absolutely no security of the elementary kind — the ordinary protection of life, limb and property which one takes for granted in a civilised community. There was evidence of fear in those streets, and of real risk in walking them, especially at night. And the reason for this lack of security seemed to me equally manifest. There were plenty of social workers, but no police. I do not say the area is not policed; obviously it is. But the perennial, 24-hours-a-day, ubiquitous and admonitory presence of police protection is clearly absent. The police lack the money, they lack the men, above all they lack the encouragement from on high. Ordinary law-enforcement has the lowest priority of all under the present Government, and the fact is beginning to show.

Now in one sense this is a curious thing to happen under a Labour government, which professes to seek to free us from the fear of want and the fear of unemployment. Is not the fear of violence and lawlessness equally important? Might it not in some cases be even more important?

Labour's false sense of priorities is all the more surprising in that crime menaces the poor most of all. They cannot afford security devices and alarms, and they live in areas where crime tends to be endemic. Social workers may be able to teach delinquents to play, and give advice on day care, but they are not much good at stopping a man from being murdered, or preventing a rape, or theft or simple vandalism. Labour has forgotten that the rule of law is central in any true system of social security.

I felt this even more strongly when I visited Liverpool last month. For Liverpool is a pretty lawless city, yet it has been the object of more social and political activism, and subsidies and subventions and theorising and, above all, planning, than almost any other city in the kingdom. Like Glasgow − its chief rival for violence − it has been practically planned to death. Yet curiously enough, it is not dead. It is a living city, and in some respects a majestic and noble one; and what continue to make it majestic and noble are precisely those elements which fall outside the sphere of collectivised planning and political activism. Virtually everything which is wrong with Liverpool and its surroundings − such as the total disaster of the Kirkby 'overspill' town − is the result of political collectivism. Virtually everything which is right is the work of individuals and groups operating outside the political system.

Soaring above this windy city is the new Anglican Cathedral Church of Christ, which will finally be completed in October. Just after the turn of the century the supposedly sectarian and bigoted Protestants of Liverpool had the wit to employ a 22-year-old Roman Catholic called Giles Gilbert Scott, and he designed them a church of stupendous size and breathtaking magnificence. It has taken more than 70 years to build, and people ought to flock to Liverpool from all over the world just to see it.

In the beauty of its stone, the quality of its craftsmanship throughout, the audacity of the concept and the sheer grandeur of its execution, it is to my mind the finest building erected anywhere in this century. It can even rival Durham and York as our greatest artefact in stone. It represents the culmination, and I suppose the final expression, of the cathedral tradition introduced by Constantine the Great when he set up the first church of the Holy Sepulchre in Jerusalem.

Its triumphant existence is, to Catholics, even more poignant in that, just down the road, a cathedral conceived on a yet more munificent scale, by Sir Edwin Lutyens, which was to have had a dome even bigger than St Peter's in Rome, and dazzle the world by its Romanesque-Byzantine glory, had to be abandoned after the war. It was then realised its construction was far beyond the resources of the people who would worship in it; a watershed, I fear, in the history of Western civilisation (and Christianity). Only the crypt was built, though that in itself staggers the visitor with its splendour. Above it was erected a circular tent-like church, with a high spiked lantern redeemed solely by its spectacular coloured glass. The cathedral was built to a strict budget, laid down by that practical prelate, the late Cardinal Heenan, and looks it. Unkind locals call it 'Paddy's Wigwam'.

It is tempting to use these two cathedrals to draw a political analogy between the solidity and self-confidence of the Edwardian world, which gave birth to one, and the restless experimentation and meretricious values of the world we live in, which produced the other. But that would be to miss the whole point. The reader, recalling my remarks about the municipal palace at Hillingdon, and contrasting them with my praise of the Anglican cathedral at Liverpool, may be tempted to fling back in my face my question: *Cui bono*? What, and whose, purpose is served by the splendour of either.

My answer is that the difference is profound, and goes right to the heart of the human condition, and Britain's sadness and sickness today. The Hillingdon palace, brilliantly designed though it is, is a monument to an illusion. It says to the beholder: the ills of the world are curable; man is a perfectible creature, the master of his destinies; by social effort and collective action, the things which make him unhappy can be progressively removed; and the way to do this is to allow the political process to enter into more and more aspects of our lives.

Now this doctrine is false. It has, of course, always been false. But our generation, and our children, are being obliged to rediscover falsehood for themselves, through painful experience. The message of Scott's Cathedral is the reverse. It says that man is an imperfect and fallible creature, prone to self-deception and self-destructive arrogance, fond of erecting houses of cards which crash about his head. His only hope of progress is by accepting the limitations and weaknesses of his own nature, bearing them constantly in mind in all his plans, and seeking guidance from something less corruptible and more absolute than himself, whether it be moral principles or an omnipotent deity. We need not believe in a Christian god, or any god, to get this message for Britain today. Indeed, within sight of the cathedral, it is written in the pathetic fabric of the city and its surrounds, in the shattered plans and ruined buildings of political hyperactivism.

And if we need any further proof, we have only to go down to the Liverpool waterfront and take the boat to Belfast. There, indeed, is an object lesson in the destructive futility of politics. For a whole decade, Belfast has eaten, drunk and breathed politics and nothing else. More than 1,000 people, during those 10 years, have died in the name of political activism. The political activists have come in all shapes and colours, and mouthed innumerable slogans, and kept the gunmen inspired, happy and busy in their work. But the political activists have not brought a single new factory to Ulster, or created one new job, or built any hospitals or houses − or even repaired the ones their words helped to burn. It is the political quietists who have done these things.

The ravages of political activism in places like Belfast and Liverpool, and the East End of London, testify to the folly of imagining that the ills of mankind are remediable by public solutions. But they should not, and must not, undermine our faith in democracy. On the contrary, political activism gets out of hand precisely when the democratic process is weakened, and especially when it is weakened deliberately by the party in power and its powerful allies outside.

That is what has been happening in Britain over the past four years. For us, the road to recovery − the road away from suicide − begins with the restoration of the democratic spirit.

There is still a general belief, at least among their members, that the Labour Party, and the Labour movement generally, are fundamentally democratic organisations, committed to one-man-onevote and majority decisions. This is a dangerous illusion. The Labour

movement consists of a number of oligarchical organisations, supposedly with a mass base, but in practice run by very small numbers
of people who sustain themselves in power by exploiting the institutional machinery and the apathy of the multitude.

It is, for instance, very characteristic of most British trade unions
that little or no attempt is made to secure a high turn-out at union
elections. Press coverage, which arouses the interest of members and
encourages a higher vote, is almost invariably resented as 'gross
interference in the internal affairs of the union'. Some unions forbid
candidates to campaign actively. Others have fiercely resisted the introduction of the postal ballot. The tendency is for the existing
machine to select the new general secretary and then ensure he is
elected. Thus oligarchy perpetuates itself.

The actual number who vote in vital union elections is a disgrace to
a movement which professes belief in democracy. When Jack Jones
was elected general secretary of Britain's biggest union, the TGWU,
out of 1,418,140 members only 529,546, or 37 per cent, voted. Jones
got 334,125 of these. Thus, on the basis of less than a quarter of the
votes of the members, he secured for life (i.e., until retirement) a job
which, according to one opinion poll, made him the most powerful
man in Britain.

Jones's successor, the present general secretary, Moss Evans, was
elected by less than half of a 39 per cent poll − one-fifth of the
members. When Hugh Scanlon was elected president of the
Engineers, only 11 per cent of the members voted. David Basnett,
elected general secretary of the GMWU for life, was the beneficiary
of the union's 'block' branch ballot system − the candidate who gets
the majority of the votes of those attending the branch meeting is
credited with the votes of all its members. Officially, then, nearly 90
per cent of the branches voted. The number of individual members
who actually voted was perhaps less than 10 per cent.

Men elected for life on such narrow suffrages do not hesitate to
lecture the rest of us on what 'the people' want and what
'democracy' requires. Moss Evans, who, like most trade union
leaders, noisily deplores the interest of newspapers in union
activities, has already put forward detailed proposals for controlling
the press, which would include 'a practicable code of objectivity,
balance, fairness and accuracy, to govern presentation of news and
opinion' and 'a means of policing and enforcing any such publicly

agreed criteria'. He seeks to legitimise this scheme for press censorship by invoking a democratic entity he vaguely defines as 'the public'. Thus:

The public are entitled to protection from abuse of this power to influence it. Those who possess these powers must be required to exercise them within the terms of an 'operator's licence'. The qualification for holding such a licence must be the acceptance and practice of clearly defined standards of responsibility and accountability.

When it comes to the point, however, 'the public' is simply brushed aside since, he adds, 'TUC policy has already defined the instruments necessary to the attainment of these ends.' As 'the public' in practice means the TUC, when it comes to censoring the press we may well beware of Mr Evans's other threat: 'And we must insist upon real public control of television and radio in order to give the public freedom of expression.' We know what that means!

Until the 1960s, the tendency of the trade union bosses to bully and domineer the Labour movement was to some extent balanced by the vigour of the constituency parties and the independence of Labour members of Parliament. Both have declined together. Party membership has shrunk to the point where it is rare for a constituency party to have more than 20 or 30 active members; and in these circumstances it has become increasingly easy for small groups of totalitarian Marxists to take over control, and harass or replace their member.

The process has been greatly facilitated by the ending of the system of 'proscribed organisations', which prevented those who rejected parliamentary democracy from holding Labour membership and taking part in constituency activities. Ending the ban opened the gates to the fascist Left. Equally important has been the emergence on the National Executive Committee of a large built-in left-wing majority, which effectively withdraws from social democrat MPs protection, under the party constitution, from the assaults of small totalitarian groups. Most social democratic Labour MPs now tread very warily indeed. On libertarian issues their voices are prudently silent, and often they feel obliged noisily to applaud the latest example of trade union thuggery. The social democrats have lost the battle for the Labour Party, and they know it.

Among the triumphant militants of the Left there is less and less attempt to disguise where they stand on the democratic rights of ordinary people. Assuming, as they do, that political activism is the only morally worthwhile activity in life, they must necessarily believe, and they do believe, that political activists are more morally worthy than the rest. Just as, among the trade union bosses, there is a conviction that the votes of non-active members should not be allowed to count, so on the political wing of the movement there is a growing tendency to despise what is contemptuously referred to as 'head-counting democracy'. Those who support it (i.e., Margaret Thatcher) are denounced as 'populists'.

The new, anti-democratic mood of the party was neatly summed up at last year's party conference in a striking piece of Newspeak: 'We believe,' said a speaker, 'in the Democracy of the Committed.' Of course, the speaker does not believe in democracy at all. He believes in oligarchy, an oligarchy of political activists and zealots who impose their views on the rest of the community by their ability to manipulate the democratic machinery. All men are equal, but the Committed are more equal than others.

There is in the new Labour Party a deep, growing and bitter distrust of ordinary people, a distrust born of a declining share of the popular vote, of by-election disasters, loss of control in former local government strongholds but, above all, of Labour's manifest failure to make its collectivist policies attractive. In an ideological sense, the British working class has rejected Labour; and the Labour fanatics resent it. They feel that the workers are not worthy of them, and therefore must be 'guided' into worthiness. Hence 'the Democracy of the Committed'.

This feeling of resentment is particularly acute during a period of Labour government (and failure). I am reminded of Brezhnev's remarks at Delhi airport, after a visit to Mrs Gandhi's dictatorship, when he was asked about the freedom of the press and other liberties: 'Such things should not be allowed to destroy the relationship of trust and affection which must develop between a Socialist Government and the people.'

But if Labour activists no longer trust the people, they place increasing reliance on the mob. Mob politics have now become an important part of Labour Party activism, a real and satisfying substitute for democracy by argumentative persuasion. Labour cannot get the people to come to meetings, but it can raise mobs, a strategy powerfully facilitated by the penetration of the party by the fascist Left. It is significant that the greatest and most sustained effort by the Labour movement over the past four years was the siege of Grunwick. Here, indeed, was the Democracy of the Committed operating at street level. It mattered not that a majority of the Grunwick employees wanted to work; or that the inhabitants of the area, who had their streets and gardens trampled by 'committed' hooligans and covered in filth, loathed and feared the invaders; or that the courts steadfastly supported the management. The object was to win by force: mob politics.

What killed the campaign was TV. For TV showed millions of horrified viewers, day after day, what the Grunwick workers and the people who lived nearby were having to put up with; and the message eventually got through to James Callaghan in Downing Street, who then used all the arm-twisting techniques at which he is a master, to halt the campaign. The message went back: 'Don't frighten the voters. If you want to do that sort of thing, wait until after the election.'

Not, I hasten to add, that Callaghan is a believer in 'counting heads' democracy; no 'populist' he. Tammany Jim is a man of the machine, the caucus, the quiet talk behind closed doors, the little deal behind the Speaker's Chair. He has inherited, and improved upon, Harold Wilson's notion of making Labour 'the natural party of government'; and that certainly cannot be done by democratic means. What Callaghan has been doing, and encouraging his cabinet colleagues to help him to do, has been to transfer as many areas of power as possible from elective institutions to non-elective ones, controlled by ministers.

A small but very significant example is what has been happening on the 'regional water authorities'. Most people will have noticed a huge increase in their water rates this year. This follows a decision by the Department of the Environment, under which local councils, which used to collect sewerage charges themselves, are no longer allowed to do so. Instead the charge is collected by the water authorities, which of course are non-elective. This switch of taxation from an elective to a non-elective body − which itself costs £10 million just to 'administer' − means that ordinary people have absolutely no sanction against overcharging (water authority charges themselves have been rising on average by 16 per cent a year). They cannot sack the members of the water authorities because they are appointed and removed solely by ministers.

The water authority scandal is only one example of the manner in which more and more important activities are being shifted outside the aegis of our constitution, beyond the control of the elective Parliament, and into the hands of secretive, irresponsible bodies, whose members are hired and fired by ministers under no control whatever. Water authorities are, of course, Quangos. They are a tiny part of a huge and rapidly growing system of government patronage which, as its extent and details become known, can fairly be called the biggest scandal in Britain today.

I first heard the word 'Quango' at a political conference in Australia, and, finding it a useful term, brought it back to Britain. It stands for 'Quasi-Autonomous Non-Governmental Organisations'. They are quasi-autonomous because, in effect, they are subject to no parliamentary control; they have to operate within their statutory authority, and the ministers can harass them; otherwise they are on their own. They are non-governmental because they are not ministers or civil servants.

The point about not being ministers is important, because it means they are not subject to the numerical and financial limitations which − thank God! − prevent a Labour prime minister from putting every single member of the Parliamentary Labour Party on the 'payroll vote'. They can thus, in practice, be created and expanded at the whim of the minister. And this is exactly what has been happening.

I used to think that the Quango scandal was a comparatively minor problem, to be tackled chiefly under its 'Jobs-for-the-Boys' aspect. But in recent months Mr Philip Holland, MP for Carlton, has been making a determined, and increasingly successful, effort to drag the truth out of ministers − and we can now discern a growing threat to constitutional government and the democratic process.

Of course, there is no doubt about the 'jobs-for-the-boys' aspect. The amount of political patronage in this country (excluding committees and, of course, excluding civil servants) is simply enormous − much greater than it was in the heyday of Whig corruption. If Sir Robert Walpole were to make a tour of the Quango scene, he would emerge a very envious fellow. For instance, some 16 cabinet ministers appoint 17,944 members to some 765 bodies. A great majority of these are unpaid or part-timers, but the total emoluments still tot up to £8,983,000. The Prime Minister, in addition, appoints (or rather advises the Queen to appoint) 66 members to 20 bodies, at a cost of £756,000 in pay, and this is in addition to ministerial, ecclesiastical and Civil Service appointments, 13 academic appointments not paid from public funds, and the governor, deputy governor and directors of the Bank of England.

In one year alone, up to May 1977, ministers made 1,113 appointments. How many of these are genuine Quangos is hard to discover. We are in one of the great arcane areas of government operations, whose secrets are much more enthusiastically preserved by Labour ministers than those of the Ministry of Defence. The key text is the 'Directory of Paid Public Appointments Made by Ministers'. But this has two limitations. It does not give the names of the Quango-holders, and as it was published in 1976 it is now hopelessly out of date. It will be interesting to see if the Government can be bullied into reissuing it, updated, before the election. There is also the 'List of Members of Public Boards'. This actually gives names, but only of those boards described as 'of a commercial character', and it is accurate only up to April 1, 1977. Any further facts have to be extracted by skilful use of parliamentary question time.

What does emerge is that the Quango system is expanding very rapidly. Mr Holland calculates, at a rough guess, that there are 900 true Quangos, costing the public £20 million a year (pay plus expenses). But they are increasing all the time. The system in no way reflects the cuts in other forms of government expenditure: quite the reverse. Quangos breed Quangos, and they are themselves in constant osmotic expansion. Thus the Central Arbitration Committee of the Advisory, Conciliation and Arbitration Service, set up under Labour's Employment Protection Act of 1975, and one of the most sinister institutions in the country, had in 1976 a chairman (parttime, paid £6,625), a deputy chairman and a panel of 25 members. By November 1977, it had expanded to a chairman, 18 deputy chairmen and 63 members (including Mick McGahey), all of them paid.

Again, take the Price Commission, another sinister body (set up by Ted Heath). In 1976 it had a chairman (full-time, £16,580), a part-time deputy chairman on £7,548, two part-time members on £3,432 and three on £1,716. It has since expanded to a chairman (£18,000), three part-time deputy-chairmen on £6,500 each, and 12 part-time members at £3,600. Thus the number of 'jobs' has increased from 6 to 16 and the cost to the public, salaries alone, from £34,424 to £80,700.

Who benefits from the Quango system? The Tories believe that the bias is increasingly towards the Left since, with Labour making the choice, any Tories appointed are usually of Peter Simple's Jeremy Cardhouse breed; 'impartial' academics usually turn out to have a long record of service to 'progressive' causes, and industrialists tend to be mesmerised by Labour's reckless use of the honours systems, of which (naturally) Quango-holders are the prime beneficiaries. Be that as it may, it is impossible to quantify the political bias because the full information is not yet (and if Tammany Jim has any choice in the matter never will be) available.

What can be said is that certain people have done rather well. On May 2 this year Mr Holland asked the Employment Secretary if he would list the full-time occupation and part-time government appointments held by each part-time member of Acas. In a written reply the Department's Minister of State, Mr Harold Walker, said he had no complete records. But some interesting facts emerged.

As one might expect, the Old Emperor himself, described in *Hansard* as 'Mr J. L. Jones, CH, MBE, retired from full-time occupation', tops the poll (as of May 2, 1978). In addition to membership of Acas, the Minister said Mr Jones was also: member, UK National Commission for Unesco; deputy chairman, National Ports Council; member, Iron and Steel Advisory Committee; member, National Economic Development Council; member, Overseas Labour Consultative Committee; member, EEC Economic and Social Committee; member, British Overseas Trade Board; member, Anglo-German Foundation for the Study of Industrial Society; member, Board of the Crown Agents; member, National Advisory Council on Employment of Disabled People; and member, Royal Commission on Criminal Procedure. (After the publication of this list, Mr Jones announced that he was no longer a member of five of these bodies and would shortly retire from two more).

No one, so far as the information goes, can quite match Jones's 13 Quangos. But his old deputy, Harry Irwin, has nine, Hugh Scanlon has five and Sir George Smith, general secretary of the Union of Construction, Allied Trades and Technicians, has a healthy seven.

The actual chairman of the Central Arbitration Committee, Professor J. C. Wood, CBE, described in *Hansard* as the Professor of Law, Sheffield University (this presumably means his full-time occupation), is also a strong performer, since he is chairman of the Boot and Shoe Repairing Wages Council, chairman of the Laundry Wages Council, chairman of the Licensed Residential Establishments and Licensed Restaurant Wages Council, chairman of the Road Haulage Wages Council; member, Legal Studies Board, Council for National Academic Awards; member, Review of the Police Negotiating Machinery; member, ILO Committee of Experts on the Application of Conventions and Recommendations; member, Committee of Enquiry on Police Pay; and finally member, Mental Health Review Tribunal – a total score of 11.

The shameless manner in which these boards have been allowed to proliferate is not the most serious aspect of the matter. Many of them have judicial or quasi-judicial functions. That is, they interpret, lay down, administer and enforce the law. They do so on an evergrowing scale. Thus Industrial Tribunals increased from an average daily number of 57 in 1976 to an average daily number of 77 last year. This figure has certainly since risen substantially. Each has a legal chairman and two lay members. The Lord Chancellor and the Department of Employment jointly select the legal members, but the Department selects the other two and it pays all three. What has happened to the independence of the judiciary? These are very important courts, but they have much more in common with Star Chamber or the other prerogative courts than a constitutional court.

Moreover, they are not the only ones: a huge and growing number of boards – many set up by Labour since 1974 – act partly as courts, despite the fact that ministers alone select their members and pay their salaries. This return to prerogative 'justice' is the greatest assault upon the rule of law in Britain since the days of Charles I. It is not surprising that it should have accelerated under a Government whose members insult the judges and underpay the police.

No doubt the instinct of Margaret Thatcher, faced with the Quango scandal, is to do what Malcolm Fraser did in Australia, when he came to power after the disastrous Whitlam Government – sack the lot. Fraser's massacre of the Quango system set up a fearful wailing among Labour's placemen and Australia's Legion of the Great and Good; but it does not seem to have done the slightest harm to Australia, and it is a tempting example to follow. Alas, Tories like patronage, too, and Mrs Thatcher is under strong pressure from some colleagues not to throw away the goodies which she, and they, will need in power. In any case, some of the boards (perhaps a quarter) are undoubtedly necessary and many Quangos are perfectly' legitimate.

But the least Mrs Thatcher can do, and what she undoubtedly will do, is to bring the system back under democratic control by ensuring that a parliamentary committee – and it must be an experienced and tough committee – has the power to scrutinise and if needs be veto ministerial appointments. This will be the first step in dismantling the monstrous system of patronage and seizing back some of the territory lost to democracy in recent years.

Indeed, one important theme I expect to see developed by Mrs Thatcher during the coming campaign is 'Back to Democracy'. It matters little whether she and those who think like her are called 'populists' or no. Power has been slipping away from the people because Labour activists do not trust them; and political activism itself is profoundly anti-popular, since it tends to give the people exactly the opposite of what they want. Two outstanding areas where this can be demonstrated are housing and employment protection.

In housing, doctrinaire political activism has inflicted enormous injury on the ordinary working people of Britain by insisting, over three decades, that the sale of council houses to tenants was a cardinal sin against socialism. Council tenants have thus been wholly deprived of the right to make the capital gain of owning and selling a property – probably the only chance most of them have ever had of acquiring a significant sum of money for their old age, or indeed saving at all. Labour is now weakening on this point, but the damage has been done.

Moreover, it continues to inflict bad housing on the poor by passing restrictionist statutes, which reflect the venom of Labour militants but do not have the effect intended (often the opposite). One of the worst pieces of legislation ever to be enacted by Parliament was Labour's 1974 Rent Act, which broadly speaking, extended the anti-landlord provisions of unfurnished to furnished accommodation.

A study published in the June issue of the *Economic Journal* by Duncan Maclennan, on the effects of the Act in Glasgow (a key area it was intended to benefit), shows that it actually reduced the availability of rented accommodation, and so increased homelessness. The position would have been even worse had landlords not been able to change the nature of the tenancy, and so escape the Act's provisions:

If the 1974 Rent Act was intended to discourage private renting further, it can be said to have been an unequivocal success . . . furnished sector tenants, at least in Glasgow, are trapped between the effects of the Rent Act and intransigent policies on municipal letting . . . it is already clear that formal attempts to reduce landlord power result in supply reduction, increasing excess demand, and may increase the actual power which landlords have over their tenants.

Now the interesting thing is that no one in the Labour Government took the trouble to discover whether tenants of furnished accommodation actually wanted the Act. That, brothers, is definitely *not* what Labour Government is about. The political activists wanted the Act, political activism demanded it; and so the Act was passed. The fact that the tenants suffered in consequence does not enter into Labour calculations because class warfare must come first.

Much the same could be said of the Employment Protection Act, another scandalous piece of Stalinist legislation. The evidence piles up daily that it is actually increasing unemployment, since the sheer weight of the legal and financial responsibilities it thrusts upon employers, to say nothing of the legal terrorism of its Industrial Tribunal system, deters them from taking on labour, and encourages them to get rid of it at the first opportunity. In Liverpool now there is even a proposal to suspend the operations of the Act in a desperate effort to cut the dole queues. Ordinary people, so far as we know, did not want this Act; but it was willed by the trade union bosses and the Labour militant elite, and it was therefore drummed through Parliament and enforced with total ferocity.

The same analysis applies to two other industrial issues, of great importance, which now face us: workers' share in management, and worker-participation in shareholdings. On both, there is a democratic answer and an undemocratic answer. The undemocratic answer on worker-control, as adumbrated by the infamous Bullock

Report, would effectively give the right to appoint worker-directors to the trade union bureaucracy, and so strengthen still further the powers and privileges of this unrepresentative oligarchy. The democratic answer would allow all the people at the workplace freely and fairly to elect their own worker-directors for the factory.

Again, on worker-shareholding, the undemocratic answer, demanded by the trade union bosses, is for all the worker-shares to be 'held centrally' and 'administered' by the trade union bureaucracy. The democratic answer is for each worker to hold shares in the company which employs him, and actually be given the bits of paper into his hands.

What is remarkable is that, on a growing number of such questions, where the rights and future of ordinary people are at stake, it is the Conservative Party which is now firmly taking the democratic line, and it is the Labour oligarchs, placemen and militants who are resisting it. Perhaps the Tories ought now to call themselves the Democratic Party. It is an idea worth considering, for the cleavage goes right across the spectrum of political issues, and it marks a great watershed in British political history. That is why the forthcoming general election is so serious.

Travelling around Britain, one is conscious of a faint, if still sluggish, stirring of the economy. After four years of Labour stagnation, we actually got 2 per cent growth (at an annual rate) in the first quarter of this year – a sign that Callaghan and Healey are doing their cynical best to engineer some sort of a pre-election boom. A recent political-economic model of the United Kingdom, devised by Bruno S. Frey and Friedrich Schneider, shows the arithmetic of the Cabinet's motivation.

A rise in the rate of inflation by 1 per cent, they found, reduces the Government's Gallup Poll lead by 0.6 per cent; an increase in unemployment by 1 per cent reduces the Government's lead by 6 per cent. Conversely, an increase in the growth rate of disposable real income by 1 per cent increases the lead by about 0.8 per cent. Hence: 'If the Government's lead falls below a critical level, policy instruments are used in an expansionary fashion, i.e., expenditures are raised while taxes are reduced.'

This is the thinking behind Healey's Budget and other measures. The Bank of England's latest *Quarterly Bulletin* refers to 'a clearly abnormal increase in real incomes'. Abnormal? I'll say: it's election year. Average earnings are now rising at an annual rate of 14 per cent against price rises of 7 per cent.

This degrading little operation, which must mean future inflation and unemployment, and is designed solely to save the seats and jobs of Labour politicians, is being financed by the pre-emption of North Sea Oil – so Labour 'option papers' about what we are to do with the oil money are academic; it is already being spent, hand over Healey's fist. Here is one final example of how Labour governs in the interests of Labour activists and oligarchs rather than the common people. And that is one further reason why the coming election will be, above all, about the future of our democracy, and the constitutional rule of law in Britain.

CHAPTER 10

Britain's own Road to Serfdom

In the autumn of 1978 there were still many timorous voices urging the Conservative leadership that the party could not hope to win an election unless it renounced any desire to curb the power of the unions. In my address to the Conservative Political Centre meeting, held during the party conference in October, I argued that a future Conservative government would have no choice but to fight union power.

It is commonly, and unthinkingly, supposed that the extinction of democracy and individual freedom in this country could only be achieved as a result of military defeat and foreign conquest, or by a political coup organised by totalitarian forces. Not so. There is a far more insidious and specifically British road to serfdom – and we are following it. That road consists of the gradual relinquishment of control by the democratic and parliamentary process, and its replacement by self-perpetuating oligarchies.

Now it may seem paradoxical to speak of the relinquishment of parliamentary control at a time when some refer, and rightly refer, to the 'elective dictatorship' of Parliament. This is a phrase used by Lord Hailsham in his recent and admirable little book on our troubles (*The Dilemma of Democracy*); and I agree with it. But the two notions are not in conflict: on the contrary – they are part of the same process. Lord Hailsham is right to claim that parliamentary sovereignty cannot, and should not, be absolute, since there can be no constitutional authority whatever for legislation which overrides our natural sense of right and wrong. But I would add that absolute parliamentary sovereignty must be, *a fortiori*, restricted when the House of Commons is itself unrepresentative and is manifestly defying the democratic will.

Our country, our constitution and our Parliament have been immeasurably damaged, over the past four years and more, by the perpetuation of a government which has no true democratic mandate. The present Labour Government began life as a minority government in the spring of 1974. It achieved a tiny Commons majority in the autumn of that year, soon lost in calamitous by-election defeats.

But even at the 1974 high point in its fortunes, it only secured the votes of 29 per cent of the electorate. It nevertheless proceeded to pass a series of highly contentious, class-combative and destructive Acts of Parliament. These include, to name only four, the Trade Union Acts of 1974 and 1976, the 1974 Rent Act and the 1975 Employment Protection Act. These Acts have inflicted serious damage on our economy and in some cases on our liberties. All are unpopular. Not one of them − and there are half a dozen more in the same category − could conceivably have received public endorsement in a referendum. Yet they have become the law of the land, and they have been enforced with enthusiastic venom.

Since then the Labour Government has lost its majority. But it has ignored repeated defeats in Parliament. It has proceeded to govern, using its executive powers to the full − well, indeed, beyond the traditional spirit of the constitution − with the assistance of various fringe parties, which have nothing in common with Labour, or indeed with each other, beyond a well-justified fear of facing their electors. Mr Callaghan, in a recent address to the nation, characterised by cynical mendacity and a manifest contempt for parliamentary democracy, indicated that this process would continue. We are now, therefore, entering the fifth year in which the composition of the House of Commons and, still more, the attitudes, philosophy and conduct of the Government, are wholly out of touch with the democratic nation.

This is, in itself, serious and destructive. It indicates, for one thing, that the Labour Party is losing faith in democracy. It no longer wants to play the democratic game according to the rules, in their spirit or even in their letter. The new, anti-democratic mood of the party was summed up at last year's party conference in a striking piece of Newspeak: 'We believe,' said a member of the party's national executive, 'in the Democracy of the Committed.' Of course the speaker does not believe in democracy at all. He believes in oligarchy – an oligarchy of political zealots and activists who impose their fanatical views on the rest of the population by their ability to manipulate the democratic machinery. All men are equal, but the Committed are more equal than others.

There is in this new Labour Party a deep, bitter and growing distrust of ordinary people. This distrust is born, of course, of Labour's declining share in the popular vote, harrowing by-election defeats and the loss of former strongholds in local government. But it is born, most of all, of Labour's manifest and overwhelming failure to make its collectivist policies attractive. In an ideological sense, the British working class has rejected Labour, and the Labour fanatics resent it. They feel that the workers are not worthy of them and therefore must be 'guided' into worthiness. Hence the 'Democracy of the Committed'. It is this hatred of ordinary people born of rejection which is the emotional foundation of the new fascist Left.

Unfortunately, Labour's retreat from democracy coincides with the operation of other forces in our society which are moving strongly in the direction of oligarchy. Since the early sixties, and particularly in the last four years, there has been an explosion in the executive power and patronage of ministers. There has been a rapid and uncontrolled growth of bodies, and government employees, virtually outside the control of Parliament, and subject largely to the personal *diktat* of Labour ministers.

Last month, the Civil Service Department published, or rather printed, since it is not on sale and is difficult for the ordinary citizen to obtain, a remarkable document called *Survey of Fringe Bodies*, which it had commissioned a retired civil servant, Mr Gordon Bowen, to prepare. These fringe bodies, or Fribs as I call them, are not, as a rule, the same as Quangos. Many of the largest and most important of them ought to be part of the Civil Service but are not so, because that would mean subjecting them to normal Civil Service controls, and a diminution of direct ministerial power over them.

Hence the growth of Fribs has been accelerating. In 1900 there were only 10. By 1949 there were 84. By 1965 there were 150. By 1975 there were 235. By now there are many more – for the period of this

Labour Government has seen the fastest growth in the Fribs of any time in our history. Unfortunately, Mr Bowen's survey only takes in the figures up to 1975, so the most sinister aspects of the story have not yet been revealed. Even so, the facts of his survey are astonishing. Already, by 1975, the Fribs employed 184,000 people – equal to 25 per cent of the total staff in the Civil Service, industrial and non-industrial. If we exclude defence, the Fribs are equal to 40 per cent of the entire Civil Service. We have thus, in effect, acquired a second bureaucracy, already nearly half the size of the official one, and much more susceptible to direct ministerial influence and patronage.

This sinister *doppelgänger* of the Whitehall bureaucracy is spending money, most of it from the taxpayer, on a colossal and growing scale. Even in 1974-5, total expenditure by Fribs was £2,367 million. How much is it now? I do not know. That is something Conservative Members of Parliament must use the Commons mechanism to find out – and they will discover it is exceedingly difficult. In 1975, for instance, the principal Fribs controlled by the Department of Employment, namely the Manpower Services Commission, the Employment Service Agency, the Training Services Agency and Remploy Limited, and the Industrial Training Boards, spent over £350 million. Now these agencies are the means whereby the Labour Government, in its desperation, seeks to perform cosmetic surgery on the unemployment figures, and if there is one area where Frib activity has been increased, in numbers of employees and, above all in money spent, it is this one. I would guess that this group of Fribs are now spending well over half a billion pounds a year, and quite possibly more.

How is a Frib created? It is the easiest thing in the world. Of course, you can create one by an Act of Parliament, with all the opportunities for public exposure, detailed debate and reasoned amendment thereby offered. Many Fribs are so created. But as the report says, 'The simplest way in which a fringe body can be established is a Minister's Administrative Act.' All he has to do is to make known his decision to set up the Frib, and he does not even have to do this by a statement in Parliament. In fact no less than 27 Fribs have been set up by Minister's Administrative Act.

And what a rich field of patronage follows! In 1975, no less than 171 chairmen of Fribs, many of whom get large full- or part-time salaries and enjoy pension rights and compensation for loss of office, were appointed by ministers. The Prime Minister appoints 18 himself and in addition, through the Queen, a further 16. And what about the members of the boards, of whom there are thousands? 'In almost all instances,' says the report, 'board members are appointed by the responsible minister.'

This is not merely patronage, it is power – power beyond the dreams of Whig avarice! Where, in the 18th century, men like Walpole and the Duke of Newcastle handled scores, or at the very most a couple of hundred jobs, the Labour bosses deal in thousands. And what we have here is not merely a question of 'jobs-for-the-boys'. What is, perhaps, the most serious aspect of the matter is that many of the proliferating Quango boards have judicial or quasi-judicial functions. That is, they interpret, lay down, administer and enforce the law. And they are doing so on an ever-increasing scale. Thus, Industrial Tribunals expanded from an average daily number of 57 in 1976 to an average daily number of 77 last year. This figure has almost certainly since risen substantially. Each has a legal chairman and two lay members. The Lord Chancellor and the Department of Employment jointly select the legal member, but the Department selects the other two, and it pays the stipends of all three. What has happened to the independence of the judiciary? These are very important courts, which can have an enormous impact on the lives of individuals, and indeed on the welfare of firms employing thousands. But they have more in common with Star Chamber, and the other prerogative courts abolished by Parliament in the 1640s, than with a constitutional court.

I am alarmed to see that the Lord Chancellor, far from taking steps to bring these courts properly within the judicial safeguards of our constitutional system, is actually planning to enlarge their scope. According to a report in *The Times* last month, he is preparing to make use of the powers given him under the iniquitous Employment Protection Act to give Industrial Tribunals jurisdiction to hear claims from employees related to breaches of their contract of employment. And there is a collateral proposal, or at any rate a speculation, that employees going before a tribunal in such circumstances will be entitled to the full resources of the legal aid scheme – at present they can get only £25-worth of free legal advice in an Industrial Tribunal case.

It is no reflection on those who sit on Industrial Tribunals to say that many employers have no confidence in the whole system which they regard as part of the class-warfare being waged against management by the Labour Government. To extend the jurisdiction of the courts, and to make recourse to them cheap and easy, will inevitably be seen as a further blow aimed at management. Some people, and I am one of them, believe that the savagery of the Employment Protection Act and the Industrial Tribunals it brought into existence, actually deters firms, especially small firms from taking on labour — and thus is a source of unemployment.

Here, then, is a case where Quangos are not merely expensive, but do actual harm to the economy. It would be very interesting to get more evidence of the impact of Quangos and Fribs on our lives. But the whole subject is submerged in an obscurity which ministers find particularly convenient. What, you may ask, is the difference between a Frib and a Quango? There is no difference of an absolute nature. Some can be classified as both, or either. Generally the Quangos are smaller, employ fewer people, and spend less money. On the other hand, they often enjoy judicial or quasi-judicial powers — itself an affront to our notion that the judiciary is completely independent of the executive. And jobs on Quangos often carry great prestige. But both systems have grown up so fast, and on such a scale, and in such an atmosphere of secrecy, and with so little parliamentary supervision, that ministers can hide behind and within the sheer complexity of the monsters they have created. But, though it *is* possible to distinguish between Fribs and Quangos, the things they have in common are perhaps more important. Both types are very largely outside the control of Parliament. Both enormously enhance ministerial power and patronage. And both are the means whereby the ruling elites of the country can be corrupted and reconciled to the oligarchic principle.

Now this brings me to the trade unions. In a recent attack on Margaret Thatcher, Mr Michael Foot accused her of being in the clutches of a mad professor, Professor Hayek. I must say, I would not describe Mr Michael Foot himself as being an outstanding example of rationality, or even sheer sanity. He says that Professor Hayek is mad because he 'hates free institutions'. And by free institutions, Mr Foot means, it turns out, the British trade unions. Mr Foot is a consummate political humbug, but for the minister who

forced through Parliament legislation which is universalising the
closed shop to identify free institutions with British trade unions is,
even by Mr Foot's standards, an outstanding piece of impudent and
sanctimonious hypocrisy. I don't think even Jim Callaghan could
beat it.

Now it is perfectly true that at one time the unions might have been
classified as a check on the executive. They might once have been
seen as a countervailing power to the overweening might and arrogance of central government. But this is true no longer. The huge
growth of government patronage, the proliferation of the system of
Fribs and Quangos, have in effect destroyed the independence of the
trade union movement. Of all the ruling elites in Britain, the one
which has benefited most from the workings of Fribs and Quangos is
the group of big trade union bureaucrats. How can a union official
be said to be independent when he sits, by ministerial appointment,
and subject to ministerial removal, on half a dozen public boards,
and earns several thousand pounds a year thereby – possibly much
more? If an MP's independence is assumed to be undermined by his
holding an office of profit under the crown, why should a trade
union boss be immune? Is it supposed that all trade union bosses are
sea-green incorruptible? Are any?

By dint of careful parliamentary questioning, Mr Phillip Holland
MP has begun to discover the sheer scale of the trade union involve-
ment in government patronage. I name no names. I don't think there
are any particular villains. The trade union bureaucrats as a whole
have accepted the system, and wallow in it. Indeed, they quarrel with
each other if they don't get their fair turn at the trough. In May 1978,
past and present officials of one union were reckoned to have 27 state
appointments between them. A single union boss had 13 at one time;
another had, or has, 9, a third 8. Two officials of one big union hold
11 between them. And in 1977, according to government figures, 39
members of the TUC General Council held the grand total of no less
than 180 state jobs. These are not jobs for which particular qualifications are demanded – more's the pity. They are not jobs filled by
competitive examination, or by a rigorous process of selection by independent commissions. They are sheer, old-fashioned, Whig
personal patronage, of the most shameless and oligarchic kind. And
the manner in which they are filled is destructive alike of personal independence and the national interest.

But unfortunately, the integration of the trade union bosses with the oligarchical system of government patronage corresponds to the deepest instincts of these gentlemen. After all, they are oligarchs themselves. They have, themselves, for many years operated in their own unions oligarchical systems of which they are the principal beneficiaries. With one or two rare exceptions, British trade unions have nothing to do with democracy. They are not free institutions. They are bureaucratic machines, operating on a self-perpetuating basis. For one thing, they often elect their highest officials for life — a procedure known elsewhere only to Latin-American dictators and African tyrants. And such life-term officials are usually elected by less than 25 per cent of the members — sometimes by less than 10 per cent — in a process whereby the self-perpetuating machine simply turns out the vote in the big factories. Public campaigning, press publicity, TV and radio appearances — all the campaigning activities we associate with democracy — are discouraged, in some cases forbidden and severely punished.

Far from being free institutions, British trade unions, with some notable exceptions, are organisations where true freedom of discussion is virtually banned. To question the nature, practices and performance of the union and its bosses can be an offence under its rules. A typical rule book allows the union's bureaucrats to expel any member guilty of what it calls 'conduct whether in connection with [the union], the trade, or otherwise, which is, in the opinion of the committee, directly or indirectly detrimental to the interests, welfare or reputation of the union'. An examination of the rule books of 80 unions, representing 94 per cent of the TUC's general membership, found that 66 rule books contained a clause of this kind.

And, remember, these days, under the closed shop regime, expulsion means instant loss of employment without compensation or legal redress — even without, if some Labour ministers had their way, unemployment pay or supplementary benefits. Thus huge power over the lives and happiness of individual men and women is vested in tiny, irresponsible oligarchies. It is the very essence of the British trade union system.

And of course the union oligarchies need this power to inspire fear. They do not want any barrack-room lawyers on *their* patch. They have too much to hide. A recent investigation by Christopher Story of the annual financial returns filed by trade unions reveals a horrifying tale. The unions are getting very rich, at the expense of their members. The income of the 25 unions investigated by Mr Story rose from £62 million in 1974 to nearly £110 million in 1977 − a whopping increase of 76.5 per cent − financed very largely by a huge, 90 per cent increase in members' subscriptions, an increase, over the four-year period, much higher than the inflation rate.

The true story cannot be told, for the filing regulations, laid down by the Labour Government, are so lax as to permit the concealment of huge sums of money. But it cannot be too strongly emphasised that British unions, with some exceptions, are run in the interests of their bureaucrats, not their members. Some unions pay out no benefits at all, others trivial sums. In many big unions the amount paid out in benefits is much less than 10 per cent of subscriptions − sometimes as low as 2 or 3 per cent. Often, benefits paid to members are less than financial benefits received by full-time officials. Thus in 1975, the cost of privileged mortgages to the officials of one public service union was £259,308 − the benefits paid out to members only £148,390. Union bureaucrats have never had it so good. They shower upon themselves brand-new office blocks, cars and chauffeurs, holiday homes and every kind of tax-free perk. It is significant that, of total expenditure by these 25 unions last year, nearly 70 per cent went on 'administrative expenses' − that is, on the bureaucrats and their system − and only 8.2 per cent went on benefits to members. The union bureaucrats, in fact, are a parasitic oligarchy, feasting on the British working class.

But they show no sense of shame when such facts are published. On the contrary: they ignore these investigations, or denounce them as a lying conspiracy, 'got up by the press' and by 'the enemies of the working class'. They are totally single-minded in their pursuit of power. Their next major objective is undoubtedly the fulfilment of the proposals laid down in the infamous Bullock Report, which might be described as a blueprint for massive extension of the oligarchical principle and the naked reality of the corporate state. The Bullock Report would effectively give the right to appoint 50 per cent of the worker-directors, in all large and medium-sized British private-sector firms, to the trade union bureaucracy, who would, of course, pick these unelected oligarchs from among their own numbers − and so strengthen still further the powers and privileges of this unrepresentative group. It is said that the Bullock Report is too outrageous to be implemented. Don't you believe it. It has the support of the trade union bosses, and if one thing is certain, should the Labour Party win the forthcoming election with a working majority, it is that these proposals will be made into law. What is equally likely, in my view, is that parallel proposals for workers' participation in shareholdings, under which all worker-shares would be 'held centrally' and 'administered' by the trade union bureaucracy, would also be enacted as legislation should Labour win at the polls.

And would the process stop there? It would not. I have already pointed out that the union bosses reject detailed and documented criticism of their anti-democratic behaviour as a 'conspiracy of the press'. But they are not content with this accusation. They intend to do something about it. Proposals for 'controlling the media' are already floating around the Labour Party. They are in fact foreshadowed in the Labour Government's recent White Paper on broadcasting. The trade union oligarchs would go very much further. Last year, Moss Evans, who succeeded Jack Jones as the most powerful man in the trade union movement, made detailed proposals for censorship of the press. He asked for a 'code of objectivity' to 'govern presentation of news and opinion', together with what he was pleased to call 'a means of policing and enforcing any such publicly agreed criteria'. He added, speaking on behalf of the union bosses: 'Our standpoint therefore is clear. The public' − by which of course he means the trade union bureaucracy − 'are entitled to protection from abuse of this power to influence it. Those who possess these powers must be required to exercise them within the terms of an "operator's licence". The qualification for holding such a licence must be the acceptance of clearly defined standards of responsibility and accountability.' What are these to be? 'TUC policy has already defined the instruments necessary to the attainment of these ends.'

Now the last sentence is perhaps the key one. Although the 'public' is dragged in to provide some kind of specious democratic justification for this insolent proposal to censor the press, in fact the public is to play no part in the decision-making process. Nor, you will note, is Parliament. No: Mr Evans is arrogantly emphatic: 'TUC policy has already defined the instruments necessary'. It is the union bosses, and the union bosses alone, who will determine how our free press is to be destroyed.

But this is only part, is it not, of the general contempt the oligarchs have for the parliamentary process and the principle of universal suffrage? Censoring the press is a practical example of how 'the Democracy of the Committed' would work. But it is not the only one. The oligarchical, anti-democratic spirit is gradually taking over the Labour Party and the trade union movement. It expresses itself in the manner in which long-serving Labour MPs, whose own belief in parliamentary democracy is unquestionable, are turned out of their seats by tiny conspiracies of left-wing fascists. It expresses itself in the way organised mobs – sometimes paid mobs – are used in an attempt to overturn majority votes, as in the Grunwick affair. Most of all, it expresses itself in the brutal, impudent and increasingly shameless refusal to accept electoral verdicts.

We had a foretaste of this in the illegal determination of many trade union bosses to destroy the Conservative Industrial Relations Act, which was passed by a democratically elected parliamentary majority. Since those days, the position has grown steadily more serious. The closed shop legislation, and its savage enforcement, has led to a rapid extension of unionism, especially in the public sector and above all among civil servants and local government employees. There is now a growing demand, among the bureaucrats of Civil Service and local government unions, that they be allowed to participate in the formation of policy, and its execution. We have already seen, in some hospitals, attempts by those who claim to represent the lower-paid workers to determine hospital policy, even at its highest levels – including the medical levels – and corresponding attempts to destroy those hospitals, when these unconscionable claims have been resisted. We have also seen, following Conservative successes in the local elections this year, attempts by militant members of local government unions to resist, by the use of the strike weapon, the legitimate plans of Conservative councils to put through the policies for which they were elected.

We have here, then, in embryo, a claim on the part of the union oligarchs to have and exercise a veto on the democratic process itself. According to the view of these men – and it is a view spreading rapidly among the public sector union militants – the verdict of the electors is not decisive. Not at all. It is merely the basis for a discussion, in which they have the right to participate. This claim has already been put forward at the local government level. How long will it be before it is put forward at the parliamentary level?

In fact, has it not already been put forward? We had the spectacle, last month, of the Trade Union Congress behaving like a Labour election rally, with David Basnett, its president, openly, vociferously and brazenly committing the whole resources of the unions to securing a Labour victory. This is a new and most sinister development. For if institutional trade union power is to be flung openly into the scales on behalf of Labour, what is the corollary, when Labour loses? It is that trade union power, as exercised by its oligarchs, and irrespective of the wishes of its members, will be flung openly, systematically − and in the end violently − against any Conservative government, or indeed against a government of *any* complexion which does not receive the endorsement of the union bosses.

This is the negation of democracy. This is the rejection of universal suffrage, the denial of the elective principle and the repudiation of the very notion of a representative Parliament. It is in fact the high road to the one-party state.

It is sometimes said that the country can no longer afford to elect a Conservative government, for fear of a devastating conflict with the unions. It is likewise said, as a consequence of this fear, that the Conservatives must trim their sails accordingly, modify and tone down their programme and beliefs, and so cobble together a series of attitudes and proposals which will satisfy the union oligarchs and receive their contemptuous stamp or approval. But this is arrant and indefensible cowardice. It is appeasement in its most naked and shameful form. It is total and unconditional surrender to the very forces which are bent on destroying our democracy and removing freedom from our land.

To accept such an appeaser's argument would, I believe, destroy the Conservative Party, and the two-party system with it. But the chief victim would be the nation as a whole. Those of us in Britain who still believe in democracy, and are prepared to work and fight for it, are not going thus to surrender our responsibilities. We must face the truth, ugly though it is. We *are* travelling down the road to serfdom, in a characteristic British manner, inches at a time, so that it is difficult to determine the speed or even the direction of the movement. But we are travelling nonetheless, and perhaps faster than we realise at present. There *are* forces in our society bent on destroying our freedoms. They are more powerful than they were five years ago; far more powerful than ten years ago. Their aims are clear. *They* are in no doubt as to what they intend to do. *They* have no hesitations, or second thought. You may be sure, *they* will not appease *us*. Are we to allow them to take away our democracy without a struggle?

There can only be one answer. The Conservative Party is now the great — the only — repository of freedom in this country. It is the democratic party; the party of individual freedom, the party of the rule of law. It is the last line of defence we possess. The Conservative Party, when returned to power, must use that power to halt and reverse Britain's march to serfdom. It must use that power responsibly, prudently and wisely. It must not seek controversy and dispute. But it must not run away from either. Above all, it must show courage — the courage to do what it knows to be right, and the courage to fight and overthrow what it knows to be wrong.

CHAPTER 11

Pillars of Society

Early in 1979, with the outcome of the forthcoming election still very much in doubt, I wrote another series of articles for The Sunday Telegraph, *this time examining those traditional underpinnings of social stability − the Civil Service, the law and the church − and finding that their support left a great deal to be desired.*

Not long ago I walked along the Albert Embankment and reached the point, marked by a little wrought-iron bench, from which, as one gazes across the Thames, the full architectural glories of the Houses of Parliament can be seen.

From the customary landward side, Sir Charles Barry's majestic concept is fragmented by the need to incorporate the fourteenth century splendours of Westminster Hall. But from across the river, the audacious symmetry of this classical exercise in Tudor Gothic dominates the horizon, so that towers and pinnacles, roofs, windows, buttressing and every tiny decorative flourish, fall into place within the scheme, and the onlooker is overwhelmed by the relentless power of this monument to democracy and the rule of law.

The river was ice-still; the sky pewter; no one about. It was the day Labour's policy-planners first used the sinister and paradoxical phrase, 'Prolonging the life of Parliament', and I realised that the coming of 1984 might be sooner than I had thought.

How fragile is our free and open society? How easily might it yield to assault from within? It is wrong to see these questions only in political terms. True, Parliament is both the keystone and the canopy of our democratic edifice: once it is captured and demolished, nothing that remains would be much worth preserving. But Parliament does not, and should not, stand alone in protecting us. Society also rests on those great pillars of state which reinforce and underpin the workings of universal suffrage: an objective and incorruptible Civil Service, an independent judiciary and legal system, and the notion of public morality institutionalised in the established Church.

We take these pillars for granted, and that, in one sense, is a measure of their strength. But are we deceived? Are the pillars of society weaker than we had assumed, and incapable, in their decay, of sustaining the confidence we place in them? I have been examining these questions and getting some disturbing answers.

In what is both the most cynical, and most elegant, book on the subject, *The Spirit of British Administration* (1966), Charles Sisson, a poet as well as a bureaucrat, describes the civil servant as 'a man who has been trained to a practical operation . . . nothing less than the preservation of the State'. That, of course, is the object of the British Civil Service. But in a growing number of ways, it now resembles less a sustaining pillar than a juggernaut which has lurched out of control.

The Civil Service, as the pivot of a centralised English monarchy – the first in Europe – goes back to Anglo-Saxon times. As early as 1086, in *Domesday Book*, it produced a demonstration of administrative power of which no other European court was capable. Our Exchequer records go back to 1130, and are continuous after 1154. For more than a millennium English administration successfully maintained an unimpeachable currency – the true test of good government.

But it is only in the past 60 years that bureaucracy has taken over. In mid-Victorian Britain, what Carlyle contemptuously dismissed as 'that Continental nuisance' did not exist. The census of 1851 showed that there were then only 75,000 public employees – against 932,000 in France – the great majority of them working in Customs and Excise and the Post Office. Only 1,628 clerks and officials manned the central departments of civil government. Decisions were taken by politicians.

When the young Queen Victoria asked Lord Palmerston what was meant by 'bureaucratic influence', he told her that this sprang from the loose organisation of Continental regimes, where executive power fell into 'irresponsible hands'. 'In England,' he continued, 'the Ministers who are at the head of the several Departments of the State, are liable any day and every day to defend themselves in Parliament, and in order to do this, they must be minutely acquainted with all the details of the business of their offices, and the only way of being constantly armed with such information is to conduct and direct those details themselves.'

The precise point at which Big Government lurched out of control, and the Civil Service transformed itself into a massive and irresponsible bureaucracy, is impossible to determine. On January 1, 1978, there were no fewer than 737,984 people manning the Civil Service proper. This figure was actually down on 1977, but the drop is almost entirely accounted for by defence cuts. In most cases the civil departments continue to expand. Over the past decade, those employed by Health and Social Security rose from 69,580 to over 96,900, Inland Revenue from 65,020 to 84,962 (it will pass the 90,000-mark in 1979). Home Office from 23,497 to 32,952 and Customs and Excise from 17,806 to 28,845.

In addition to the three-quarters of a million in the Civil Service as such, there were, in 1975, some 235 fringe bodies or Quangos. These organisations employed a further 184,000 people, that is 25 per cent of the Civil Service as a whole.

We have, then, not much under a million civil servants of one kind or another, constituting not only an uncontrollable mass but a powerful political pressure group in its own right. However, the best way to examine the question of control is by looking not at manpower but at expenditure. For all practical purposes, our modern system of government finance was invented by Peel and Gladstone in the mid-nineteenth century. Gladstone rightly perceived that public spending was central to the whole well-being of a nation. 'An excess in the public expenditure,' he said, 'beyond the legitimate wants of the country, is not only a pecuniary waste, but a great political and, above all, a great moral evil. And it is characteristic of the mischiefs that arise from financial prodigality that they creep onwards with a noiseless and stealthy step, that they commonly remain unseen and unfelt until they have reached a magnitude absolutely overwhelming.' (Speech to the House of Commons proposing a Public Accounts Committee, 1861).

The nightmare against which he warned has now overtaken us. The various departments of state have the spending of over £40,000 million of our money, and total public expenditure (including the nationalised sector) rose from £4,582 million in 1946 to nearly £60,000 million in the mid-1970s, at which point it was almost 60 per cent of our gross national product.

Whether there is a critical percentage of GNP at which public expenditure threatens to destroy the economy is debatable. What is certain is that in 1975-6 some kind of magic limit was passed, panic set in, and a bedraggled and humiliated Government went, rattling its begging tin, to the IMF.

Since then, overall cuts in expenditure have been imposed; but there is absolutely no evidence that public disbursements have been brought under fine control. On the contrary, the relative calm of the past two years has been brought about almost entirely by the appearance of North Sea oil in the balance sheet. We are, in brief, living on capital – and all the symptoms of bureaucratic prodigality continue to make their appearance.

The extent and nature of public wastefulness cannot be comprehended by a single intelligence; it can only be illustrated. The Health Service alone bristles with scandals. In November last year the Commons was told that in the 18 months after the 'reorganisation' of the Health Service, the number of administrative and clerical staff increased by 20 per cent, and the middle and higher management grades by a third. The Public Accounts Committee confessed itself unable to understand how the cost of the new Royal Liverpool Hospital rose from £12 million to £50 million, and why it was still three years late; it found the high cost of London's teaching hospitals a mystery, and drew attention to 'large unexplained differences in running costs between these hospitals and others'.

Many of the failures of the public service to give taxpayers value for money spring from the follies of Government and the sheer quantity of badly conceived and badly drafted Bills.

Yet a high proportion of the waste cannot conceivably be blamed on policies and politicians, and must be placed squarely on the shoulders of the Civil Service. Several very senior bureaucrats, both active and retired, have insisted to me in recent weeks that the total amount of taxpayers' money spent cannot be reduced without cutting commitments.

They agree that the public sector is too large − too large, they add, for the talent available, let alone the cash. They agree wholeheartedly that spending must be cut. Where, therefore − they ask − is policy to be changed? They are adamant that cash-cuts can only reflect cuts in services. This, of course, is the line they have sold successive governments, including this one, over the past 20 years. But it is false; and demonstrably false. Let us take one example.

In 1967 Leslie Chapman, a senior civil servant in the Ministry of Works (now the Property Services Agency), was appointed regional director for the south of England. He was very experienced, very cost-conscious and, best of all, very determined. He resolved to carry out a detailed survey of all the depots for which he was responsible, with a view to cutting down maintenance and, if possible, other costs.

The knack, he found by experience, was never to take documents or statements on trust, and never to be fobbed off with such phrases as 'general maintenance work' or 'routine maintenance work', which he found were universally employed to justify the existence of scores of highly paid craftsmen and the spending of thousands of pounds in materials. He discovered that it was only by employing experts in the various trades, to make specific and detailed investigations of what was going on in their respective disciplines, that the true nature of waste could be exposed. His first proper survey, of the Royal Army Ordnance Corps Depot at Bicester, Oxfordshire, revealed that a third of the maintenance costs, and as much as half the direct labour force employed, could be saved immediately. This survey became the basis for others, and eventually the region cut £3.5 million from an original budget of £10 million.

Mr Chapman cut direct labour from 4,000 to 2,000, without any ascertainable reduction in performance. He saved £30,000 a year by abolishing the car service and getting staff to use their own. He sold off as much land as he was allowed and, in some cases, simply knocked surplus buildings down, thus saving the cost of maintenance: 'For the delicate surgery of trimming surplus fat from government property holdings, nothing is as effective as a bulldozer.'

He discovered certain laws of administrative folly, one of which he called 'the-do-it-yourself syndrome'. He noted that 'this causes quite rational people to believe that, if the organisation does something itself, it really isn't costing anything at all, and certainly not very much'. In one small area around Aldershot he found civil servants running a gravel pit, a saw-mill, a sign-writing centre, a foundry, joinery and wood-working shops, a machinery maintenance shop, a printing business and nurseries for shrubs and trees. All these jobs could be performed privately for less cost.

The really shocking aspect of Mr Chapman's story is not that he found it possible to save a total of £12 million over a seven-year period in a single region of one comparatively small government department, but that the authorities, when apprised of his new methodology, reacted with indifference, even hostility.

Discouraged, Chapman retired from the service at the end of 1973. Before he left, he wrote to the deputy secretary, Department of Environment, enclosing a fully documented account of the savings scheme, and adding: 'I believe I owe it to the services, and indeed to the tax-paying public . . . to see that these matters and their implications are ventilated and action taken to see that there is no recurrence.' A copy was sent to Sir William Armstrong, then head of the Civil Service. The deputy secretary replied, five months later, saying that he had inquired into the matter: 'Your view was that priority should be given to maintenance economy reviews on the lines you had instituted in your region. What is apparent is that you did not succeed in convincing your colleagues that this was necessarily the most productive approach.'

Sir William's office replied more briefly: 'I write to acknowledge your letter and enclosures of December 20 to Sir William Armstrong. These have been read with interest. Yours sincerely.' Sir William then went on to a life peerage, and the chairmanship of one of the Big Four banks (not mine, I'm glad to say). Mr Chapman went on to write a book called *Your Disobedient Servant*.

Control of public finance is at the very centre of Parliament's history and activities. At times in the past (e.g., the 'Good Parliament' in 1376), the Commons has acted with savagery towards public servants who mishandled the revenues. 'This month ends,' wrote Pepys fearfully in September, 1666, 'with my mind full of government and concernment how this Office will speed with the Parliament, which begins to be mighty severe in the examining our accounts and the expense of the Navy this war.'

Parliament's interest was often drastic, but it tended to be spasmodic, and in 1861 Gladstone created the House of Commons Public Accounts Committee to keep a continuous check. He also created, over a period, the system known as 'Treasury Control', which is subordinate to parliamentary control but is the precursor and concomitant to it.

Under the dual system of Treasury and parliamentary control, public spending is processed in three phases. First, any expenditure requires the prior approval of Parliament, by the vote on the Annual Estimates. Second, Parliament votes the Appropriation Act, which provides the supply for particular purposes. Third, Parliament, through the Comptroller and Auditor-General (at present Sir Douglas Henley) and the Public Accounts Committee, exercises what is called *post-obit* control, to ensure (in theory) that Parliament's instructions have been carried out.

It sounds foolproof. In fact the system has, for all practical purposes, collapsed. At the heart of our public finances, the envy of the world for centuries, there is now the administrative equivalent of a celestial Black Hole into which countless millions vanish.

Part of the blame rests with the Treasury Control method itself. One of its features is that the permanent secretary of each department is also its accounting officer, and personally responsible for clearing its accounts with the Treasury and the PAC. Thus 44 over-burdened men are responsible for accounting for £40,000 million a year. Originally they all served for part of their careers in the Treasury and kept in close touch with it, running the departments for many years. Now they often lack Treasury experience, and anyway are constantly shifted from one department to another, though it takes at least a year for a top official to familiarise himself with a department's accounts. The result is that they are not, and in fairness cannot be, held personally responsible, as the system demands.

But if financial control within departments has broken down, it is improbable that the Treasury, its own historic structure overwhelmed by the growth of public spending, will be able to impose discipline. It is still less likely that the Public Accounts Committee, which is a group of non-professionals unsupported by a staff of accountants, can put matters right. All it can do is to let out occasional bellows of rage. Often, indeed usually, it does not even know the right questions to ask; and it is simply not equipped to pursue a line of inquiry to the point where the real, awful truth begins to emerge.

For this the individual members are in no way to blame. It is, by
Commons standards, a strong committee, and Edward du Cann is an
experienced and exemplary chairman. But both its powers and
resources are totally out of date.

As a result there are enormous areas of government finance into
which PAC investigations are blocked. Edward du Cann complained
bitterly to the Commons on December 4 that, although the National
Enterprise Board and the British National Oil Corporation had
received authority from Parliament to spend a combined total of
£1,600 million in the current year, the Comptroller and Auditor-
General was flatly refused access to their books. Access to the
Housing Corporation's books has also been denied. In the case of the
Crown Agents, the failure to exercise supervision allowed public servants to act illegally for a whole century, and eventually to create a
financial catastrophe.

By comparison with the auditing systems operated by the federal
governments of the United States, Australia and Canada, for instance, ours is grotesquely inadequate and reeks of a period when
government spending was less than £100 million a year.

Reform is resisted in great part because the Labour Party, as a
whole, confuses two quite separate issues: the attempt to avoid waste
and the attempt to cut welfare services. There is, in fact, no connection between the two − or rather it is demonstrable that effective
financial control would make most cuts in welfare services which
even Labour governments are forced, in the end, to impose, wholly
unnecessary.

But emotionally and psychologically Labour MPs (as a rule) cannot bring themselves to tackle public finance at its roots, and even
Tory MPs who are willing to spend the enormous amount of time
and energy required to master the subject often find themselves in
lonely isolation.

Attempts at reform often blow up in their proponents' faces, and
actually make things worse. The Fulton Committee on the Civil Service, which reported in 1968, made a large number of recommendations. But neither the Wilson nor the Heath Government implemented them as a whole. Instead the Civil Service was allowed to
adopt the ones it liked and tread water on the others. It got better
pensions, 'planning units', a Civil Service College (including a

splendid mansion in the heart of the stockbroker belt, in which I once stayed in considerable comfort), greater attention to the career-development of public servants, expanded departmental manage-ment services and, not least, the creation of a new Civil Service Department.

These various goodies all involved taking on more staff, and as the corresponding economy measures were ignored, the net result is that the Civil Service has expanded by 100,000 since Fulton sat. The crea-tion of the CSD, far from improving the general management of the service, has merely allowed all concerned to slide away from their responsibilities. When Labour MP Michael English tried to find the answer to the question: 'What Department of State is responsible for determining the efficiency of other Departments of State?' he could not get a unanimous response. Some thought the Treasury, others the CSD and yet others believed each department monitored itself — a nice pickle. The truth is, no one did — or does. The great Whitehall Leviathan is, in all essentials, a monster without a head.

Efforts to control the bureaucratic growth, from the inside, by Government, by Parliament, by Royal Commission and by the Press, all seem unavailing. Resistance to control from the inside is, in fact, growing. The old Whitley Council system of negotiating pay and conditions, which worked well for over 50 years, is being pushed aside, as the Civil Service unions are politicised and radicalised.

Last month, the moderates in the largest union, the Civil and Public Services Association, scored a striking victory, winning a majority on the executive by 16 to 10, after earlier elections, which had given the left extremists control, had been invalidated.

But this was an uncovenanted success, for as a rule, apathy and non-attendance play into the hands of the left-wing militants. There are 1,100 major branches of the CPSA. The largest, Long Benton in Newcastle, the central administration of the Health and Social Security Department, has 9,500 members. But average attendance at union meetings is 70; so the Marxists control it. It is the same elsewhere. The Socialist Workers' Party, the International Marxist Group and the Workers Revolutionary Party control 17,000 votes; the Marxist wing of the Labour Party some 35,000 votes; and the CP 37,000. This coalition of 89,000 votes is usually enough to ensure left-wing control.

What is more, the Left is pledged to continuing expansion of the

Civil Service, especially through the NHS, where its grip is strongest. Leftists support flat-rate increases, because their aim is a one-class Civil Service, in which the top policy-planners will be obliged to belong to a mass union. Part of their growth policy is to expand the public sector, and thus create new Civil Service jobs and more union members.

In various ways, the militants are seeking to influence the actual policies of the departments in which they work. In short, we are not very far from the stage when an incoming Conservative Government might find it difficult to get its orders obeyed (as has already happened at the local government level). The alleged anti-Labour bias of the service has been reversed − with a vengeance.

The emergence, over the past 20 years, of an uncontrollable and increasingly politically motivated bureaucracy is a threat to society on many fronts. It devalues Parliament and the democratic process. It makes firm economic management virtually impossible, and undermines the very existence of the private sector. Not least, it erodes the freedom of the ordinary citizen.

It is of the nature of the state to be devoid of pity, and to be more brutal to the individual than any private corporation, however vast. 'The heartless character of the official,' writes Sisson, 'is of a kind with the ultimate heartlessness of all government.' He cites Pontius Pilate as the archetypal administrator: 'The steps he took to still a particular local clamour were more or less what the Service required, and he washed his hands with a civilising regret.'

The English system of law grew up in the virtual absence of a bureaucracy, against a political background of what the historians term 'self-government by the King's command' − the best form of regime, looking back on it, that history has to show. Hence our law cannot effectively cope with the sudden emergence, over a single generation, of an oppressive bureaucracy.

We have no system of administrative law; no constitutional courts. Question Time in the House, which represents the ancient right to petition the Crown, has become a noisy mockery. The Ombudsman has proved a tragic disappointment. Most people feel a sense of Kafka-esque helplessness in the face of the state machine.

In the past 10 years Parliament has passed more column-inches of statutes than in the whole of the nineteenth century; and most of these statutes are merely foundations on which the bureaucrats erect a gigantic edifice of regulations. Every year, between 1,000 and 1,600 statutory instruments, of which MPs have no knowledge, are issued. The *First Special Report from the Joint Committee on Statutory Instruments*, published last year, deplored the way in which ministers and their departments by-pass Parliament by issuing such instruments, which lay legal obligations on citizens who have absolutely no idea the instruments exist, let alone know of their detailed terms.

The committee charged those concerned with a 'cynical disregard' of individual rights; it demanded that all delegated legislation be detailed, specific and self-explanatory, and should not depend on the exercise of ministerial or departmental discretion. But why should its voice be heeded, when the far more powerful complaints of the PAC are ignored?

The French, who have groaned under bureaucracy throughout their history as a people, have a despairing phrase for it: *'Seul le pouvoir arrête le pouvoir.'* In Britain, by contrast, the traditional resource of the individual harassed by the state has been the Common Law.

In his *Confessions* St Augustine asks: 'What are States without justice but robber-bands enlarged?' In England it is, by tradition, to the Common Law that the subject turns when he wants protection from the robber-state or, indeed, from any powerful and oppressive body. Milton in *Areopagitica*, set modest limits to the justice which Englishmen claim: 'That no grievance ever should arise in the Commonwealth, let no man in this world expect; but when complaints are freely heard, deeply considered and speedily reformed, then is the upmost bound of civil liberty attained that wise men look for.' I doubt if Milton's criteria can be met today: the law is a very uncertain pillar of society.

It is also an immensely complex business. The Royal Commission which is inquiring into legal services has already collected volumes of evidence seven feet high, and is not within sight of reporting. Yet legislation continues to pour out: an average of 3,000 pages of it every year, plus 10,000 pages a year of subordinate regulations. Lord Gardiner, the former Labour Lord Chancellor, calculates that the permanent Law Commission, which he set up to examine, repeal or consolidate legislation, has already succeeded in cutting the number of old statutes by 2,000. But he is the first to admit that we legislate too freely, and that our legislation is too difficult: 'We have the most complicated legislation of any country.'

The international legal consultant, Sir William Dale, has compared a number of English statutes with their precise equivalents in other countries. He finds that ours are twice as long and half as clear. Lord Gardiner blames the parliamentary draftsmen, who are literally a law unto themselves, employ an abstruse legal diction and are quite capable of turning down a Bill drafted by a leading jurist.

That, however, is a comparatively small point. Much more important is the absence, in Britain, not only of any system of administrative courts to curb the excesses of an ever-swelling bureaucratic state, but of any basic system of rights to which the individual can turn when his liberty is threatened. In the case of the trade unions, for instance, the resources of the Common Law have been progressively blocked by a whole series of statutes passed in the unions' interests by Labour majorities, and culminating in the ferocious laws of 1974 and 1976.

These laws invest the unions with privileges once enjoyed by medieval churchmen. An individual cannot bring an action for damages against union officials engaged in 'industrial action', whether or not they are in breach of contract: it is doubtful whether he can even sue them for libel, no matter what they say; and an individual who loses his livelihood as a result of a closed shop agreement under the 1974 Act has no redress in law against either employer or union, and is entitled to no compensation whatever.

In almost all free countries with written constitutions such laws would rapidly be invalidated by the courts. Even in England, judges try to use the Common Law to protect oppressed victims. But each time they discover a hole in the statutory iron curtain, Labour governments rush in to plug it: thus a new union privilege Bill is on the stocks to make the successful defence constructed by the Grunwick management illegal. Blackstone's famous definition of English equity, as a system 'by which the meanest individual is protected from the insults and oppression of the greatest', simply does not apply any more.

There is a growing movement, led by Lord Hailsham, to produce and pass a Bill of Rights which would, as he explained to me, operate at every level in the judicial process, from the magistrates' court to the House of Lords. This would help to curb what he terms the 'elective dictatorship' of Parliament. The campaign has acquired urgency in the light of the evident determination of Labour to abolish the Lords, since thereafter there would be nothing to prevent a Labour government with a majority of one from prolonging the life of Parliament indefinitely or, indeed, abolishing elections altogether.

Such a Bill of Rights was introduced in the Lords last year and a Select Committee appointed to examine the question. It reported that a Rights Bill might not give all the protection needed, since the doctrine of parliamentary sovereignty, and of the superior power of the most recent statute, means that no Parliament can bind its successor, or even itself. This may not be so. Some great jurists, such as Austin, have argued that 'speaking accurately, the members of the Commons House are merely trustees for the body by which they are elected and appointed; and consequently, the sovereignty always resides in the King, peers and the electoral body of the Commons.' Hence a Bill of Rights, passed by Parliament and endorsed by a referendum, might well be upheld by the courts as superior to any subsequent statute of an ordinary kind. In any event, it would constitute an indelible marker of Rubicon. The breaching of such a Bill would constitute the transition from constitutionalism to tyranny.

The issue is not supposed to be a party one; but of course it is. The present Lord Chancellor, Lord Elwyn-Jones, says he is opposed to such a step on the grounds that it would not solve our constitutional problems. Similar noises are made by other legal luminaries of the centre-Left. The truth is that both the trade unions and the Labour Left are flatly opposed to any Bill which will, or even might, curb their future freedom of action.

In the meantime the judges do their best, as they have always done. It was no accident that the greatest of Common Lawyers, Chief Justice Coke, was the ideologue of the Parliamentarians against Charles I. Indeed, most of our fundamental 'human rights' are judge-made – for example, the presumption of innocence, no obligation to testify against oneself, fair hearing, peaceful assembly, freedom of association and freedom of the press.

Despite attempts by Labour governments to legislate against Common Law rulings in favour of individuals, the resources of the Common Law are very great. Over the past generation, English judges have proved very skilful at drawing on them – in, for instance, the Gouriet case against the postal workers, the Laker case, the Tameside education dispute, the invalidation of Home Office policy over radio-TV licences, and in the field of race relations and trade union law.

Lord Denning has taken the van in this rich and creative period of English law; so successfully, in fact, that he feels a Bill of Rights would do more harm than good, and bring judges into politics. Lord Elwyn-Jones agrees with him. 'It is as disagreeable to be tried by Ministers as to be governed by judges,' he says – a neat little lawyer's maxim not incompatible with a certain amount of fence-sitting. Lord Gardiner adds: 'I don't mind judges making law, but I don't want them involved in matters which impinge on party politics.'

To such arguments Lord Hailsham has a crisp reply: 'Judges cannot choose the work they do; they have to come to a decision one way or another on all litigation which is brought before them. If they assume jurisdiction they are in politics; if they decline jurisdiction they are in politics. All they can hope to be is impartial.' To judge by the November 29 House of Lords debate on a Bill of Rights, the bulk of the senior judiciary supports Lord Hailsham.

Hatred of 'judges' law' runs deep in the Labour Party, and is based on the same collectivist reasoning which leads it to oppose a Bill of Rights. Many Labour and TUC leaders have been brought up on Harold Laski's *Parliamentary Government in England*, which argues that 'The judges interpret the "rule of law" as though they are themselves the masters of a "higher law" than that of the sovereign legislator'. Hence the savage criticism of individual judges by Labour MPs and, most disturbing of all, a more generalised attack by Mr Callaghan's deputy, Michael Foot, which has so far been allowed to pass without public rebuke by the Lord Chancellor.

The biggest threat of all comes from the unions, who see judges as class enemies as well as barriers to further union power. A recent confidential report prepared for the TUC criticises the judges, especially Lord Denning, for limiting the effects of the 1974 and other pro-union statutes; it speaks of 'the worrying disposition on the part of important elements in the judiciary to limit their scope', and cites as 'cause for concern', for example, Beaverbrook Newspapers v Keys, in which the Court of Appeal ruled that a print union was not entitled to forbid the printing of extra copies of the *Express* when the *Mirror* was on strike (since reinforced by a further Court of Appeal decision in the Press Association 'blacking' case on December 21). In the past such noises emanating from the union bosses have usually been a prelude to a demand for government action.

The unions are particularly incensed that the Employment Protection Act, which weighted decisions in Industrial Tribunals heavily against the employer, is no longer working to plan. This Act is a particularly villainous piece of class legislation, and the tribunals are highly unsatisfactory as courts of justice; in the view of many managers, they actually cause unemployment, by deterring small and medium-sized businesses from taking on new labour. Nevertheless, employers are learning to work them by engaging increasingly expert counsel, and the Employment Appeals Tribunal has, to the fury of the unions, cut the number of successful cases of unfair dismissal by about one-third since 1975, chiefly by producing four rulings: that the Act should not unreasonably impede management in the running of a business, that tribunals should not apply their own test of unfairness, that a dismissal cannot be unfair if it is in accordance with the appropriate procedure, and that, even when incorrect procedure is used, a dismissal can still be fair if the results would have been the same.

The unions complain that while employers retain counsel, the union officials who represent dismissed workers lack legal training. Now here we begin to get at the heart of the coming battle between the Left and our independent legal system. If unfairly dismissed workers need legal help, the obvious answer is that legal aid should be extended to Industrial Tribunals. At present, legal aid is not available for such purposes, largely for financial reasons. Responsible legal opinion, including the Law Society, says that it should be made available. But the unions are opposed, partly because it would benefit non-union workers, who are not now represented at all, and partly because even union members might often prefer independent lawyers to union officials.

The TUC submission to the Royal Commission insists that, if money is available, it should go not to legal aid but to what it terms 'existing agencies which provide primary law representation' – that is, to the unions themselves. This is also official Labour Party policy. Indeed, one of the next great strides forward in union power is to be the creation of a huge body of trained 'para-legal' union officials, whose scope will be progressively extended by the opening up not only of tribunals and appeals tribunals, but of genuine courts of law, to this type of representation. It is, in fact, a sizable wedge which the unions intend to hammer into the legal profession and the entire system of justice.

Hence the training of union officials in technical legal matters is an increasingly important issue, partly because the TUC intends to get the taxpayers to finance it, and not least because the extreme Left is moving in on the operation. The *Slough Observer* reported at the end of last year efforts by Slough College 'to conceal from the public the fact that special courses for trade union shop stewards were being run by lecturers who were either members of the Communist Party or the holders of 'extreme Left-wing views'.

The interest of the extreme Left in the legal system, as a means of penetrating the citadels of power, goes back to the 1960s when 'radical' students began to move from the sociology faculties, which they dominated and largely discredited, into the study of law.

When these new law graduates marched out of the universities, an institution providentially emerged to give them employment and scope for their fervour: the law centre. This concept, like much else in the civil rights field, was developed from American experience, where 'neighbourhood law firms' and 'public interest law firms' have led the campaign for deprived minorities, especially blacks, at local level. The first British law centre was opened in North Kensington in 1971 and there are now about 35, mainly in working-class areas of big cities in England and Wales. They are supported partly by doing work under the Legal Aid fund, partly by the Lord Chancellor's Department, but mainly (and in some cases almost entirely) by local authority money.

Law centres have already aroused furiously conflicting views, both inside and outside the legal profession. Some local authorities, especially those which fell to the Tories last year, dislike them intensely. The three in Wandsworth are now costing the ratepayers £168,000 a year, and their total bill comes to £250,000. The leader of the new Tory council, Dennis Mallam, says: 'I am not happy with the way the centres are run. They are OK for helping individuals, but I get worried when I see the centres going into political areas like support for the Grunwick strike.'

The Society of Conservative Lawyers says it is 'greatly concerned' at the political role which many LCs see for themselves, and that 'at certain LCs only people with pronounced left-wing views will be considered for employment'.

The best way of judging the law centres, perhaps, is to examine their methods and objects as set out in their submission to the Royal Commission. Each LC is supposedly controlled by the local 'deprived community', but the Law Centres Working Group, which made the submissions, claims to speak for all of them.

They are, for example, bitterly hostile to the legal profession, as now constituted: 'In our present society there is little we can do to prevent a majority of professionals being middle-class. What we need to do is to put these skills at the disposal of the community, without simultaneously injecting middle-class values.' They want their funding to be provided by central government, since they regard local authorities as potential or actual enemies and, though democratically elected, totally unrepresentative of the 'deprived communities' for whom they claim to speak.

Reading this remarkable submission, I got the distinct impression that the law centre 'movement' is no longer a legal welfare institution but is essentially directed to effect radical changes in society, at public expense, and in accordance with predetermined ideological principles. Its hostility to the existing democratic system is revealed by its contemptuous attitude to local authorities, though doubtless it intends, if possible, to establish such a grip on the 'deprived' that it can deliver blocks of votes. It aims, in fact, to become a state within a state.

At present, LCs require a Law Society waiver of its rule against 'touting' in order to publicise their activities, and in return for this they agree not to trade in divorce, probate and conveyancing (the private solicitor's standbys), crimes committed by those over 21, or personal injuries of a grave nature. The Society of Conservative Lawyers wishes to extend this system of control. It objects strongly to 'the refusal of many LCs to act for landlords and employers, no matter how impecunious they may be'. It supports the proposal by the Law Chancellor's Advisory Committee that a uniform code and system of accountability be introduced, and to this end it suggests a special type of practising certificate.

The point of this plan, of course, is that it puts the LCs firmly under the control of the profession. And here is the nub of the whole problem. The law may not be a very popular profession among the public. But the more I examine its institutions, and the threats now mounted against them, the more convinced I am that the independence of the judiciary — so vital to us if a future Labour regime attempts to tamper with our parliamentary institutions — itself rests very largely on the independence and self-government of the profession, based on the Bar Council and the Law Society.

The law centre movement, if allowed to expand without controls, menaces our legal system because it does not, on political grounds, respect the obedience to the rule of law which is the basis of professional conduct. Yet already it forms what could become the nucleus of a state legal profession, and as such part of the mainstream of the Left's collectivist assault on the Open Society.

Several strands of left-wing strategy converge in new plans to create a National Legal Service, on the lines of the NHS. They are put forward by the TUC which wants a Secretary of State for Justice, sitting in the Commons and not necessarily a lawyer, charged with 'general responsibility for the legal system, including a co-ordinated policy in the field of legal services'. And this plan is echoed, with variations, in evidence submitted by the Society of Labour Lawyers. They, too, want a Minister of Justice and, in the long term, a Legal Services Scheme, which would administer state legal aid, just like the NHS, on a basis of right and need, not of income.

It would be controlled by a Legal Services Commission, a kind of Superquango, which they describe as 'An independent corporation', funded by the Government and accountable, through a minister, to Parliament. They do not explain how the Commission can remain independent if its members are appointed, and dismissed, by the Government. Indeed, they seem more anxious to limit, than to protect, the independence of the law, since they want lay placemen and quango-mongers not only on the Commission but 'sitting on the central committees of the profession — the Senate of the Inns of Court and the Bar and the Council of the Law Society'.

One stands aghast at the thought of the blundering bureaucratic monster which would eventually emerge if, as Labour planners are determined, such schemes become law. Even as it is, judges and barristers are furious at the way in which the national courts service, set up following the Beeching Royal Commission to administer the crown courts, is working in practice.

They say it is becoming a huge, impersonal bureaucracy, increasingly staffed by civil servants quite inexperienced in case-work: some of the lay administrators, it is claimed, already consider themselves far more important than judges. One QC claims that officials put in charge of 'taxing' fees have never been in court in their lives: 'The slower and more incompetent you are in preparing a case and the longer it takes in court as a result, the more you get paid.'

It all sounds horribly familiar. The old assizes and quartersessions, which the crown courts replaced, appeared old fashioned, as does so much to do with the law. But they worked independently.

What alarms lawyers about the idea of a nationalised legal system is not merely the gigantic burden of costs it would place on the taxpayer, the huge increase in litigation it would undoubtedly bring about, and the paralysing delays which would inevitably follow, but the fear that lawyers would become state officials and that private practice, as in the field of health, would gradually be eliminated. The judges would then become little better than bureaucrats themselves, and a central pillar of the Open Society would simply disappear.

As one QC put it to me, 'The only thing we could then do would be to get on our knees and pray.' But would that do any good either? Does the Church, the last of our pillars, offer any reassurance?

One of the most spectacular sights in England today is York Minster. This is by far the largest and most majestic of English medieval churches, and in the past decade, at prodigious cost, it has been cleaned and restored from pinnacle to crypt, its foundations renewed, its bosses and effigies repainted, its brasses burnished, its walls and buttresses strengthened and its furnishings repaired and re-gilded, to the point where it is, perhaps, in a better state than at any time in its long history.

To my mind, it is an ocular reminder that the Church of England, derided and mocked though it often is, remains a great force.

Yet it is manifest that this ancient pillar of society, the very heart and pearl of the Establishment, is not what it was. At the beginning of the century there were 23,670 Anglican clergymen, serving a population in England and Wales of 30.6 million. By 1976, with the population 70 per cent higher, the clergy had dropped to 12,056.

Within this general downward curve, the figures for ordinations have fluctuated. Dr Coggan, the Archbishop of Canterbury, told me recently: 'The number of men coming forward for ordination is now on the upgrade — and they are good men, too!' Looking ahead to the 1980s the indications are that the Church, ordaining 200 – 300 full-time parish clergy and about 500 'auxiliary parochial ministers' a year, will keep its congregations served. But the *Church of England Yearbook 1978* provides sombre evidence that the enthusiasm of the laity, in so far as it can be quantified, has declined: baptisms, at 232,000 in 1976, have fallen by a fifth since 1973; those attending Sunday services in 1976, at 1,252,000, by a tenth over the same period; while confirmations fell from just over 190,000 in 1960, to under 100,000 in 1976. The 1977 figures, just released, show some improvement: church attendances, communicants and confirmations all increased marginally, but baptisms are down again.

There is no getting away from the figures, particularly since they are underscored by evidence from other Christian churches. In 1975 A.E.C.W. Spencer, formerly in charge of the Newman Demographic Survey, shocked the English Catholic hierarchy by calculating that the number of 'alienated' Catholics has risen from 249,000 in 1958 to over 2,600,000 in 1971. 'What emerges,' he wrote, 'is that the Catholic folklore that "once a Catholic, always a Catholic" . . . was substantially true of England and Wales in the late 1950s: it had altogether ceased to be true by the early 1970s.'

Of the other Christian churches, the largest, the Methodist, has suffered a huge drop in membership. Lord Soper, the most prominent of the Methodist leaders, sadly summed up for me the whole pattern of Christian decay: 'When I was a boy, people at least knew the name of the church they stayed away from. Now, they don't even know that.' Membership of the Free Churches has fallen by 92,000 in the past three years.

The Anglican Church, of course, has now lived with this problem for a considerable time. The Church emerged in its existing form in the mid-sixteenth century, at the beginnings of a big upsurge in population, and it is not at all clear whether Anglicanism ever established a firm grip on the urban population – its roots are rural. Certainly, it was never a majority church in the towns created by the Industrial Revolution, and the figures available from the 1851 census onwards indicate that a majority of the nation has not worshipped in the Established Church for well over a century. Anglicanism has tended to be a middle- and upper-class religion, except in the countryside, where it transcends the class barriers.

Its weaknesses, however, did not begin to show until after 1914, when the dislocations of war, and the disruptions of settled habit, first revealed the ravages of secularisation. Since then the Church has gone through endless self-analysis, heartsearching, renewals and reforms.

Savage criticism poured in from all sides, most of all from within; and as the sixties turned into the seventies, it became more radical and insulting.

It seems to me that nobody can fairly accuse the Anglican authorities of not taking these, and many other, criticisms to heart. In recent years they have undergone never-ending humiliations, gyrations and somersaults in their desperate efforts to appease the groundlings. Bishops have scoured their dioceses for working-class ordinands. Proponents of the proletarian-style 'South Bank Religion', such as the Rev Hugh Montefiore and the Rev David Sheppard, have been given sees. The bishops, as it happens, are the only discernible category of human beings in Britain whose incomes have actually been reduced in nominal, as well as real, terms in the present century (the Archbishops of Canterbury and York receive only £9,628 and £8,405 respectively, though both are to get a modest rise in April, if the Department of Employment sanctions it).

Bishops have not precisely been stripped of all power and authority, but they have been made to feel pretty small. During a recent Lambeth Conference, styles of address were debated, and a resolution passed: 'The Conference recommends that the bishops, as leaders and representatives of a servant Church, should radically examine the honours paid to them in the course of divine worship, in titles and customary addresses, and in style of living, while having the necessary facilities for the efficient carrying on of their work.' The *Handbook, 1978* adds: 'Consequent on this resolution, a more informal trend is becoming the norm and whereas formerly a bishop would have been addressed as "my Lord" and a dean as "Mr Dean", it has become more normal to address a bishop in speech as "Bishop" and a dean as "Dean".

The change in style reflects a real decline in espisopal authority. Some 26 out of 43 full bishops sit in the House of Lords: Canterbury, York, London, Winchester and Durham by right, the others by seniority. But their ecclesiastical powers have been gradually whittled away. So insignificant have they now become that the Government has relinquished the right to appoint them. Bishops Young of Ripon and Walker of Ely were the last Prime Ministerial appointments. The PM still has a power of veto, exercised through Colin Peterson, Secretary for Appointments to the Prime Minister and Ecclesiastical Secretary to the Lord Chancellor. But the picking is now done by the Church's own Crown Appointments Commission, which came into existence in 1977; sending Montefiore to Birmingham was its first piece of bishop-making.

In theory the Church of England has become a kind of democracy. In practice it is a supine and sluggish bureaucracy, haphazardly run by oligarchs. Debates at the thrice-yearly General Synod are often lively, but its legislative system, linked to those of individual diocesan synods, makes any kind of strong leadership or coherent policy almost impossible. Thus in 1972, the unification scheme with the Methodists, worked out by experts over 16 years, was accepted by the three Houses (bishops, clergy and lay people) by votes of 34 to 6, 152 to 80 and 147 to 87; nevertheless, since the rules required a two-thirds majority in all the Houses and an overall majority of 75 per cent, the measure failed.

Last autumn the motion to permit the ordination of women failed in the General Synod because, though it was passed by the bishops and laity, the clergy rejected it. The system is so complicated that, even had this first hurdle been jumped, some 52 more votes (according to my calculations), all affirmative and some by two-thirds majorities, plus an Act of Parliament, would have been required before women could have become priests — the whole taking at least five years.

Other symptoms of the bureaucratic disease are appearing. There is already talk of a staff college for ecclesiastical bureaucrats — St George's House, Windsor, being the embryo of such an institution.

Constitutional and bureaucratic checks on leadership now extend right through the Church. And of course one reason why bishops are losing their authority is that they are too busy being bureaucrats. Mervyn Stockwood, Bishop of Southwark, whom I went to see in his palace — sorry, house — in Tooting Bec, gets very worked up on this point: 'There are endless committees, I'm notorious for avoiding Synods. Why? They mean 15 days blocked straight away. I was chairman of the Revision Committee for the new baptismal service, and even with me in charge it took up six whole days. This comes of trying to make the Church more democratic. The professional laymen, who adore ecclesiasticism, take over – and they are steeped in the ethos of Tunbridge Wells.'

Accompanying this dispersal or even denial of authority, so alien to the manner in which Jesus and the apostles conducted their ministries, is an embarrassed and apologetic tone of voice which has become perhaps the most striking characteristic of up-to-date Anglicanism. The Church of England's motto is no longer *semper eadem* but 'We Are All Guilty'. The ferocious assaults on its social structure have not in fact succeeded in eliminating middle-class dominance, as the merest glance at the names of those who sit on its main committees amply reveals: but what they have done is to make the Church's leaders feel abysmally guilty about their social origins, imperial past and white skins.

Hence there are periodic orgies of self-abasement, one occurring last December when Anglican churches throughout Britain celebrated the 30th anniversary of the Declaration of Human Rights. In Westminster Abbey, the Rev Harry Morton, General Secretary of the British Council of Churches, referred to what he was pleased to term the 'anti-history' of the Christian community in the area of human rights. 'I remember,' he intoned, 'what European Christians have done to the Jews, culminating in the holocaust, the Conquistadors to the Amerindians, the Puritan Fathers to the North American Indians; I remember the slave trade and the white settlers of South Africa, the settlers of Australia and New Zealand . . . I make an act of contrition on behalf of the British Churches.'

The tragedy of this ignorant kind of claptrap is not only that it ignores the long and ultimately triumphant struggle of the Latin Church to eliminate European slavery and, later, of the Evangelicals, assisted by the Royal Navy, to destroy the slave trade all over the world, but that it fails utterly to understand the moral theology of Christianity, and the doctrinal insistence on individual freedom which made these historic movements possible.

Indeed, so anxious are many Anglican 'opinion-formers' to iden-tify themselves with what they think to be progressive notions, that they find themselves applauding policies which are quite incompat-ible with basic Christian doctrine. A shocking case in point is the adoption by the synodical 'Board of Social Responsibility' – by far the worst offender, in this respect – of a statement pledging the support of Anglican consciences for the closed shop. The motion eventually adopted by the General Synod last February was not quite so enthusiastic — it had some qualifications — but both these documents were gleefully flourished by British Government lawyers when three British Rail victims, sacked without legal redress or compensation under closed shop provisions, took their case to the European Court of Human Rights at Strasbourg.

And this is not the only occasion when the desperate search for modernity has played straight into the hands of sheer evil. The role of the World Council of Churches — in which Anglican opinion is a formative voice — in giving moral encouragement and financial support to African terrorist movements is an atrocious sin against justice of infinitely greater consequence than those for which repentance is so often expressed.

As it is, by accident or design, much damage has been inflicted, over the past decade, by church policy in three crucial areas: the liturgy, doctrine and moral teaching. The liturgical changes have undoubtedly caused enormous distress among the Church's more faithful supporters. The truth is that Coleridge's phrase, 'the willing suspension of disbelief', applies as well to religious as to poetic faith and demands a hieratic language. To make matters worse, the Church which has produced the prose of Cranmer, Hooker, the King James Bible, the Caroline divines and Newman, is going through an arid literary phase. Modern churchmen tend to express themselves with gruesome mateyness ('not the kind of thing to set the pew on fire') or to devalue by overuse once-powerful words ('caring', 'heartening'), or to harp on inapt theological terms ('In many parishes, hermeneutics, thanks to the National Evangelical Congress, has become a word in day-to-day use').

'One's understanding,' said the Bishop of Liverpool recently, 'of priorities in the Gospel and in Church life are [sic] influenced very heavily by the socio-economic experience of life.' There are vogue words like 'praxis' ('doing the truth', whatever that may mean), jargon — 'a tent-making ministry' (good), 'the folk-church inheritance' (bad) — and a wide spread of euphemisms, like 'liberation theology' (justification of murder) and 'non-illusory faith' (agnosticism).

Hence the replacement of the Book of Common Prayer and the Authorised Version by the leaden committee-vernacular of 'Series 3' has dispirited and demoralised the faithful, and has been aptly compared to the work of property-developers wrecking an old cathedral city.

Nor is it just the verbal forms and sacramentals which are being cast away. The desire to modernise at almost any cost operates most powerfully in the realm of basic doctrine. It can do so, of course, because the Anglican Church is not dogmatic. As Jan Coggan says in *Far From the Madding Crowd*, 'A man can belong to the Church of England and bide in his cheerful old inn, and never worry his mind about doctrines at all.' It stands for what Bishop Patrick called 'virtuous mediocrity . . . between the meretricious gaudiness of the Church of Rome and the squalid sluttery of fanatic conventicles'.

Against this background, the Church has had to relax even the slender defences against heterodoxy it once possessed. Since 1975, those being ordained no longer have to confess belief in the Thirty-Nine Articles. They make, instead, a Declaration of Assent.

All the same, until the publication in 1977 of *The Myth of Christ Incarnate* by a variety of clergymen, academics and trendsetters, most of us thought that belief in Christ's divinity was not only an essential part of Christian doctrine but, in one sense, the whole of it. The Incarnation of God in Christ is the one event in history which stands altogether outside the cultural values of humanity. Christianity without Incarnation is nothing; it has no significance whatever. Nevertheless, this volume of essays, in which the doctrine is, with varying degrees of enthusiasm, abandoned, was published. I spent half an hour or so, on BBC2, cross-questioning one of its leading spirits, the Rev Don Cupitt, Dean of Emmanuel College, Cambridge, and came to the conclusion that his views were closer to a liberal form of Judaism than any form of Christianity I could discern. But I was impressed by his grasp of TV terminology.

The disintegration of doctrine has, inevitably, been followed by a clouding of the moral vision. In the early sixties, it was argued, by those who wished to disembarrass the criminal law of its less tenable moral assumptions, that it was possible to make an absolutely clear distinction between what was 'legally wrong' and 'morally wrong'. Thus, homosexual behaviour between consenting adults, to cite a typical example, was considered inappropriate for legal prohibition. But we were told that reforming the law would in no way legitimise the sin.

What in fact has happened is a clear demonstration that it does.

Not only do laws reflect morals; morals reflect laws — or their absence. The recent moral drift has now given a new meaning to George Herbert's celebrated definition of Anglicanism, 'neither too mean, nor yet too gay'.

I do not know whether any Anglican clergyman goes as far as the American Jesuit, Fr John McNeill, who claims: 'The homosexual is here according to God's purpose. God has divine purpose in so creating human nature that a certain percentage of human beings are homosexuals.' But certainly many now qualify their condemnation of 'the abominable crime'; an official 'working party' on homosexuality has been unable, so far, to reach agreement; a recent Student Christian Movement book, *Is the Homosexual my Neighbour?*, suggests that the Church should offer social acceptance to homosexuals and encourage them to form permanent relationships, and it accuses Christians who try to break up such unions of 'excruciating mental and emotional torture'; and, finally, the cleric who suggested that Jesus was probably a homosexual, too, has now been made a bishop.

These various attempts to accommodate the Church to 'the modern world' (or some such abstraction) evidently generated a good deal of resistance, all the more angry for its lack of articulation. 'Nothing in the world,' wrote Victor Hugo, 'is more powerful than an idea whose time has come.' The truth of this observation was happily discovered by Dr Edward Norman, Dean of Peterhouse, when he devoted his Reith Lectures last year to a restatement of Christian spirituality and a reasoned but ringing condemnation of the way in which Anglicans — and not only Anglicans — had allowed their Church to be penetrated and guided by secular values, and in particular by the values of a distinctive and reprehensible political philosophy. The rebuke was well merited and overdue — hence all the more rapturously applauded by ordinary Christians.

I doubt if those who preach 'the social gospel' and 'liberation theology' will display much penitence, however. They are far too strongly entrenched in the apparatus of the Church, and far too deeply indoctrinated with the dialectic and vocabulary of guilt-religion, to surrender to this modern 'First Blast of the Trumpet'.

All the same, Norman has effectively reminded us that there is more than one stream in Anglicanism, and that its power and influence should not be judged solely by the frantic efforts of its modernising element to keep up with the latest twists and turns in the conventional wisdom of our age.

'I agree,' said the Archbishop of Canterbury to me recently, sitting in his Lambeth Palace study, 'there has been too much stress on the Third World and not enough on the next world. Of course the trouble is, when we say things about the Third World we are reported. But not when we talk about the next world.'

Dr Coggan is in all essential respects a much more characteristically Anglican figure than Dr Stockwood (or Dean Norman, for that matter). He is temperamentally well equipped to manage a Church which has been described as '11,000 separate corporations, each with its own freehold', and still give a sense of leadership. Since becoming Primate he has moved marginally towards the centre, as is right, but his churchmanship has an old-fashioned relish to it. He sees the Christian as a man of privilege but also and primarily as a man under obligation, by virtue of faith and grace.

If St Paul were alive, he says:

I think I can see him growing increasingly impatient with talk about a charter of *rights*, and bringing us back, with inexorable logic, to the need, rather, for a charter of *duties*.

You and I must both die one day. I want to know how to die. I want to be able to teach other people how to die. There *is* a judgement day, and we must prepare ourselves for it. We have duties. I feel this very strongly. Duty is a stern word. But then there is an element of iron in the Christian ethic which is very important.

Dr Coggan, rightly in my view, stresses the predicament of man, which he sees as the consequence of the Fall. He denounces the cult of greed:

I am not blaming the unions solely, but all strata of society. We are all infected with greed. This is what St John calls 'the Sin of the World' – another name for Original Sin. Original Sin explains much about modern society. There is a flaw in human nature. A Christian society does not accept the progressive moral betterment of man. There is no kind of Utopia into which we shall gradually glide. On the contrary, a great deal of Biblical literature suggests we are heading for a final crash. It is this knowledge which saves Christians from disillusionment.

It is just as well that the high priest of our national Church gives no countenance to the notion of inevitable human progress. The Church is still a pillar of society, and a formidable one too; but it should not be a support of received opinion or a plinth for card-houses. It does not deal in earthly Utopias, knowing them to be false and, if relentlessly pursued, diabolical. Its coinage is immutable principles, often unwelcome to the sovereign will of peoples — or of those who claim to speak for them.

Walking in the shadow of Westminster Abbey not long ago, I reflected that it was not by accident that Edward the Confessor's great church, which still holds his bones, was placed a mere stone's-throw from Parliament. For it was Christian priests who set down in writing our earliest laws, those of Aethelbert of Kent; clerics who created and manned the Chancery at Westminster, and later, the Exchequer beside it; and it was in a royal chapel, St Stephen's, that the House of Commons first found a home.

Throughout our history, the Church has accorded, or refused, its benison to secular governments. Should other pillars fall, let us pray that it remains erect to remind us that a nation's sense of justice is indestructible.

PART THREE

The Libertarian Alternative

CHAPTER 12

Has Capitalism a Future?

This is a speech I gave at a conference of financiers and investment managers in New York, organised by the publication Bank Credit Analyst. *It aroused a surprising amount of attention, and shortened versions of it were published in the* Wall Street Journal, Die Welt, The Times *of London and other newspapers across the world. I give here the full, original text.*

Let us begin by defining our terms. By 'capitalism' I mean large-scale industrial capitalism, in which privately financed, publicly quoted corporations, operating in a free market environment, and with the back-up of the private enterprise money market, constitute the core of national economies. This is a fairly broad definition, but I think it will do.

The first thing to be noted is that this phenomenon is pretty recent. I would date it, in its earliest phase in England, only from the 1780s. It is thus less than 200 years old anywhere. As a widely spread phenomenon, it is barely 100 years old. Seen against the grand perspective of history, capitalism is a newcomer. We now possess some knowledge of economic systems going back to the early centuries of the third millennium BC. It is possible to give, for instance, an outline account of the economic structure of Egypt under the Old Kingdom, about 2,700 BC. Our knowledge of how civilised societies have organised their economic activities thus covers a stretch of more than 4,600 years. And in only about 200 of those years has industrial capitalism existed. The next point to note is the remarkable correlation between the emergence of industrial capitalism and the beginnings of really rapid economic growth. Throughout most of history, growth rates, when we have the statistical evidence to measure them, have been low, nil or minus. A century of slow growth might be followed by a century of decline. Societies tended to get caught in the Malthusian trap: that is, a period of slow growth led to an increase in population, the outstripping of food supplies, followed by a demographic catastrophe, and the beginning of a new cycle.

There were at least three economic Dark Ages in history, in which a sudden collapse of the wealth-making process led to the extinction, or virtual extinction, of civilised living, and the process of recovery was very slow and painful. The last of these three Dark Ages extinguished Roman civilisation in Western Europe, in the fifth century AD. It was not until the thirteenth century that equivalent living standards were again achieved − the recovery thus took 800 years. Society again fell into a Malthusian trap in the fourteenth century and again recovery was slow, though more sure this time,   as intermediate technology spread more widely, and methods of handling and employing money became more sophisticated. Even by the first half of the eighteenth century, however, it was rare for even the most advanced economies, those of England and Holland, to achieve 1 per cent growth in any year. And there is a possibility − I myself would put it higher − that mankind would again have fallen into a Malthusian trap towards the end of the eighteenth century if industrial capitalism had not made its dramatic appearance.

And it *was* dramatic. By the beginning of the 1780s, in England, an unprecedented annual growth rate of 2 per cent had been achieved. During that decade, the 2 per cent was raised to 4 per cent. This was the great historic 'lift off', and a 4 per cent annual compound growth rate was sustained for the next 50 years, on average. Since this English, and also Scottish, performance was accompanied by the export of capital, patents, machine tools and skilled manpower to several other advanced nations, the phenomenon soon became international.

Figures indicate the magnitude of the change that industrial capitalism brought to human society. In Britain, for instance, in the nineteenth century, the size of the working population multiplied fourfold. Real wages doubled in the half century 1800−50, and doubled again, 1850−1900. This meant there was a 1,600 per cent increase in the production and consumption of wage-goods during the century. Nothing like this had happened anywhere before, in the whole of history. From the 1850s onward, in Belgium, France, Austria- Hungary, above all in Germany and the United States, even higher growth rates were obtained; and feudal empires like Japan and Russia were able to telescope a development process, which in Britain had stretched over centuries, into a mere generation or two.

The growth rates of 12 leading capitalist countries averaged 2.7 per cent a year over the whole 50-year period up to the First World War. There was, it is true, a much more mixed performance between the wars. The United States, for instance, which in the 44 years up to 1914 had averaged a phenomenal 4.3 per cent growth rate, and which in the seven years up to 1929 had increased its national income by a staggering 40 per cent, then saw its national income fall 38 per cent in the mere four years 1929 – 32.

But following the Second World War, growth was resumed on an even more impressive scale. In the 1950s, for instance, the 12 leading capitalist economies cited before had an average annual growth of 4.2 per cent. In Germany it was as high as an average of 7.6 per cent. In all the West European economies, the rate of investment in the 1950s was half as high again as it had ever been on a sustained basis. In several such countries it was over 20 per cent of the GNP; in Germany and the Netherlands it was 25 per cent, in Norway even higher. Moreover, this high capital formation took place not at the cost of private consumption, but during a rapid and sustained rise in living standards, particularly of industrial workers. These tendencies were prolonged throughout the 1960s and into the 1970s. So far as the mature economies were concerned, the second industrial revolution, 1945 – 70, was entirely painless – and largely so even in Japan, where even higher investment and growth rates were sought, and obtained, to catch up with the United States and Europe.

In short, after nearly five recorded millennia of floundering about, in relative or absolute poverty, humanity suddenly, in the 1780s, began to hit on the right formula: industrial capitalism. Consider the magnitude of the change-over in the last 200 years or less. The wealth of present-day West Germany is notorious. In the year 1800, in the whole of Germany there were less than 1,000 people with annual incomes of $1,000 a year or more. Or again, take France. France now has more automobiles per capita even than Germany, and more second homes per family than any other country in Europe. In the 1780s, four-fifths of French families spent 90 per cent of their incomes simply on buying bread to stay alive.

Industrial capitalism, judged simply by its capacity to create wealth and to distribute it, is thus a phenomenon unique in world history. It could be argued that it is the greatest single blessing ever bestowed on humanity. Why, then, is the question asked – has capitalism a future? Because capitalism is threatened, and we feel it to be threatened: the question is not academic. The idea has got around, and it is widely believed, especially among young people – above all among young people who like to think they are well educated – that industrial capitalism is unpopular, and always had been; that it is the work of a tiny, interested minority who have thrust it upon the reluctant mass of mankind.

Nothing, in fact, could be further from the truth. The storage economies of remote antiquity were often hideously unpopular. So was the slave-based economy, combined with corporatism, of the classical world. Agricultural feudalism was certainly unpopular; and mercantilism had to be enforced, in practice, by authoritarian states. But industrial capitalism from the very start received the demonstrable approbation of the masses. They could not vote in the ballot box, but they voted in a far more positive and impressive manner, with their feet. And this for a simple reason. The poorest member of society values political freedom as much as the richest and the well educated – that is my belief. But the freedom he values most of all, the freedom which means most to him, is the freedom to sell his labour and skills in the open market. It was precisely this that industrial capitalism gave to men for the first time in history. Hence it is a profound error of fact, in my view, to see what Blake called the 'dark, satanic mills' of the Industrial Revolution, as the enslavement of man. The factory system, however harsh it may have been, was the road to freedom for millions of agricultural workers. Not only did it offer them an escape from rural poverty, which was deeper and more degrading than anything experienced in the cities, but it allowed them to move from status to contract, from a stationary place in a static society, with tied cottages and semi-conscript labour, to a mobile place in a dynamic one. That was why the common man voted for industrial capitalism with his feet, by tramping from the countryside to the towns, in enormous numbers, first in Britain, then throughout

Europe. And tens of millions of European peasants, decade after decade, moved relentlessly across the Atlantic in pursuit of that same freedom, from semi-feudal estates and smallholdings in Russia, Poland, Germany, Austria-Hungary, Italy, Ireland, Scandinavia, to the mines and factories and workshops of New York, Chicago, Pittsburgh, Cleveland and Detroit. It was the first time in history that really large numbers of ordinary people were given the chance to exercise a choice about their livelihood and destiny, and to move, not as a member of a tribe or a conscript soldier, but as free individuals, selling their labour in the open market.

They voted for industrial capitalism with their feet not only because they felt in their bones that it meant a modest prosperity for their children and grandchildren – and on the whole they have been proved abundantly right – but because they knew it meant a new degree of freedom for themselves.

Indeed, the success of industrialisation, despite all its evils, continues to persuade countless ordinary men and women, all over the world, to escape the poverty and restraints of rural status society and to enter the free labour markets of the towns. Hence the growth of the megalopolises all over the world – Calcutta and Bombay, Teheran and Caracas, Mexico City and Djakarta, Shanghai and Lagos, Cairo and Johannesburg; there are now literally scores of million-plus cities all over the Third World. This never-ending one-way flow from countryside to city is plainly a voluntary mass choice, for most governments fear and resent it and many are attempting, sometimes savagely but always ineffectively, to halt or reverse it. It is more marked in the free market economies, but it is marked everywhere. Short of evacuating the cities by force and terror, as is now apparently being practiced in parts of South-East Asia, there is no way to stop this human flood. There seems to be an almost irresistible urge in human beings to move away from the status society to contractual individualism – the central feature of industrial capitalism. And this operates even in totalitarian societies, as witness the efforts, for instance, of the Chinese and Polish governments to limit the urban explosions they are experiencing.

If industrial capitalism is both unique in its wealth-producing capacity, and also has the endorsement of a popular mandate, why is it under threat? And who is threatening it? Let us look at five principal elements. The first, and in some ways the most important, is that the free enterprise idea is losing, if it has not already lost, the intellectual and moral battle. Not long ago I went into Blackwells, the great bookshop at Oxford University. I wandered over the huge room which houses the books on politics and economics, and having been disagreeably surprised by what I saw there, I made a rough calculation. New books extolling the economic, social and moral virtues of communism and collectivism – and there were literally hundreds and hundreds from all over the world – outnumbered books defending free enterprise, or merely seeking to take an objective view of the argument, by between five and six to one. Now this overwhelming predominance of collectivism was not due to any sinister policy on the part of Messrs Blackwells, which is a highly efficient capitalist enterprise. It was a marketing response to demand, on the part of students and teachers. And this was Oxford University, not one of the new slum universities of recent years, some of which have been virtually shanghaied by Marxist factions, but one of the free world's greatest centres of learning, where the battle of ideas is fought under the best possible conditions.

There can be no doubt that the intellectual and moral assault on free enterprise, and the exaltation of Marxist collectivism, which is such a striking feature of the 1970s, is directly related to the huge expansion of higher education, put through at such cost to the capitalist economies, in the 1960s. Now there is in this a huge and tragic irony. For in the 1950s, the decade when the university expansion was planned, it was the prevailing wisdom, among the leading thinkers of the West, that the growth of higher education was directly productive of industrial growth – that the more university graduates we turned out, the faster the GNPs of the West would rise. This was the thesis outlined by President Clark Kerr of Berkeley, in his 1963 Godkin lectures at Harvard, and it was a thesis put forward, with immense effect in Britain, by Sir Charles, now Lord Snow. Kerr said: 'What the railroads did for the second half of the last century, and the automobile for the first half of this century, may be done for the second half of the century by the knowledge industry: that is, to serve as the focal point for national growth.' And Kerr added that more graduates would not only mean a bigger GNP but act as a reinforcement for middle-class democracy, with all its freedoms.

To speak of the 'knowledge industry', however, was to ask for trouble. Knowledge is not a manufactured commodity. There is knowledge for good and knowledge for evil, as the Book of Genesis says. The 1960s, during which most Western nations doubled, and in some cases trebled, their university places, did not reinforce democratic freedoms, or enlarge the GNP or strengthen the free enterprise system. They produced the students' revolts, beginning in Paris in 1968; they detonated the Northern Ireland conflict, which is still harassing Britain. They produced the Bader-Meinhof gang in West Germany, the Red Brigades in Italy, the Left Fascist terrorism of Japan. They produced an enormous explosion of Marxist studies, centered around the social sciences, and especially sociology, and a new generation of university teachers and schoolteachers, dedicated by faith and by a sort of perverted religious piety, to the spread of Marxist ideas. It is true, of course, that student unrest, as such, has quietened down. But the steady diffusion of ideas hostile to our free system continues remorselessly. Industrial capitalism, and the free market system, is presented as destructive of human happiness, corrupt, immoral, wasteful, inefficient and above all, doomed. Collectivism is presented as the only way out compatible with the dignity of the human spirit and the future of our race. The expanded university threatens to become not the powerhouse of Western individualism and enterprise, but its graveyard.

There is a second threat, what I call 'Ecological Panic'. Now this movement, again, began with the best intentions. I well remember when Rachel Carson's work, *Silent Spring*, first appeared in the *New Yorker*, and the surprise and concern it rightly aroused. We were tending to ignore some of the destructive side-effects of very rapid industrial expansion. The wave of concern that followed was justified, and the steps then taken, notably the clean air policies, and the policies for cleansing lakes and waterways, have been spectacularly successful. Thanks to smokeless fuel, London fogs, which were real killers, have been virtually eliminated. The last really serious London fog was in 1952. The Thames is now cleaner, and has greater quantities of fish, and more varieties in it, than at any time since before the days of Spenser or Shakespeare. Similar successes are now being registered in the United States, which adopted such legally enforceable remedies somewhat later than Britain did. These are examples of what can be done by thoughtful, unemotional, systematic and scientifically justified application of conservation and antipollution policies.

But most of these were put in hand before the ecological panic started. Once ecology became a fashionable good cause, as it did in the late 1960s, reason, logic and proportion flew out of the window. It became a campaign not against pollution, but against growth itself, and especially against free enterprise growth − totalitarian communist growth was somehow less morally offensive. Everyone should read Professor Wilfred Beckerman's *In Defence of Economic Growth*. Beckerman is one of the best of our economists, and was a member of the Royal Commission on Environmental Pollution; he knows the subject better perhaps than any other working economist and his book is a wonderfully sane and lucid summary of the entire subject. I have never yet been able to persuade any committed ecology campaigner even to look at this book. Of course not: they have a faith, and they do not want to risk it. One of the most important developments of our time, I would argue, is the growth, as a consequence of the rapid decline of Christianity, of irrationalist substitutes for it. These are not necessarily religious, or even quasi-religious. Often they are pseudo-scientific in form, as for instance the weird philosophy of the late Teilhard de Chardin. The ecology panic is another example. It is akin to the salvation panic of sixteenth century Calvinism. When you expel the priest, you do not inaugurate the age of reason − you get the witchdoctor. But whereas Calvinist salvation panic may have contributed to the rise of capitalism, the ecology panic could be the death of it.

If the restrictions now imposed on industrial development had operated in eighteenth century England, the Industrial Revolution could not have taken place. It would in effect have been inhibited by law − as of course many landowners of the day wished it to be − and in any event legal requirements would have eliminated the very modest profits by which it originally financed itself. We would still be existing at eighteenth century living standards, and wallowing in eighteenth century levels of pollution, which were infinitely worse than anything we experience today − if you want to see what they were like, visit the slums of Calcutta or Djakarta.

As it is, the ecology panic has been a potent destructive force. The panic-mongers played a crucial role in persuading the Middle Eastern oil producers, especially Iran, to quadruple the price of oil in the autumn of 1973, the biggest single blow industrial capitalism has suffered since the Wall Street crash of 1929. That was the beginning of the profound recession from which we have not yet emerged. In the end, as was foreseeable at the time, the huge rise in oil prices did not do anyone any good, least of all the oil producers. But it ended the great post-war boom and robbed Western capitalism of its tremendous *élan*, perhaps for good. As Browning put it, 'Never glad confident morning again.' And it is significant that the ecological lobby is now striving desperately, with fanatic vigour and persistence, to prevent the development of nuclear energy, allegedly on the grounds of safety. It is a fact, a very remarkable fact in my view, that throughout the West (we have no figures for Russia or China) the nuclear power industry is the only industry which over 30 years has contrived to avoid a single fatal industrial accident. Its record is unique, and has been achieved by the efforts of the industry itself, and the responsible governments, without any assistance from the ecolobby. But of course the lobby would like a few fatal accidents: that would suit their purposes very well. In Britain recently, we had a long, public enquiry, what we call a statutory enquiry, into whether or not it was right to go ahead with the enriched uranium plant at Windscale. The enquiry was a model of its kind. The ecoloby marshalled all the scientific experts and evidence they could lay their hands on. At the end the verdict was that there was no reason whatever why the programme should not proceed. Did the ecolobby accept the verdict? On the contrary. They immediately organised a mass demonstration, and planned various legal and illegal activities to halt the programme by force. Some members of the lobby are Communists, and their motives are obvious. But the mass of the movement, in the United States, Britain, France, Germany and Italy, so far as I have been able to observe, is not politically motivated. It is simply irrational: but irrationality is an enemy of civilised society, and it can be, and is being, exploited by the politically interested.

A third factor in the future of capitalism is the growth of government. Industrial capitalism, or rather the free enterprise economy, and Big Government, are natural and probably irreconcilable enemies. It is no accident that the Industrial Revolution took place in late eighteenth century England. It was a period of minimum government. Of all the periods of English history, indeed of European history, it was the time when government was least conspicuous and active. It was the age, unfortunately very short, of the night-watchman state. As a matter of fact, the Industrial Revolution,

perhaps the most important single event in human history, seems to
have occurred without the English government even noticing. By the
time they did, it was too late; happily − otherwise they would probably have stopped it.

It is almost inevitable that government, particularly an active, interventionist government, should view free enterprise with a degree
of hostility, since it constitutes a countervailing power in the state.
The tendency, then, is to cut free enterprise down to size, and this
may be done in a number of ways. In the United States the
characteristic technique is government regulation and legal harassment, and this of course has been far more pervasive and strident
since the ecolobby swung into action. In Britain the technique is both
through direct assault − nationalisation − and slow starvation. In a
way, nationalisation is ineffective, since it allows the public to make
comparisons between the performance of the nationalised sector and
that of the free sector, nearly always to the latter's advantage. Starvation is more insidious. By this I mean the progressive transfer, by
taxation and other government policies, of resources from the private
to the public sector.

In 1955 for instance, public expenditure in Britain as a proportion
of the GNP was 41.88 per cent. By 1975, 20 years later, it has risen to
nearly 60 per cent. Moreover, this rise was accompanied by a record
budget deficit of about 22 billion dollars, itself a further 11.5 per cent
of GNP. Of course the taxation had to be provided, and the deficit
serviced, by the private sector. We have, then, an Old Man of the Sea
relationship, in which the parasitical Old Man is growing bigger, and
poor Sinbad smaller, all the time. The shrinking productive sector
has to carry the burden of an ever-expanding, loss-making public sector. Thus Britain's nationalised steel industry will lose 1,000 million
dollars this year, and it has just been authorised by statute to borrow
up to 7 billion dollars, guaranteed by government and taxpayer. Now
the interesting thing is that in Britain the public sector, and the Civil
Service, generally, are now paying higher wages, providing better
conditions, and giving larger pensions, which in a growing number of
cases are index-linked, and so inflation proof, than the private sector
can possibly afford. And of course they are financing these goodies
out of tax-guaranteed deficits − that is, from the dwindling profits
of the private sector. This is the starvation technique. When a private
firm goes bust, provided it is big enough, the state takes over, the

losses are added to the taxpayer's bill, and the private sector has one more expensive passenger to carry.

In this technique, the fourth factor, the trade unions, play an important part. In Britain it is demonstrably true that the legal privileges of the trade unions, which virtually exempt them from any kind of action for damages (including, now, libel), lead directly to restrictive practices, overmanning, low productivity, low investment, low wages and low profits. Thus trade union action tends, in itself, to undermine the performance of industrial capitalism as a wealth-creating system. In Britain, for instance, the trade unions can rightly claim that capitalism is inefficient, because they make sure it is inefficient. Ford workers in Britain, using exactly the same assembly line machinery as in West Germany, produce between 20 and 50 per cent less automobiles. ICI Chemicals, one of the best companies in Britain, nevertheless has a productivity performance 25 per cent lower than its Dutch and German competitors. A recent analysis shows this is entirely due to overmanning and restrictive practices. The private sector is now threatened by two further union devices: the legally enforced closed shop, which compels the workforce to join designated unions on pain of dismissal without compensation or legal redress; and new plans to force firms to appoint up to 50 per cent workerdirectors, these worker-directors to be appointed not by the workforce themselves, nor even necessarily from among them, but by and from the trade union bureaucracy. This has to be seen against the explicit policy of some groups within the unions of driving private sector firms to bankruptcy, by strikes and harassment, so that the state will then have to take them into the public sector.

Of course what is happening in Britain will not necessarily happen elsewhere. But certainly if the Bill now before the Senate giving unions much wider and more effective powers to organise goes through, the United States will be well launched on the road Britain has travelled; and there are many other ways in which the present US administration seems determined to follow Britain's example. The West Germans, too, are now beginning to adopt some of the institutions which flourish in British trade unionism, notably the shop stewards' movement. Businessmen all over the free world may despise the performance of British industry. But trade unionists all over the world admire and envy the power of British trade unionists and are actively seeking to acquire it for themselves.

Let us end with a word of warning. I have said nothing of the fifth threat in industrial capitalism and the free enterprise system — the threat from without. But of course this is bound to increase as the military superiority of the Soviet Union over the United States is reinforced. I have never thought that the Communist system would triumph by a direct assault. I have always assumed that it would first establish an overwhelming military predominance and then, by pressure and threats, begin to draw the political and economic dividends of it. If the United States opts out of the competitive arms race with the Soviet Union, while providing, as she supposes, merely for her own defence, then we must expect to see this fifth threat hard at work winding up industrial capitalism and free enterprise all over the world.

Thus, when we ask has capitalism a future, the answer is: it all depends on the United States. West Germany and Japan, it is true, have strong free enterprise economies; they also have a tradition of state capitalism, and would adapt themselves with surprising speed and readiness to a new collective order. France already has a huge public sector, and a long tradition of *dirigisme* or *étatisme*. All three are Janus-faced. Britain, I believe, is profoundly anti-collective, and will remain so if it continues to be given the choice. But its private enterprise system is now very weak, and its business and financial elites are demoralised and defeatist. I myself think that capitalism will survive, because of its enormous intrinsic virtues as a system for generating wealth, and promoting freedom. But those who man and control it must stop apologising and go on to the ideological offensive. They must show to ordinary people that both the Communist world, and the Third World, are parasitical upon industrial capitalism for their growth technology, that without capitalism, the 200 years of unprecedented growth that have created the modern world would gradually come to an end. We would have slow growth, then nil growth, then minus growth; and then the Malthusian catastrophe. In short, those who wish to maintain the capitalist system must endeavour to teach the world a little history, and remind it, and especially the young, that though man's achievements are great they are never as solid as they look. If man makes the wrong choice, there is always another Dark Age waiting for him, round the corner of time.

CHAPTER 13

Is there a Moral Basis for Capitalism?

This is the edited version of a paper I delivered at Airlie House, Virginia, in May 1979 at a conference on politics and morals organised by the American Enterprise Institute and Syracuse University.

It takes nerve these days to suggest there can be a moral basis for capitalism, let alone to argue that capitalism provides, on the whole, the best economic structure for man's moral fulfilment. No day passes without a prominent clergyman denouncing the gross immorality of some large capitalist concern; and in most schools children are encouraged to hold their noses when such notions as 'profit' and 'private enterprise' are discussed.

Such attitudes, it seems to me, are confused. They are based on a lack of understanding of the relationship between man's moral development, and the way in which he organises his society. We can and do achieve moral maturity under any kind of economic and social system, including those we find morally repugnant. Indeed, history suggests that societies specifically contrived to promote morality rarely succeed. Such earthly Utopias tend to become theocracies, and theocracies – whether the temple-states of antiquity, Calvin's Geneva, or the Ayatollah's Iran – traffic in a spiritual intolerance which does violence to mind and body. The core of man's moral condition is the free will he is bidden to exercise. Hence the question we should begin by asking is: What social system is most conducive to developing the informed conscience which enables man's free will to make the right choices?

The first thing to note is that the articulated concept of the individual conscience, though always buried in our nature, took a very long time to emerge. The earliest recorded societies did not recognise that every human being has a unique personality endowed with self-consciousness and a free will. In the Ancient Egypt of the Old Kingdom, in the first half of the 3rd millennium BC, religious and political doctrine revolved around the assumption that only the Pharaoh was a complete personality. His life and fate embraced that of all his subjects. They engaged in the infinite labour of building his tomb-pyramid not from compulsion but almost certainly with enthusiasm, because they believed that their salvation was subsumed in his: if his funeral and tomb arrangements were satisfactory, they would be carried into eternal life along with him.

Only very gradually did the ancient Egyptians 'democratise' their idea of a Last Judgment, in which each human being was separately weighed in the scales of eternal justice. The great American Egyptologist, Professor James Breasted, has called this discovery 'the dawn of conscience'. And it was an important human discovery as well as a religious one, for it implied that every individual was responsible for his or her actions and therefore, in a moral sense, free. The implication was first properly understood by the Jews, who probably derived the idea from the Egyptians. The Jews (as the earliest parts of the Bible indicate) had, like other primitive societies, a strong belief in collective virtue and crime, and in collective rewards and punishments. These beliefs were very persistent, and the Jews were still trying to shake them off long after they became rigorous monotheists. Only in the two or three centuries before the birth of Christ were they really beginning to work out their theory of the immortal soul and the Last Judgment. At roughly the same time, the Stoic philosophers in the Greek world were developing the idea of the individual conscience, a necessary adjunct to the concept of free will.

The two sets of ideas were made for each other, and Christ and his great interpreter St Paul were the inheritors of this new collection of thoughts about the human individual. The New Testament, which outlines their philosophy, is essentially libertarian and individualistic, since it asserts that the unique personality of each individual, as reflected in his moral choices, is infinitely more important than anything else about him — class, colour, status, sex, or nationality.

The essence of Judaeo-Christian teaching — leaving out their conflicting notions of the actual mechanism of salvation − is that every man or woman, by the mere fact of his or her humanity, is a party to what I call the Divine Contract. The Divine Contract comes into operation at the age of understanding and terminates with earthly death, at which point judgment is given as to whether its terms have been fulfilled − and the inevitable consequences follow. The essence of the Divine Contract is that it is an individual bargain between God and Man. There is nothing collective about it. Each man and woman determines the fate of his or her soul, and the terms of each contract are identical. Judaeo-Christianity, therefore, is based on absolute individuality and on total spiritual equality. In the Divine Contract, all are equal before the law, and each is wholly responsible for his or her actions.

In Christianity in particular, this paramountcy of the individual was reinforced by the Greek concepts which underlay Pauline theology. The tragedy, however, is that Christianity became the official religion of the Roman Empire only after the classical spirit of the Graeco-Roman world had spent itself, and only after the acknowledgement of the individual had been submerged beneath an Oriental despotism. Christianity was married to and appropriated by the Late Empire, which was in all essentials a corporate state. Not only did it possess legally enforced class distinctions but it organised its subjects by trades and occupations, which they were compelled to follow by law, and to which their descendants were likewise bound. The corporation was all; the individual was nothing. Such rights as a man had, he acquired by virtue of his class and trade, not by his existence or merits as an individual human being.

The Dark Ages and the Middle Ages were thus dominated by a collectivist philosophy. Christianity gave men and women moral individuality, but society took it away on the material plane. Men went through life as members of sharply differentiated categories: they spoke and dressed as such, and were judged as such in the courts. It was very difficult to change class, occupation, even place of residence. They were locked into a system − for life; indeed, they were seen and saw themselves as mere living components of a collective social body. The image of society as a body or *corpus*, rather than a collection of individuals, each complete in themselves, dominates the thinking of the pre-modern world.

The concept is illuminated by the story of De Montfort taking a heretic city during the Albigensian crusade. Turning to his spiritual adviser, a Cistercian abbot, De Montfort asked him how his soldiers, who had orders to slaughter the heretics and spare the rest, would be able to tell them apart. 'Oh, kill them all,' replied the abbot. 'God will know his own.' Only God had the capacity to recognise the individual. Spiritually, the individual was paramount; in earthly terms he was buried in the collectivity.

Yet Christianity, with its stress on the individual, did carry with it the notion of inalienable rights, slowly though it matured. In Western Europe, missionary Christian bishops collected, purified, codified, Latinised and set down in writing the laws of the barbarians, and invested them with spiritual authority and sanction. By its work on these law codes, Christianity implanted the concept of the rule of law: a rule which, for the Church's own protection, could be invoked even against the state. The Christian Church needed a law which was even stronger than the state: and it got such a law. Of course, it was thinking in terms of its own corporate rights: but the notion of the rule of law was progressively extended to cover and underpin the rights of the individual.

By a similar process, the idea of freehold property was established. The freehold was unknown to barbarian Europe; indeed, it was only imperfectly developed in Imperial Rome and Byzantium. The church needed it for the security of its own properties, and wrote it into the law codes it processed — wrote it, indeed, so indelibly that it survived and defied the superimposed forms of feudalism. The instrument of the land deed or charter, giving absolute possession of land to a private individual or private corporation, is one of the great inventions of human history. And, taken in conjunction with the notion of the rule of law, it is economically and politically a very important one. For once an individual can own land absolutely, without social or economic qualification, and once his right in that land is protected — even against the state — by the rule of law, he has true security of property. And once security of property is a fact, the propensity to save — which (as Keynes noted) is exceedingly powerful in man — is enormously enhanced, and not only enhanced but translated into the propensity to invest.

We see, then, that the Dawn of Conscience, the idea that the individual has an absolute freehold in his own soul, foreshadows the dawn of capitalism. Capitalism is based on the system of possessive individualism, in which individual men and women, as well as tribes, crowns, states or other political and social corporations, own absolute freeholds in property and manage and dispose of them freely. Likewise, the notion of equality before the judgment of God foreshadows the notion of individual equality before the law of man.

These concepts are very much interdependent. Individual freehold is impossible without the rule of law, with its necessary implication of equality before the law, and its guarantee that the law will uphold individual property rights even against state prerogative. England and Holland were the first states in which such rights were effectively established, and legal certitude is the precondition of capitalist enterprise. As Professor Hayek puts it in *The Constitution of Liberty*, 'There is probably no single factor which has contributed more to the prosperity of the West than the relatively certainty of the law which has prevailed there . . . .'

The establishment of the individual freehold is not the only way in which Christianity made capitalism possible. Like the Judaism on which it is based, it is a historical religion, generated by a definite historical event and proceeding towards a definite historical goal. Its thrust is thus linear, not cyclical: time is of the essence of its machinery, and it insists on preparedness; its constant exhortation is that 'We know not the day nor the hour'. Its morality stresses the saving principle of worldly pleasures deferred for the sake of future felicity, and it proceeds by a regular accounting of vice and virtue towards a final audit and a celestial dividend. It is no accident that the monks of the West first produced a system of regular working hours, governed by exact computation of time, and the tolling of the bell. Indeed, most historians now agree that the roots of capitalism lay in the ethics of Christianity long before the advent of Calvin and his 'salvation panic'. The Merchant of Prato was inscribing, at the head of each page of his accounts, 'For the Greater Honour and Glory of God', long before Protestantism was born. But, in my view, the notion of freehold possession was by far the most important Christian contribution to the emergence of capitalism.

Indeed, I would go so far as to argue that without individual freehold a capitalist system cannot develop. But, once you have individual freehold, with its concomitant developments of the rule of law and equality before the law, the development of some form of capitalism is not only likely but virtually inevitable. The connection between Christian morality and capitalism thus centres essentially around the role and importance of the individual.

We can see this connection being worked out in history. In the later Middle Ages, and especially in the towns, the Christian notion of the individual conscience gradually broke through the corporatist carapace of society. As the towns grew in size and importance, as men changed their class and occupation – and fortunes – more rapidly, a new spirit of individualism was bred: people were increasingly judged and rewarded on their merits and efforts, not their status. In art the true portrait emerges, and not just of the rich patron: the crowd scenes of a Hieronymus Bosch or a Breughel show a sharpening focus even on the faces of humble folk. In the sixteenth century we get the first true biographies and the first plays based upon the development of character. Individuals leap out at us from the pages of the historical records. The moralistic writings of Erasmus for the first time link the Christian notion of the individual conscience to the spirit of individual enterprise.

The new individualism inevitably threatened the social structure, based as it was on class privilege and the absolute right of status. In the English civil wars of the 1640s, the House of Commons, which represented the institutionalised individualism of property, overthrew the concept of the king as head of the body-corporate. It was the end in England of the medieval corporate state.

But in one sense, individualism threatened the political rights of property also. In the political debates – of which we have a marvellous verbatim record in the Clarke Papers – between Cromwell and some of his generals, officers and men, held in Putney church in 1647, that was the point at issue: did a man have political rights by virtue of his property, his stake in the country, as Cromwell and his supporters maintained, or did he have rights by virtue of his personality, the fact that he was a free, adult human being, a simple individual, as the radicals demanded?

At the time, the argument went in favour of property, but in the long run the logical thrust of Christian moral individualism was irresistible. The civil wars, by dissolving the old corporate state, necessarily began a process of economic emancipation of the individual, which was just as important as giving him political rights. In the eighteenth century, as property triumphed over hereditary class and status, new ways of evaluating property and protecting it by law began to emerge. The law of industrial patents, which was now developed in England, made it possible for the first time for a man to obtain a true commercial reward for his inventive skill and investment in research — a notable and historic victory for the gifted and industrious individual. By introducing a new and dynamic element into the economy, it was one of the principal contributing factors to the Industrial Revolution, which began to transform the world from the 1760s onwards.

Another important extension of the notion of individual property was the breakdown of the Laws of Settlement, which sought to control the free movement of labour, and were in fact one of the last relics of the old corporatism.

Adam Smith, in his great treatise on how wealth is created, was quick to grasp that this represented the economic emancipation of the ordinary working man. It allowed him to escape from the grip of a status society to one in which rewards depended on a freely negotiated contract, enabling him to realise the value of the only freehold property he possessed — his energy and skill. Throughout history, argued Smith, governments, lords and guilds had sought to prevent ordinary poor men from seeking work in the best market. Yet, he added,

The property which every man has in his own labour, as it is the foundation of all other property, so it is the most sacred and inviolable. To hinder [a poor man] from employing his strength and dexterity in what manner he thinks proper without injury to his neighbour is a plain violation of this most sacred property.

As Smith grasped, the notion of the individual freehold embodied a political as well as an economic freedom: at bottom, political and economic freedom are inseparable. The political freedom to vote as you please is largely meaningless without the economic freedom to work where you please. Once a man is free to make contracts for his own labour, he will soon begin to demand the right to make contracts with his political masters too. It is no accident that the Industrial Revolution and the creation of the capitalist economy based on freely contracted labour were rapidly followed by the development of democracy in the West.

One might say that capitalism, far from dehumanising man,

allowed him at last to assume the full individuality which Christianity had always accorded him as the possessor of a distinctive moral conscience and an immortal soul. Just as the notion of freehold property was implicit in the notion of the free will, so the wage contract was implicit in the divine contract. The advent of capitalism both reflected and advanced the emergence of the individual human personality. In the West, we are so used to being brought up and treated as individuals that we tend to take the concept of individuality for granted. Yet it is a comparatively modern idea — no older than capitalism; scarcely older than the Industrial Revolution. For most of history the great majority of ordinary people have been treated by the authorities as if they were a congealed mass, without distinctive personalities, let alone individual rights and aspirations. For democracy to evolve, it was first necessary for society to recognise that it was composed of millions of individuals, not undifferentiated groups classified merely by occupation and social status.

It was with the rise of capitalism that ordinary people acquired names. Not, of course, the names they were given at birth, and by which they were known among the narrow circle of their family and neighbours, but hereditary family names which, in combination with their given names, provided them with a specific identity.

Family names were originally dynastic, reserved for kings. Only very slowly did they spread down to the aristocracy and then on to the gentry. Most of those peasants who voted for industrial capitalism with their feet acquired names in the process, along with their residence and immigration papers. As recently as the First World War soldiers in the Russian army below the rank of senior NCO did not have names on the official record, only numbers. Only in the nineteenth century did most of the governments in Europe pass laws encouraging or compelling the adoption of family names. Denmark, for instance, passed such a law as late as 1904; the Turks did not do so until 1935.

More than to any other force, then, we owe the acknowledgement of our individuality to capitalism, to the notion of what has been well called 'possessive individualism'. And individualism is rooted in the Judaeo-Christian doctrine of conscience and free will. Free will implies choice: the moral function of society, the way in which it best serves the moral needs of the individuals who compose it, is when it facilitates the process of choice, permits consciences to inform themselves, and so offers the individual the greatest possible opportunity to fulfil his part in the divine contract. That, essentially, is the moral basis of capitalism. Capitalism, strictly defined as a purely economic device, is morally neutral. But capitalism, based as it is on the legal rights of individual freehold, creates a multiplicity of power-centres, rival to that of the state. Hence, it is a matter of historical observation that capitalism tends to promote − and, in my contention, must promote − liberal-democratic political systems; and such systems are not morally neutral; they are morally desirable, for they offer the individual the element of choice through which his free will matures.

By contrast, socialist societies, pursuing Utopia and a positive moral framework, inevitably restrict this choice. I no longer believe, as I once did, that political freedom can be preserved where economic freedom is eliminated. As I have already argued, the existence of the right to own freehold property makes capitalism inevitable; where, therefore, it is desired to eliminate capitalism, the property freehold must be destroyed first. Capitalism, indeed, cannot be effectively destroyed without eliminating legal freehold. And without such freeholds, there can be no effective and durable rival centres of power, to keep the state in check. Monopoly, therefore, must follow, as night follows day; and where there is monopoly, there is no choice. And without choice, the free will must live in an atrophied state, in hidden darkness and danger, as it did under the most hideous tyrannies of the past. Monopoly is the enemy of morality − and so, therefore, must be the collectivist societies which promote it. The more such collectivisms proclaim or even acquire popular endorsement, the more dangerous they are. Lord Acton rightly observed:

It is bad to be oppressed by a minority but it is worse to be oppressed by a majority. For there is a reserve of latent power in the masses which, if it is called into play, the minority can seldom resist. From the absolute will of the entire people there is no appeal, no redemption, no refuge but treason (*The History of Freedom in Antiquity*, 1877).

It seems to me that the authors of the mature Judaeo-Christian system of morals − the greatest such system the world has ever seen − were right to anchor it in the *individual* conscience. There is no intrinsic morality in the majority decision: far from it. All great moralists have rightly drawn attention to the horrors of the mass or herd in action, symbolised in the terrifying New Testament image of the Gadarene swine. Sir Thomas Browne, in *Religio Medici*, warns us against 'That great enemy of reason, virtue and religion, the Multitude; that numerous piece of monstrosity which, taken asunder, seem men, and the reasonable creatures of God but, confused together, make but one Great Beast and a monstrosity more prodigious than Hydra . . . .'

A true moral system must contain a self-correcting mechanism: for Christianity it is the conscience of the individual. The strength of the system lies in its just estimate of man as a fallible creature with immortal longings. Its outstanding moral merit is to invest the individual with a conscience and bid him follow it. This particular form of liberation is what St Paul meant by the freedom men find in Christ. For conscience is the enemy of tyranny and the compulsory society; and it is the Christian conscience which has destroyed the very institutional tyrannies Christianity itself has created — the self-correcting mechanism at work. The notions of political and economic freedom both spring from the workings of the Christian conscience as a historical force.

In this process, I have argued, the decisive device is the notion of individual freehold. And individual freehold performs for capitalism the same role as the individual conscience in a Christian moral system — it is the self-correcting mechanism. So long as men can by law hold freehold property in the teeth of the state, or any other large corporation, they will successfully endeavour to get such property, and hold it; and such men will be numerous, and their tendency will be to grow. Where a multiplicity of men hold freehold property, political power must be divided and shared. And where power must be shared, and is shared, there can be no economic monopoly either. Any tendency inherent in capitalism towards monopoly — and I am not so sure that there is generally such a tendency, despite Marx's arguments — is balanced by the undoubted tendency of capitalism to promote democratic liberalism and thus parliamentary checks on monopoly power. This is the self-correcting mechanism at work again.

I am not speaking of theoretical argument, but of demonstrable practice — of history. To take only the cases of the United States and Great Britain: when in history have we had, as over the past 200 years, such outstanding examples of societies reforming themselves from within − not by revolution and violence, but by debate and argument, and by law and statute? That the first capitalist societies were rugged and ruthless, even cruel, cannot be disputed. But the value of an institution lies not in its clumsy origins but in its potentiality. The ability of capitalism to reform and improve itself is almost infinite, and logically so: for by its very nature it is not a monolith but the sum of innumerable freeholds, vested in innumerable free minds, minds which reflect the infinity of human pressures, desires and inventiveness. It is truly protean.

Indeed, its resilience, which has a moral quality because it is rooted in the free interplay of human consciences, is in marked and significant contrast to the rigidity of collectivist systems. They can be changed too − but only by force. They respond − but only to revolution. They lack the self-correcting mechanism because they do not, and by their nature cannot, accord rights to the individual conscience.

Such systems therefore lack a moral basis − not so much as ideas, but as realities − and, lacking a moral basis, they are doomed to revert to the chaos from which they sprang. Democratic capitalism, on the other hand, is destined to survive; though, being protean, its more distant manifestations would astonish us, were we alive to witness them. But democratic capitalism, I suspect, will always in some way retain the notion of the individual freehold, for it is this, the physical manifestation of the individual conscience, which gives it its economic and political strength and, not least, its moral legitimacy.

CHAPTER 14

A Tory Philosophy of Law

Shortly after the election of the Thatcher Government, I gave a lecture to the Society of Conservative Lawyers in which I looked at the long-term reforms which a Conservative government should consider, if democracy and the rule of law in Britain were to be made secure.

What particular insights and gifts of understanding does the Conservative lawyer bring to the political process? And in what particular ways is his approach useful and important at present? I start from the assumption, which I think many Conservative lawyers will share, that the political and constitutional system of this country is going through a period of risk and jeopardy. The Conservative electoral victory did not remove the long-term threat to our stability and free institutions. What it did was to give us a breathing space, during which we can prepare more effective and durable defences to meet the threat, which is certain to be resumed. In this task Conservative lawyers have an indispensible part to play.

The first thing a Conservative lawyer ought to be clear about in his own mind is the proper role of Parliament. I should begin by saying what Parliament is not. It is not a legislative device for the transformation of society. It is not a machine whereby revolutions are carried through peacefully and legally. It is not an engine of Utopia. By attempting to be these things, it merely damages its effectiveness and authority. No Conservative lawyer should entertain the view that prosperity, let alone happiness, can be brought about by Act of Parliament. Indeed, the statutory pursuit of the unattainable – such as economic equality – is certain to end in the diminution of freedom, and very likely, if pursued ruthlessly enough, to bring about the collapse of the rule of law itself.

A Conservative lawyer, I suggest, takes a sceptical view of the power of the statute, unless it corresponds to overwhelming public need and desire, and reflects fundamental moral assumptions. He is inclined to agree with Thomas Hobbes, when he said: 'The freedom of the subject is the silence of the law.' There is nothing to be proud of in the fact that Parliament turns out an average of 3,000 pages of new law every year, plus 10,000 pages of subordinate legislation. This is evidence, not of virtue, but of confusion, inefficiency and false aims.

The truth is, Parliament is not primarily a legislative asembly. It is a deliberate court for the redressing of grievances. As such it is a means whereby a society under God and under law safeguards its civil liberties. The point was admirably made by Milton in his *Araopagitica*: 'That no grievance ever should arise in the Commonwealth, let no man in this world expect. But when complaints are freely heard, deeply considered and speedily reformed, then is the utmost bound of civil liberty attained that wise men look for.' The redressing of grievances is not necessarily done by legislative enactment alone: but by the amendment or repeal of law, or by the activity – and inactivity – of government.

The phrase 'a society under God and law' is appropriate because Parliament is not the primeval legislature. It does not, and cannot, create law from nothing. Rather it inherits, and interprets, a system of moralistic law, much of which is enshrined in the organic corpus of Common Law. Hence we might define the function of Parliament as making the necessary adjustments between the system of fundamental law and the changing needs of society. Its primary function is therefore as a revising body: it is a law-making body only in a secondary sense. It cannot make fundamental law. It cannot make marriage a crime, murder a duty, or falsehood meritorious.

It is necessary to state or restate these truths, because the prevailing wisdom is to discredit notions of natural law, whether divinely inspired or otherwise. It is powerfully argued, by Professor Hart and his disciples, that there is no such thing as absolute law. It is argued that all law is relative, reflecting the assumptions of a particular society. Law is a social phenomenon, intelligible only in a social context. It can command no kind of authority outside its own terms of reference, which of course merely reflect the norms of a particular society which may well be an injust and inequitable one. And, since society changes, fundamental law changes also – indeed, ought to change, to conform with society's altered viewpoint. In this theory of jurisprudence there are no fixed points at all. It is thus not so very different from Marxism: indeed, fits Marxism very well. The conclusions it leads to are that all law is provisional and that, in a democracy, the powers of the legislature are limitless.

I believe this is a very dangerous doctrine in any circumstances, and a particularly dangerous one in Britain, where we have no written constitution and Parliament is popularly supposed to be sovereign. I say 'popularly supposed to be' because I do not accept that Parliament is absolutely sovereign. It is sovereign only within the context of an inherited system of law and morals. In 1774, Lord Mansfield said, rightly in my view: 'Whatever is *contra bonos mores et decorum* the principles of our laws prohibit, and the King's court, as the general censor and guardian of the public morals is bound to restrain and punish.' More recently, Lord Simmonds declared that Mansfield 'was asserting, as I now assert, that there is in that court a residual power, where no statute has yet intervened to supersede the Common Law, to superintend those offences which are prejudicial to the public welfare'. The assumption here, and it is a justified assumption, is that parliamentary statute is essentially a commentary upon the fundamentals of public morality as reflected in the Common Law.

This means that we must not only accept, but defend and strengthen, the notion of restraint on parliamentary sovereignty. And we should begin by dismissing the idea of the sovereignty of the Commons – an idea which has been rightly identified by Lord Hailsham as 'elective dictatorship'. I doubt if any human body can be said to exercise absolute sovereignty, and no elective house can constitute such a body. Austin rightly held the view that, in a democracy, it is not the elective representatives who constitute the sovereign body but the electors. In Britain, he wrote, 'speaking accurately, the members of the Commons are merely trustees for the body by which they are elected and appointed; and consequently the sovereignty always resides in the monarch, peers and electoral body of the Commons.'

It is right that we should bear this in mind, since it is very rare for a party holding the absolute majority of seats in a legislature to receive a majority of the votes. In May 1979, Mrs Thatcher won, in terms of plurality of votes, the most decisive majority since 1935: but she did not even get a majority of the votes cast, let alone a majority of those able to vote. Most governments have much less moral authority. In the last Parliament, the government party had been chosen by only 29 per cent of the electorate, but it enacted some very repressive and obnoxious Acts, such as the Industrial Relations Acts of 1974 and 1976, the Employment Protection Act of 1975, and the latest Rent Act. To admit the notion of unrestricted parliamentary sovereignty, effectively vested in the Commons, is to accept the proposition that our fundamental rights and freedoms can at any time be abolished or reduced by a Parliament which acknowledges no concept of fundamental and unalterable law, but acts by simple majority, conceivably consisting of a minority of Members of Parliament as a whole, representing a minority of popular votes and acting upon the command of whips who, in turn, are subject to the orders of the few men forming the Cabinet.

It is for this reason that Conservative lawyers, in my view, should actively concern themselves with the need for a reformed and strengthened second chamber. Not many people seem to realise that a Labour victory at the May 1979 election might have brought the country to a real constitutional crisis. The Labour manifesto read: 'We propose, therefore, in the next parliament, to abolish the delaying power and legislative veto of the House of Lords.' The Parliament Act of 1911, Section 2, specifically excepts 'a Bill containing any provision to extend the maximum duration of Parliament beyond five years' from the substance of the Act which deprives the Lords of their veto power. Indeed, this provision, endorsed by the 1949 Parliament Act, is the only instance in which the Lords retain a veto power. Hence the insertion of those three words, 'and legislative veto', can only have been intended to clear the way to giving the Commons the right to extend its own life indefinitely. That is point number one − a very sinister point.

Point number two is, that a Bill thus to restrict or effectively to abolish the Lords as part of the legislature would be of very doubtful legality. Some experts, such as Hood Phillips in the 1978 edition of *Constitutional and Administrative Law*, even argue that the 1949 Act is invalid. The 1911 Act is a temporary Act, enacted pending further legislation about an elective second chamber – many people forget this. It lays down a special legislative procedure. The Act the Labour Party proposed would have to use this procedure – in effect the Commons would be using the special Parliament Act procedure in order to destroy that procedure. Thus a judge might invalidate it simply by studying the words of the enactment. This is a view set out, in interesting detail, in an article in the *Law Quarterly Review*, January 1979. It indicates that Labour's plans for the Lords might involve a headlong conflict between Parliament and the courts. But it also suggests to me that Conservative lawyers should press the Government to complete the unfinished business of the 1911 Act and bring into existence a reformed and authoritative second chamber while the opportunity still exists – a second chamber designed to curb the false notion of parliamentary sovereignty by investing residual powers, of a custodial nature, in a second chamber with an unassailable popular base, and one not susceptible to the 'creation of peers' technique. This present Parliament may well be our last chance to achieve a sensible reform of the Lords as an alternative to abolition, and we should not miss it.

Secondly, we likewise have an opportunity to repulse the concept of 'elective dictatorship' by enacting a Bill of Rights. For all practical purposes, the proposal is that a Bill based upon the European Convention for the Protection of Human Rights and Fundamental Freedoms should be enacted by Parliament so that this convention will operate at every level of the judicial process. At present, under a 1966 agreement, British subjects can apply to the Human Rights Commission for relief only when they have exhausted local remedies – and in the Thalidomide Contempt of Court case the ruling of the House of Lords has been overthrown. By enacting a Bill of Rights we would enormously simplify such procedure. We would also, in my view, provide a massive check on 'elective dictatorship', and establish a procedure by which oppressive statutes might be invalidated. I know it is argued that such a Bill would not give all the protection needed, since the doctrine of parliamentary sovereignty, and of the superior power of the most recent statute, means that no Parliament can bind its successor, or even itself. But if, as Austin argued, and I would also argue, sovereignty resides in monarch, peers and electoral body of the Commons, a Bill of Rights, passed by Parliament and endorsed by referendum, might well be upheld by the courts as superior to any subsequent statute of an ordinary kind. In any event, it would constitute an indelible marker or Rubicon, the breaching of which would constitute the manifest transition from constitutionalism to tyranny.

Such a Bill would also greatly strengthen the hands of the judges, in their vital and often lonely defence of individual rights. Now if there is one characteristic which a Conservative lawyer should exhibit, it is a tendency to look with favour on judges' law, because it is linked to the notion of fundamental law. Certainly, the radical lawyer betrays himself by his hatred of this notion. The radical position was set out in Laski's *Parliamentary Government in England*:

The tendencies of the modern state run counter to the main principles upon which the Common Law has been built . . . The judges spare no pains in attacking parliamentary decisions it is not their function to criticise. They are occupied in the construction of what is hardly less than a fundamental law which they use to confine the ambit of statutes within the limits of policies they happen to approve . . . They interpret the 'rule of law' as though they are themselves the masters of a 'higher law' than that of the sovereign legislature.

This is also the view of the relativists. Professor Hart writes: 'The manipulation by English courts of the rules concerning the binding force of precedent is perhaps more honestly described . . . as a successful bid to take powers and use them.' Judges are presented as obstacles to progressive policies by Ronald Dworkin, Hart's disciple and successor as Professor of Jurisprudence at Oxford. He writes: 'Arguments of principle are arguments intended to establish an individual right; arguments of policy are arguments intended to establish a collective goal. Principles are propositions that describe rights; policies are propositions that describe goals.' Hence, he says, judges' law tends to protect rights; legislators' law to advance policies. (*Harvard Law Review*, 1975.)

The school of Hart, then, frequently identifies legal relativism with democracy. But the democratic-legislative process can be manipulated by radical oligarchs much more easily and universally than the law can be manipulated by judicial legislators. One thing we have learnt in this terrible century of ours is that the rule of law, with its notion of inalienable right, is a far more valuable safeguard to the individual than the delusory 'one-man-one-vote'. There are many cases in which the judges speak for the masses far more truthfully than the Government they have supposedly elected. How many times have people said to themselves, in recent years, 'Thank God for Lord Denning!'

Nor is this a new development. It was Chief Justice Coke, using the resources of the Common Law, who constructed the constitutional barriers to the prerogative tyranny of the Stuarts. It is a curious fact that, although statute law goes back to the early thirteenth century, such human rights as our law recognises are largely judge-made: the presumption of innocence, no obligation to testify against oneself, fair hearing, peaceful assembly, freedom of association, freedom of the press, the rule that an executive act springing from abuse of discretion is void, the presumption against retrospective legislation, no seizure of property without compensation, and the axiom that no crime may be committed without a guilty mind. Judges will continue to exploit the resources of Common Law principles to uphold individual rights against oppression — only recently Lord Denning gave an important judgment on the freedom of the press.

Lord Denning, indeed, says that the resources of the law are such that, in his view, no Bill of Rights is necessary. I think he underestimates the hatred of judges' law in the Labour Party and the trade union movement, the determination to undermine the notion of judicial independence — not least by extending the powers of politically appointed tribunals, opening the bench to radical academics and destroying the independence and morale of the legal profession, on which the robustness of the judiciary so greatly depends. I recently spent some time sifting through the evidence submitted to the Royal Commission on Legal Services, and some of the notions now stirring in Left-wing legal circles are hair-raising in their long-term implications. I suspect they will be party orthodoxy long before the next election. That is why I am so anxious, while there is still time, and while we have the power to do so, to underpin the rule of law and the independence of the judiciary in this country, and at the same time to curb the extremist notion of parliamentary absolutism by enacting a fundamental law of rights, and furnishing an effective second chamber to uphold it.

Of course, I am not suggesting that Conservative lawyers should encourage the universal and unremitting pursuit of rights. That is a profoundly un-conservative notion. If each one of us sought to exact the rights explicit or residual in our laws, on every occasion and to the maximum of our powers, society would collapse, and public policy would become impossible. Civilisation is the exercise of self-restraint, as Yeats put it; true, and that includes legal self-restraint. It is now fashionable to put the case for the right to civil disobedience. It is argued plausibly in John Rawle's widely praised book, *A Theory of Justice*; and last year, for instance, I found myself arguing against this proposition with Professor Dworkin, on television. He has written a fashionable book, *Taking Rights Seriously*. But if everyone took his rights as seriously as Professor Dworkin advises, civil government would become impossible and we would exchange the rule of law for the rule of Rentamob. The voluntary foregoing of rights is an essential element in Conservative legal philosophy. That is why I regard with such suspicion the community law centres, one of whose fundamental assumptions is based on a maximist attitude to rights – that they must be exacted always and to the limit, regardless of the cost to the community. A litigational society, it seems to me, cannot produce an extension of rights; it can only end in producing a conflict of rights, since the sum of all our notional rights is greater than the amount of freedom available to accommodate them.

That is why I am opposed – and I think all Conservative lawyers ought to be opposed – to the suggestions put forward to the Benson Commission by the Society of Labour Lawyers for a state legal service on the lines of the National Health Service. They argue that 'there are certain basic legal rights, which should be protected at the public expense' – I notice, however, that they are opposed to a Bill of Rights – and they put forward the principle that, if rights are guaranteed by law, 'effective means of enforcing them should also be provided'. Since they define such rights as 'security in home and employment, minimum income, right to liberty and freedom from physical attack and injury', rights, I would argue, that no state can truthfully guarantee and no legal system effectively enforce, they are, in fact, putting forward the perfect formula for the litigational society. We were told recently in the press of the case of the Irish valetudinarian, who has done no work since 1946 and has cost the British National Health Service over £1 million in unnecessary operations and treatment. I shudder to think what compulsive litigants, who I suspect are potentially far more numerous, would do with the Labour's universal legal scheme.

Of course I am not suggesting that the present system is acceptable, or that the action of Conservative lawyers in Parliament should be confined to erecting defences against legislative abuse. On the contrary, I suggest they have also an important positive role to play in promoting justice. No Conservative believes in economic equality as an aim of policy. But equality before the law is not merely a legitimate, it is an indispensable part of Conservative philosophy. Here, I suggest, there is an enormous field for Conservative endeavour over the next few years. One important aspect of equality before the law is equality of access: here, certainly, communal concepts such as the law centres have a part to play. But the notion of equality of access means – does it not? – that law centres should not demand the political credentials of those they employ – as some certainly do at present – or decide whom they should help by virtue of status – thus ruling out, as most of them do, assisting landlords or employers, however exiguous their means. Equality of access also implies a more realistic attitude to rules of legal aid generally, but I am sure Conservative lawyers need no convincing on this point.

More central to the notion of equality before the law, however, is the existence and abuse of legal privilege. The outstanding examples of legal privilege in our time are the huge and growing immunities of trade unionists to civil and criminal actions. This collection of privileges – comparable in their scandalous extent to the legal privileges enjoyed by the medieval Church on the eve of the Reformation Parliament – constitute the greatest legal issue of our time and, properly understood, the greatest political and economic issue of our time. I do not believe that Britain's economic recovery is possible unless this issue is tackled. I do not believe that the present Conservative Government can possibly succeed in its aims unless this issue is tackled. This is the issue which constitutes the chief challenge to the wit and ingenuity of Conservative lawyers. And they might begin by asking one or two fundamental questions. First, by what principle are individuals refused all legal redress for damages inflicted on their property, their health, the education of their children, or any other assessable tort by trade union action? What moral justification is there to legitimise behaviour on the part of trade unionists and their officials which, in any other context, would be judged criminal? Third, by what fundamental right is the labour monopoly exercised by closed shop unions exempted from all our monopoly and fair trading legislation?

It seems to me that the time has come to subject these, and related, questions to extensive debate, and Conservative lawyers have unrivalled qualifications for beginning it. Let us, then, regard the new Parliament as a constitutional and political assize in which the defence of individual freedom will be systematically and powerfully reinforced − and the pretensions of collective privilege rigorously scrutinised and curbed.

PART FOUR

Civilisation and Violence

CHAPTER 15

The Age of Terror

This article, published in the New Statesman *in November 1974, marked the point at which I first became aware of the deadly threat that terrorism posed to civilised society, and the need to alert public opinion to its horrifying importance.*

Step by step, almost imperceptibly, without anyone being aware that a fatal watershed has been crossed, mankind has descended into the age of terror. While we have taken infinite pains to avoid the catastrophe of a thermonuclear war, the international community has allowed itself to be corrupted into accepting something scarcely less horrible: the indiscriminate murder of the innocent in the pursuit of political ends. Week by week, the number and scale of the attrocities increase. With each outrage, the cries of protest become fainter, the efforts to punish less assured, the defences against barbarism more contemptible. Dark forces have inched their way into the lighted circle of civilisation, and have become established as normal phenomena to which society must accommodate itself. The language has been adjusted accordingly, and terrorist murders are presented as 'guerrilla executions'. It is now part of the routine duties of heads of government to negotiate personally with killers, with the object of releasing convicted criminals as expeditiously as it can be arranged.

Governments, like our own, do their best to tighten up internal safeguards against gunmen. What Roy Jenkins calls his 'Draconian' measures against the IRA may make it easier for the police to arrest individual terrorists and may even – though this is much more doubtful – diminish the number of incidents. But neither an increase in police powers nor the reintroduction of capital punishment can solve the terrorist problem itself. That would require a complete reversal in the drift of international opinion, and co-ordinated measures to deny political gunmen a hearing, money and supplies all over the world. Of this there is no sign. Indeed, efforts to devise international sanctions against terror have now been tacitly dropped.

Worse still, terror has been accorded recognition and honourable status. The United Nations, theoretically the chief custodian of international order and civilised standards, has extended a welcome and privileges to the most active, ruthless and successful of the terror gangs, as a preliminary to giving it full membership. Its spokesman, the architect of a thousand crimes, has been received with howls of rapture. The representative of the Israelis, his actual and potential victims, has been virtually silenced: thus, in the 1930s, did the screaming pack of Italian fascist journalists shout down the voice of Ethiopia in the doomed League of Nations. Few question the credentials of Arafat and his killers; the fact that he has imposed himself on the Palestinian refugees by fear and violence is ignored. He had the indispensable pass-key to an Assembly mesmerised by racialism and force: the ability to kill with impunity.

According to its rules, Arafat has no more place in the UN than the head of the Mafia, who can match him in successful crime and perhaps has a wider constituency. But Arafat fits more convincingly the mythology of the modern world, which has replaced negotiation and debate by guns and explosives. And in the UN, of course, he finds many agents of his peers: military gangsters and expert racists, men skilled in the politics of torture and butchery, who have devoted their lives to the destruction of democracy and the courts. More and more, the UN begins to resemble, and sound like, a thieves' kitchen: Mr Arafat should be at home there. More to the point is the question: why do the powers still attached to civilised standards continue to give it their countenance?

Here we come to the essence of the argument. No state throughout history has had completely clean hands. What marks the progress of civilisation is the systematic recognition of laws, the identification and punishment of crime, and the reprobation of the offender. A civilised society is one which sees the evil in itself and provides means to eliminate it, where the voice of conscience is active. The horrific record of Britain's indiscriminate bombing of Germany is in part redeemed by the protests of Bishop Bell in Chichester. The brutalisation of Vietnam by the United States is balanced by the critical millions who eventually brought it to an end. We need not despair at the devastating events of our times so long as we retain the ability to distinguish between right and wrong, between law and disorder, between justice and crime, and proclaim these distinctions from the rooftops.

The tragedy of the UN is that the distinctions have been first blurred, then wholly abandoned; and that its judgments are now delivered not according to any recognised set of principles, however inadequate, but solely in response to the pressures of political and racial groupings. Racialism is condemned in South Africa but applauded in Uganda; and the fruits of aggression are denied or blessed according to the race and political leanings of those to whom they accrue. Thus the UN has become a kind of kangaroo court; far from protecting international order, it undermines it. Not even the wretched League of Nations gave a welcome and a platform to Hitler.

But it is futile to lavish abuse on the UN; it has no corporate existence; it is merely the sum of its parts. Lawless and tyrannical regimes – and there are now many scores of them in the world – will naturally seek to remould in their own image any international forum of which they are members. Their object is not to uphold law but to eliminate it. It is rubbish to suppose that an organisation of over 100 states, each with an equal vote, will reflect civilised standards. There are very few communities in the world where democracy and the rule of law still flourish. And history tells a dismal tale of their will and capacity to impose their beliefs on others. In the 1930s the democracies permitted, even encouraged by their silence and inaction, the systematic programmes of aggression conceived and enacted by Japan, Italy and Germany. Only *in extremis*, when their own very existence was threatened, did they reluctantly band together to resist.

Today the civilised powers are no less pusillanimous. They have watched impassively while the UN has betrayed its aims and torn up its charter. They have made no effort to construct collective defences against international terrorism, to punish those who practise it and deter those who give it sanctuary. The Arab decision to use the oil weapon to further terrorist aims – the first direct and unmistakable threat to the interests of the civilised powers themselves – was met with blatant cowardice, total disunity and panic attempts to strike unilateral bargains. There seems, at present, no principle that the West will not willingly sacrifice to retain the illusion of economic security. The pretensions of the EEC to form a united, beneficent and powerful force in world affairs have been cruelly exposed by the playing-card petty states of the Persian Gulf. The Israelis are under no doubt that civilised Europe will not raise a finger to prevent their extermination.

There has also been a betrayal by the Left. What should distinguish the Left is an all-embracing humanism, which places the highest possible value on life and identifies itself with those societies striving to preserve and enrich it. The Left abandoned its principles in the 1930s by deliberately ignoring or discounting the Stalinist terror, and by defending the debased form of government which made it possible. Now it is committing a new form of the same treason by endorsing indiscriminate violence as the prime weapon of political action. Let us not mince our words about this. There is now a growing number of people on the Left, in this and other advanced countries, who deliberately associate themselves with international terrorist groups, with conferences held to promote the aims of terrorism, with the supply and manufacture of explosives, and, above all, with the ideology of violence. These people claim the name of socialist, though it is characteristic of them that they regard with peculiar detestation the world's most advanced social democracy, Israel. And among their heroes is Ghadaffi of Libya, whose passion for violence is such that he favours the IRA and the UDA with almost equal approval.

How far these comparatively small groups of aggro-socialists have penetrated the thinking of the Left as a whole is a matter of opinion. But they are clearly making progress. On many matters where the conscience of the Left would once have spoken loudly and clearly, there is now an embarrassed silence. There is complete indifference to the political evolution of the Arab states – that is, the progressive elimination of anyone with a commitment to democracy. Some of those who form and organise opinion on the Left are preparing the ground for the acceptance of Israel's destruction as right and in-evitable. More important, in the long run, is acceptance that, in the pursuit of certain vaguely defined principles of self-determination, the end justifies the means, however horrible.

The voice of the Left, raised so passionately against Protestant violence and internment in Northern Ireland, has been absolutely still while the IRA has escalated its programme of bombing the innocent. Radicals who regard capital punishment with loathing are cheerfully adjusting themselves to political massacre − even of children − so long as the terrorists have the right brand-image. Some, it is true, are divided and uneasy in their own minds. A bomb which goes off and kills no one is justifiable; and it is just about permissible, though regrettable, to kill a few soldiers. But to murder a score, and injure hundreds, of uninvolved people − here the Left is silent because it does not know what to think. Yet if incidents on this scale, and greater, continue, it will slowly convince itself that they are unavoidable. Thus the corruption spreads, and the Left is in danger of allowing events to force it into a totally anti-humanist posture. Once the right of the terrorist to kill is conceded there is no logical point at which the Left can make a stand for human life. And, of course, the tacit approval of the Left is a direct and powerful incen-tive to terrorists of every persuasion to push forward the threshold of violence. Their technology improves *pari passu* with the abandon-ment of their last, lingering scruples.

The truth is that no political cause is worth the abandonment of elementary morality. Whether terrorism works varies with the case, but it can never serve an ideal. When we look back, for instance, on the hideous cruelties inflicted by both sides during the Reformation, we can see how senseless they were, and how easy it is for highminded people to commit appalling crimes in pursuit of what they believe to be the public good. But our real admiration goes to those who perceived it at the time. One such was Sebastian Castellio, who was lucky to escape burning by both Catholics and Protestants, and who pointed out in his tract for toleration, *Whether Heretics Are To Be Persecuted?*, that no certitude of righteousness justifies violence: 'To kill a man is not to defend a doctrine, it is to kill a man.'

We have come a dangerously long way from this simple maxim in recent years. So many bastions of civilisation have been surrendered to the enemy without a fight that we have almost forgotten how to arm ourselves against barbarism. We can, in fact, do it in only one way: by stating that terrorism is always and in every circumstance wrong; that it is not only intrinsically wrong but the antithesis of political idealism; that it must be resisted by every means at our disposal; and that those who practise it must not only be punished but repudiated by those who share their political aims. Anyone who cannot assent to these propositions is no socialist, and has no place on the Left. And it is only by affirming them, without equivocation, that the Left can help to guide international society back to the road of humanism and reason. I believe we shall find a growing number of allies on the way.

CHAPTER 16

The Long Arm of Justice

This article, published in the New Statesman *in July 1976, immediately after the successful Israeli raid on Entebbe, rejoiced that, while the major civilised powers remained supine under the terrorist threat, one small and valorous nation knew how to dispense justice.*

The successful Israeli commando raid on Entebbe airport brought joy to the hearts of all civilised people throughout the world, not merely because it saved the lives of over 100 innocents, extinguished their murderous captors and humiliated the despotic monster Amin, but because it demonstrated that there is still such a thing as international justice. And justice, moreover, which has a long arm. Hitherto, the international thugs who work for the so-called 'Palestinian' cause, while often hunted down individually by Israeli anti-terror units, have felt themselves reasonably secure in a number of havens, notably Algeria, Libya and Uganda. All three are military dictatorships, under regimes of terror, run by men on the borderline of sanity, officially committed to policies of international anarchy, racism and organised violence. All, while claiming irrefrangible sovereignty for themselves, systematically infringe that of neighbouring states, ridicule the laws of international conduct, train assassination squads to murder presidents and prime ministers, and actively sponsor attempts to subvert fellow African regimes with which they are in ideological conflict. All are freely armed by the Soviet leaders in their unending quest to destroy legitimacy and order throughout the world.

Uganda is a particularly instructive case. Amin came to power through violence with the approval, perhaps even the encouragement, of our know-nothing Foreign Office 'experts'. In the course of his eccentric career, he was at one time a noisy ally of Israel, and a client of their development aid service – which explains why the Israelis were so happily familiar with the topography of Entebbe airport. Then the Arabs bribed him into their camp, and he has recently become heavily dependent on their money, arms and even manpower. Amin's regime now resembles that of the late 'Papa Doc' in Haiti, with its *ton tons Macoute*, and other horrors. It has alienated every section of educated opinion in the country, and indeed the great mass of ordinary Ugandans, who may not understand the subtleties of modern politics but who can recognise an evil man who wants to lead them back into darkness and savagery.

Unable to depend on his countrymen for his personal safety, Amin has allowed a number of international terrorists, loosely attached to their 'Palestinian' paymasters, to find refuge in Uganda, and from them he has recruited his personal bodyguard. He has also allowed these terrorist groups to use Uganda as a base for operations. Earlier this year, for instance, a 'Palestinian' murder gang, armed with Soviet anti-aircraft missiles supplied by Amin, unsuccessfully attempted to shoot down an Israeli airliner, flying from Johannesburg to Tel Aviv, as it landed to refuel at Nairobi airport. Two of these terrorists, as Amin seemingly was aware, had in 1975 attempted to destroy an El Al airliner landing at Paris, The whole gang was arrested in Nairobi, and detained; and their release was part of the bargain the terrorists tried to negotiate last week.

Amin's implication in the attempted crime at Nairobi airport deepened his conflict with the Kenyan authorities, and pushed him further into the arms of the terrorists. He already has claims to large tracts of Kenyan territory, and has several times mounted acts of subversion against the Kenyatta Government – one of the last civilised regimes left in black Africa. Last week Amin suffered a blow when his ally and fellow murderer, Ghadaffi of Libya, failed in an attempt to overthrow the regime in Sudan, a contiguous northern neighbour of both Uganda and Kenya. Although a thousand mercenaries were trained by Ghadaffi for the purpose, the plot misfired, the regime emerged triumphant, and the net result was to weaken the forces of anarchy in that part of the world. It was for this reason that Amin was particularly anxious to handle the Entebbe airport affair successfully. His prestige is, in any case, waning even among the more primitive African states, and his chairmanship of the Organisation of African Unity has come to an end.

Amin's object was identical with that of the 'Palestinian' terrorists: he wanted to secure the release of the convicted prisoners held by the Israeli and other governments, which could then be hailed as a victory for Afro-Asian solidarity and, not least, for his personal authority and powers of diplomacy. That is why he agreed with the hijackers (possibly at the stage when the plan was conceived) to receive the Air France airbus at Entebbe; relieved the four exhausted hijackers, when the aircraft arrived, with 'Palestinian' terrorists from his own personal squads; provided Ugandan troops to detain and menace the terrified hostages; released all the hostages except the Israelis and the Air France crew — thus providing proof of his racist and political objectives — and made available all the military and diplomatic means in his power to bring the terrorist operations to a successful conclusion. There is abundant evidence to show that, once the hijacked aircraft landed at Entebbe, it was Amin, not the 'Palestinian' terrorists, who was in effective command.

Amin has, therefore, aligned his wretched country wholly with the forces of international terrorism, and placed it in a posture of *de facto* war with the states of Israel and Kenya. This alone would not only justify, but make meritorious and commendable, the Israeli operation to snatch the innocents from Amin's grasp, and Kenya's decision to help them do so. Was it right? asked *The Times*, fatuously. It was not only obviously right, it was essential; for the alternatives were either that over 100 hostages would die, or that more than 50 trained and convicted terrorists would be unleashed upon the world again. 'The end result is a moral and diplomatic nullity,' said the *Guardian*, demonstrating the new brand of trendy cynicism with which it has replaced its old sanctimonious humbuggery. Far from being a moral and diplomatic nullity, the Israeli operation is a practical demonstration that the forces of moral decency are no longer quite powerless in a corrupt and bewildered world, and that diplomacy need not always be confined to sordid bargains reached in UN corridors, but can be backed up by police action.

Of course, Amin will now set up a caterwauling at the Security Council, on the subject of invasions of sovereignty, natural justice, the rights of the 'emerging' nations, Israeli colonialism, and any other cliché he can contrive to gabble. Nowadays, no man of sense pays much attention to what the UN does, or does not do, still less to what it says. But it is particularly important, on this occasion, that all those nations who value the true objectives of the UN, the real substance of international law and justice, and who are genuinely committed to preserving an orderly and peaceful world, should publicly align themselves with the successful Israeli demonstration that there is no safe haven anywhere for the terrorist and his abettors. The United States has already done so. So have several other European nations and statesmen.

From the British Government and the Foreign Office, in shameful contrast, has come nothing but silence or equivocation. Blustering Jim Callaghan, who poses as a policeman and law enforcer whenever he feels it quite safe to do so, has no comment on this act of salutary justice. Foreign Secretary Crosland, himself a parachutist – though the only place he ever liberated was the casino at Cannes – betrays cowardly embarrassment. When the Government falters, it is for the House of Commons to speak for the overwhelming majority of British people, who hail the Israeli operation with admiration – and relief that the resources of civilisation are not yet exhausted.

But is is even more important that Africans, both as individuals and as governments, should repudiate Amin, and disavow his claim to epitomise their continent. There are plenty of people in the West, former supporters of colonialism, who are only too ready to believe that Africa is reverting to barbarism and savagery, and who cite Amin as their witness. In his horrifying and prophetic story, *Heart of Darkness*, set in the Belgian Congo, Joseph Conrad might have had Amin in mind when he wrote of 'his exalted and incredible degradation', and the power of the African environment to reject civilisation and recreate ancient tribal tyrannies by 'the heavy mute spell of the wilderness, that seemed to draw him to his pitiless breast by the awakening of forgotten and brutal instincts, by the memory of gratified and monstrous passions . . .' But the real Africa has a longing for civilised justice; it is both a more hopeful and a more innocent place than the Africa of Amin and his fellow despots. If the real Africa can now recover its voice, the events at Entebbe will find their place in history not just as a high adventure, nor even as a single act of international justice, but as a landmark in the maturing of an entire continent.

CHAPTER 17

The Resources of Civilisation

By October 1976, when this article was published in the New Statesman, *it was already evident that individual terrorist groups were now linking hands in their assault on civilised society. The week before, an old friend of mine had narrowly escaped assassination by the IRA, who killed instead a distinguished cancer specialist. I pleaded with the civilised world to strengthen its defences.*

At an immense gathering in Leeds in October 1881, W. E. Gladstone, perhaps the noblest man England has ever produced, and also a passionate friend of the Irish nation, said some trenchant things about Irish terrorism. His voice, one present observed, had 'the note of a clear and deep-toned bell'; and certainly his words have a striking resonance today:

If it shall appear that there is still to be fought a final conflict in Ireland between law on the one side and sheer lawlessness on the other, if the law purged from defect and any taint of injustice is still to be repelled and refused, and the first conditions of political society to remain unfulfilled, then I say, gentlemen, without hesitation, the resources of civilisation against its enemies are not yet exhausted.

Is it not time to remind the world once again that civilisation still has the resources and, more important, the will to seize its enemies by the throat? In Britain, as well as in Ulster, we face in the IRA not a nationalist movement, not a league of patriots, not 'guerrillas' or 'freedom fighters', or anything which can be dignified with a political name, but an organisation of psychopathic murderers who delight in maiming and slaughtering the innocent, and whose sole object and satisfaction in life is the destruction of human flesh. The misguided patriots who joined the IRA in the heady days of 1968 and after have melted away and have been replaced by men and women who have far more in common with Ian Brady and Myra Hindley than with old-style terrorists like Michael Collins and De Valera. Not that these last two − both saints in the Irish political calendar − can escape their share of the moral responsibility. When old Dev was laid to rest recently, with full honours civil and military, I reflected that he had played a sinister role in teaching his compatriots to prefer guns and dynamite to argument and persuasion, and that he could fairly be described as the spiritual grandfather of today's Patrick Joseph O'Gelignites and Bridget McSadists.

However, retribution is coming. There can be no doubt that the IRA terror campaign in this country has been counter-productive. Those, like myself, who once urged the withdrawal of British forces, on the grounds that this would oblige moderate elements on both sides to come together, have been persuaded by the IRA gangsters that Britain must continue to maintain order in Ulster, if necessary for all eternity − or until the Irish in their wrath rise and exterminate the IRA themselves. In the meantime, civilised society must be protected in Britain too. Last week's murder of a distinguished doctor may well prove a turning-point in persuading the British public that convicted terrorists must be executed without pity or delay.

In point of fact, 80 per cent of the public have long since needed no further proof that death is an appropriate punishment for mass terrorists both in terms of natural justice and as a deterrent. What is new, and remarkable, is that the overwhelming majority of those middle-class intellectuals who supported the abolition of capital punishment have now come round to the view that prison sentences, however long, do not offer society sufficient protection from the terrorist professionals. There is a widespread belief among the terrorists themselves that the British Government is on the verge of capitulation in Ireland, and that part of the bargain will be the immediate release of IRA 'political prisoners'. Hence, when the four monsters who exploded the bomb at Guildford were sentenced recently, the 'girl friend' of one of them, present in court, screamed at her grisly paramour: 'Don't worry – you will never serve it.' Thus no punishment at present available to the British courts acts as a disincentive to the killers, however atrocious their crimes.

The majesty of the law could, it is true, be somewhat strengthened if the Prime Minister were to make a binding statement to Parliament, couched in terms even he could not subsequently wriggle out of, that in no circumstances whatever will convicted IRA murderers be released before the completion of their sentences. But this is not enough. What the public demands, what it has a moral and constitutional right to demand, and what Members of Parliament must now, it seems to me, concede to it, is a new anti-terrorist law which makes the death sentence mandatory for those convicted of political murder. There are a number of different ways in which a statute could be framed but two characteristics are essential. First, the law must be subject to annual review by Parliament, lapsing automatically if the Commons judges its usefulness to be over. Second, it must provide, within the framework of natural justice and our customary legal safeguards, for an accelerated procedure so that the guilty can be tried, sentenced and executed before their confederates or paymasters can organise any violent interference with the course of justice. In the long history of English (and Scottish) jurisprudence there are ample precedents for avoiding 'the law's delays' in such cases; and no one need feel that a statute so framed would go against our traditions.

Whether the Government can be persuaded to take such a lead is to be doubted. Harold Wilson has never shown much inclination to organise effective action against Arab terrorists, or those whose oil-wealth finances them; and this week his tongue is raw from licking the boots of the Crown-Prince of Saudi Arabia. However, he is at least susceptible to public opinion, if it is expressed vociferously enough. Perhaps a national campaign is needed. Certainly Mrs Thatcher has the right to start putting on the pressure, and to remind the Government that bipartisanship on Ireland has its limits – and its price.

Such indications that the British Government is prepared to deploy the resources of civilisation would, moreover, have a therapeutic effect well beyond the confines of the Irish problem. For terrorism and its condonation, even encouragement, by legal governments is the greatest evil of our age, a more serious threat to our culture and survival than the possibility of thermonuclear war or the rapid depletion of the planet's natural resources. Some terrorist groups already dispose not only of vast sums of cash but of comparatively sophisticated weapon systems; how long will it be before they get their first A-bombs, especially since more than a score of countries will be producing them by the end of this decade? It may be said: no government would be irresponsible enough to hand over nuclear weapons to psychopathic murderers. Alas, this is not a James Bond fantasy but a reasonable deduction from the recent behaviour patterns of many so-called nations.

A fortnight ago the UN Social, Humanitarian and Cultural Committee – a nomenclature so rich in savage irony as to eclipse even a Swift – passed by 70 votes to 29 a resolution condemning Israel as a 'threat to world peace' and Zionism as a 'racialist and imperialist ideology'. In fact, as all educated people know, Israel, far from being a threat to anyone, stands in perpetual danger of extermination from its bloodthirsty neighbours; and Zionism is neither a racial nor an imperial but a cultural phenomenon. Of course, at the UN facts and realities do not matter. What matters is force, money and physical power.

Indeed, the UN is rapidly becoming one of the most corrupt and corrupting creations in the whole history of human institutions. How many of the delegates were actually bribed by Arab governments to vote against Israel on this occasion is a matter of speculation; but almost without exception those in the majority came from states notable for racist oppression of every conceivable hue – Iraq, for instance, has recently murdered or expelled over 300,000 Kurds on purely racial grounds – and whose common characteristics are totalitarian governments, absence of the rule of law, a fettered press, concentration camps, political murder, huge corruption at all levels, vast armed forces and impoverished workers.

Some of these states – which might more accurately be described as tribal barbarisms – have a perfectly genuine hatred for Israel. For Israel is a social democracy, the nearest approach to a free socialist state in the world; its people and government have a profound respect for human life, so passionate indeed that, despite every conceivable provocation, they have refused for a quarter of a century to execute a single captured terrorist. They also have an ancient but vigorous culture, and a flourishing technology. The combination of national qualities they have assembled in their brief existence as a state is a perpetual and embittering reproach to most of the new countries whose representatives swagger about the UN building. So Israel is envied and hated; and efforts are made to destroy her. The extermination of the Israelis has long been the prime objective of the Terrorist International; they calculate that if they can break Israel, then all the rest of civilisation is vulnerable to their assaults.

In some ways what is said and voted at the UN does not matter. There may be a case — not yet, I would say, an overwhelming one — for the United States government to cut off the UN's money, and send the whole squalid circus packing. The slab of steel and glass on the East River might then be put to some useful purpose. But breaking up the UN would not end the problem, which springs not from paper votes but from the physical supplies of arms and money which certain states are prepared to pour into the terrorist cauldron. Russia, while ferociously executing dissidents in her own midst (those who hijack Soviet aircraft unsuccessfully know they will never emerge from the KGB interrogation cellars), equips a wide variety of terrorist gangs beyond her sphere of control.

But Russia's activities at least have a certain kind of depraved rationale. Other tyrannies appear to be motivated by the sheer lust for destruction. Thus Ghadaffi, the madman who controls Libya, sends money and arms to both Protestants and Catholics in Ulster; and Amin, the Ugandan monster, is ready to provide weapons (which he recently received from Russia) to anyone interested in killing Britons, as he puts it. These savages are not ostracised by the world community. On the contrary, Dom Mintoff, the Labour Prime Minister of Malta, finds it convenient to treat Ghadaffi as an honoured ally. Amin, who is said to have beaten the Ugandan Lord Chief Justice to death, and whose murders already run into thousands, has been chosen by his African colleagues as their chairman and exemplar.

The melancholy truth, I fear, is that the candles of civilisation are burning low. The world is increasingly governed not so much by capitalism, or communism, or social democracy, or even tribal barbarism, as by a false lexicon of political clichés, accumulated over half a century and now assuming a kind of degenerate sacerdotal authority. We all know what they are; those who do not have only to peer into the otherwise empty head of an average member of the fascist Left — that men with coloured skins can do no wrong, and those with white ones no right — unless of course they call themselves Communists; that murdering innocent people for political purposes is acceptable providing you call yourself a guerrilla; that, in the right political circumstances, a chunk of gelignite is morally superior to a rational argument. The assumption is that an Armalite rifle has, as it were, a spiritual life of its own, depending on whether it is in the hands of an American (bad) or a South-East Asian (good).

In the old days the civilised powers would simply have occupied a barbarous territory like Ghadaffi's Libya, or Amin's Uganda, and set up a responsible and law-abiding government. Such operations may no longer be possible, or even desirable. But there is something to be said for replacing the UN concept by a league of civilised powers — the conditions of membership being such criteria as democratic politics, a free press, the rule of law and a determination to stamp out terrorism. Harold Wilson often drones on about Britain (under Labour) giving a 'moral lead'. Here is an excellent opportunity to exercise one, by putting such a proposal to like-minded governments.

After all, civilisation not only has a right but a positive and imperative duty to defend itself. We are the beneficiaries of the past and, more important, the trustees of the future. I was much struck the other night by a remarkably clever and funny play by Simon Gray, *Otherwise Engaged*, on at the Queen's. A decent, peaceable, reasonable minded and patient publisher plans to spend a few quiet hours on Saturday listening to his new album of Wagner. He is constantly interrupted by an endless succession of unreasonable and hysterical people who, while demanding and getting his help, subject him to sneers, reproaches, insults and even physical assault. Eventually, in perfectly rational anger, he strikes back — just once — and instantly the circle of devils dissolves and he is allowed to listen to *Parsifal* in peace.

I see this play — it may not have been the author's intention — as a powerful analogy of Western civilisation and its treatment by the rest of the world in the last quarter-century. Loaded with quite unnecessary guilt, we have given aid and comfort, and received nothing but abuse and violence. We have not won the friendship of the world beyond; all that has happened is that we have forfeited its respect.

Thus do men betray their responsibilities with the best intentions.

Has not the time come to change our strategy? What I think the rest of the world is waiting for − indeed hoping for − is some positive sign that the civilised powers are going to uphold the standards of international behaviour set by their forebears; that they are going to do so in the most systematic, relentless and comprehensive manner, and if necessary − while they still possess it − with overwhelming force. All over our tormented planet, there are millions of decent, peaceable and intelligent men and women of all religions, complexions and races, who are praying that the resources of civilisation are not, indeed, exhausted − and that the Brezhnevs and the Amins, the Ghadaffis and the Maos, the Arafats and the O'Sadists will not be allowed to take over the earth.

CHAPTER 18

The Seven Deadly Sins of Terrorism

This speech was made at the opening session of the Jerusalem Conference on International Terrorism, in July 1979, held in memory of the young Israeli colonel who had planned and led the Entebbe raid, and had perished in its last moments. Extracts from the speech were subsequently published in many newspapers throughout the world, and in the American magazine New Republic.

Before looking at the correct approach to the problem of terrorism, let us examine what I am certain is the wrong one. The wrong approach is to see terrorism as one of many symptoms of a deep-seated malaise in our society, part of a pattern of violence that includes juvenile delinquency, rising crime rates, student riots, vandalism and football hooliganism, which is blamed on the shadow of the H-bomb, Western materialism, TV and cinema violence, rising divorce rates, inadequate welfare services and poverty – an analysis that usually ends in the meaningless and defeatist conclusion that 'society' itself is to blame.

The truth is, international terrorism is not part of a generalised problem. It is a specific and identifiable problem on its own; and because it is specific and identifiable, because it can be isolated from the context which breeds it, it is a remediable problem.

To say it is remediable, however, is not to underestimate its size and danger. On the contrary; it is almost impossible to exaggerate the threat which terrorism holds for our civilisation. It is a threat which is in many ways more serious than the risk of nuclear war, or the population explosion, or global pollution or the supposed exhaustion of the earth's resources. These dangers to our civilisation can be, have been or are being, contained. The threat of terrorism is not being contained; it is, on the contrary, increasing steadily. Indeed, one central reason why it is such a formidable threat is that very few people in the civilised world – governments and parliaments, TV and newspapers, and the public generally – take terrorism seriously enough.

Most people, I fear, tend to underestimate the sheer fragility of a civilisation. They do not appreciate that civilisations fall as well as rise. They can be, and have been, destroyed by malign forces. There have been at least three Dark Ages in our recoverable history. One occurred in the third millennium BC and, among other things, eclipsed the great civilisation of the Egyptian Old Kingdom, the civilisation which built the Pyramids. Another occurred towards the end of the second millennium BC, and destroyed Mycenaean Greece, Minoan Crete, the Hittite Empire, and much else. We are more familiar with the third, which destroyed the Roman Empire in the West in the fifth century AD. It took Europe 800 years to recover, in terms of organisation, technical skills and living standards, from that disaster.

These great catastrophes had many and varied causes. But there was a common factor in all of them. They tended to occur when the spread of metals technology and the availability of raw materials enabled the forces of barbarism to equal or surpass the civilised powers in the quality and quantity of their weapons. For in the last resort, civilisations stand or fall not by covenants, but by swords.

Edward Gibbon, at the end of his great book on the *Decline and Fall of the Roman Empire*, asked: 'The savage nations of the globe are the common enemies of civilised society, and we may well inquire with anxious curiosity whether Europe is still threatened with a repetition of those calamities which formerly oppressed the arms and institutions of Rome.' Writing in the 1780s, on the threshold of the Industrial Revolution, Gibbon thought he could answer his own question with a reasonably confident negative. He rightly estimated the strength of the civilised world to be increasing, and he believed that the scientific and rational principles on which that strength was based were becoming more firmly established with every year that passed.

Now, nearly 200 years later, we cannot be so sure. The principles of objective science and human reason, the notion of the rule of law, the paramountcy of politics over force, are everywhere under growing and purposeful challenge. The forces of savagery and violence which constitute this challenge are becoming steadily bolder, more numerous and, above all, better armed. There is no need to dwell on the huge and alarming disparity between the armed forces of Soviet barbarism and those of the civilised world. More to the purpose is that arms available to terrorists, the skills with which they are used and, not least, the organisational techniques with which these weapons and skills are deployed, are all improving at a fast and accelerating rate, a rate much faster than the counter-measures available to civilised society.

In Northern Ireland, for instance, the terrorists have unquestionably strengthened their military position in relation to the security forces. In this theatre, at least, barbarism is winning ground from civilisation; and is winning ground precisely because it can turn to an international support structure. Terrorism is not a purely national phenomenon, which can be conquered at a national level. It is an international offensive, an open and declared war against civilisation itself, which can only be defeated by an international alliance of the civilised powers.

To say that terrorism is war against civilisation may provoke the objection that terrorists are often idealists pursuing worthy ultimate aims – national or regional independence, and so forth. I do not accept this argument. I cannot agree that a terrorist can ever be an idealist, or that the objects sought can ever justify terrorism. The impact of terrorism, not merely on individual nations, but on humanity as a whole, is intrinsically evil, necessarily evil, and wholly evil. It is so for a number of demonstrable reasons: let us consider the Seven Deadly Sins of Terrorism.

First, terrorism is the deliberate and cold-blooded exaltation of violence over other forms of public activity. The modern terrorist does not employ violence as a necessary evil, but as a desirable form of activity. There is a definite intellectual background to the present wave of terrorism. It springs not only from the Leninist and Trotskyist justification of violence, but from the post-war philosophy of violence derived from Nietzsche through Heidegger, and enormously popularised by Sartre and his disciples. No one since the war has influenced young people more than Sartre, and no one has done more to legitimise violence on the Left. It was Sartre who adapted the linguistic technique, common in German philosophy, of identifying certain political situations as the equivalent of violence, thus justifying violent correctives or responses. In 1962 he said: 'For me the essential problem is to reject the theory according to which the Left ought not to answer violence with violence.' Note his words: not 'a problem', but 'the *essential* problem'.

Some of those influenced by Sartre went much further. Franz Fanon was a notable example. His most influential work, *Les Damnés de la Terre*, which has a preface by Sartre, has probably played a bigger part in spreading terrorism in the Third World than any other tract. Violence is presented as liberation, a fundamental Sartrean theme. For a black man, writes Sartre in his preface, 'to shoot down a European is to kill two birds with one stone, to destroy an oppressor and the man he oppresses at the same time.' Thus the terrorist is born again, free. Fanon himself preached that violence is a necessary form of social and moral regeneration for the oppressed: 'Violence alone, violence committed by the people, violence organised and educated by its leaders, makes it possible for the masses to understand social truths, and gives the key to them.' The notion of 'organised and educated violence', conducted by elites, is of course the precise formula for terrorism. Fanon goes further: 'At the level of individuals, violence is a cleansing force. It frees [the oppressed] from his inferiority complex and from his despair and inaction.'

It is precisely this line of thought, that violence is positive and creative, which helps the terrorists to perform the horrifying acts for which they are responsible. Of course the same argument, almost word for word, was used by Hitler, who repeated endlessly: 'Virtue lies in blood.' Hence the first deadly sin of terrorism is the moral justification of murder not merely as a means to an end, but for its own sake.

The second is the deliberate suppression of the moral instincts in man. Terrorist organisers have found it is not enough to give their recruits intellectual justifications for murder: the instinctive humanity in us all has to be systematically blunted, or else it rejects such sophistry. In the Russia of the 1870s and 1880s, the most extreme terror group favoured what it called 'motiveless terror' and regarded any murder as 'a progressive action'. Many terror groups today have drifted in this direction. Once indiscriminate terror is adopted, the group rapidly suffers moral disintegration; in fact the abandonment of any system of moral criteria becomes an essential element in its training. The point is brilliantly made in Dostoyevsky's great anti-terrorist novel, *The Possessed*, by its diabolical protagonist, who argues that the terror group can be united only by fear and shared moral depravity: 'Persuade four members of the circle to murder a fifth,' he says, 'on the excuse that he is an informer, and you will at once tie them all up in one knot by the blood you have shed. They will be your slaves.' This technique is undoubtedly used in modern terror groups, where trusted and senior members of the gang are occasionally denounced as 'informers' and 'executed'. In such groups, too, women recruits are subjected to repeated rapes and are forced to take part in communal acts of sexual depravity, to anaesthetise their moral reflexes and to prepare them for making the gross travesty of their nature which their future work entails. The theory is based on the assumption that neither man nor woman can be an effective terrorist so long as he or she retains the moral elements of a human personality. One might say, then, that the second deadly sin of terrorism is a threat not merely to our civilisation, but to our very humanity itself.

The third, following directly from the first two, is the rejection of politics as the normal means by which communities resolve conflicts. To terrorists, violence is not a political weapon to be used *in extremis*; it is a substitute for the entire political process. The Arab terrorists, the IRA, the Bader-Meinhoff gang in Germany, the Red Armies and Brigades in Japan, Italy and elsewhere, have never shown any desire to engage in the political process, though the option has always been open to them. They reject democracy totally. The notion that violence is a technique of last resort, to be adopted only when all other attempts to attain justice have failed, is rejected by them. In doing so, they reject the mainstream of Western thinking, based, like most of our political grammar, on the social-contrast theorists of the seventeenth century: Hobbes and Locke rightly treated violence as the antithesis of politics, a form of action characteristic of the archaic realm of the state of nature. They saw politics as an attempt to create a tool to avoid barbarism and make civilisation possible: politics renders violence not only unnecessary but unnatural to civilised man. Politics is an essential part of the basic machinery of civilisation, and in rejecting politics terrorism seeks to make civilisation unworkable.

Terrorism, however, is not neutral in the political battle. It does not, in the long run, tend towards anarchy: it tends towards totalitarianism. The fourth deadly sin of terrorism is that it actively, systematically and necessarily assists the spread of the totalitarian state. The countries which finance and maintain the international infrastructure of terrorism, which give terrorists refuge and havens, training camps and bases, money, arms and diplomatic support – all as a matter of deliberate state policy – are, without exception, totalitarian states. The governments of all these states rule by military and police force. The notion, then, that terrorism is opposed to 'the repressive forces' in society is false; indeed it is the reverse of the truth. International terrorism, and the various local terrorist movements it services, are entirely dependent on the continuing good will and active support of police states. The terrorist is sustained by the totalitarian tank, the torture chamber, the lash and the secret policeman. The terrorist is the beneficiary of the Gulag Archipelago and all it stands for.

So to the fifth deadly sin. Terrorism poses no threat to the totalitarian state. That kind of state can always sustain itself by judicial murder, preventative arrest, torture of prisoners and suspects, and complete censorship of terrorist activities. It does not have to abide by the rule of law or any other consideration of humanity or morals. Terrorism can only get a foothold in a state like the Lebanon, or the Shah's Iran, where the executive is under some kind of restraint, legal, democratic or moral. The Shah's regime was overthrown, terrorists playing a major part in the process, not because it was too ruthless but because it was not ruthless enough. The effect of such terrorist victories is not the expansion but the contraction of freedom and law. Iran is now a theocratic horror-state, where the rule of law no longer exists; it is also a state from which terrorists can operate with safety and active assistance. Hence, the fifth deadly sin is that terrorism distinguishes between lawful and totalitarian states in favour of the latter. It can destroy a democracy, as it destroyed the Lebanon, but it cannot destroy a totalitarian state. All it can do is to transform a nation struggling towards progress and legality into a nightmare of oppression and violence.

This leads us to another significant conclusion about terrorism. Its ultimate base is in the totalitarian world: that is where its money, training, arms and protection come from. But at the same time it can only operate effectively in the freedom of a liberal civilisation. The sixth deadly sin of terrorism is that it exploits the apparatus of freedom in liberal societies and thereby endangers it. In meeting the threat of terrorism, a free society must arm itself. But that very process, of arming itself against the danger within, threatens the freedoms and decencies and standards which make it civilised. Terrorism, then, is a direct and continuous threat to all the protective devices of a free society. It is a threat to the freedom of the press and the freedom of TV to report without restraints. It is a threat to the rule of law, which is necessarily damaged by emergency legislation and special powers. It is a threat to *habeas corpus*. It is a threat to the continuous process of humanising the legal code. It is a threat to the civilising of our prisons. It is a threat to any system designed to curb excesses by the police, the prison authorities or any other restraining force in society.

Yet the seventh deadly sin of terrorism operates, paradoxically, in the reverse direction, and is yet more destructive. A free society which reacts to terrorism by invoking authoritarian methods of repressing it necessarily damages itself, as I have argued. But an even graver danger, and a much more common one alas, is of free societies, in their anxiety to avoid the authoritarian extreme, failing to arm themselves against the terrorist threat, and so abdicating their responsibility to uphold the law. The terrorists gain ground when they provoke oppression. But they triumph when they are met with appeasement. The seventh and deadliest sin of terrorism is that it saps the will of a civilised society to defend itself. Hence we find governments negotiating with terrorists, negotiations aimed not at disarming the terrorists, for such negotiations may sometimes be necessary, but negotiations whose natural and inevitable result is to concede part (or even the whole) of the terrorists' demands. We find governments providing ransom money to terrorists; we find governments permitting private individuals to provide ransom money, even assisting the process whereby it reaches the terrorists, and so goes to finance their further efforts. We find governments releasing convicted criminals in response to terrorist demands. We find govern-

ments according terrorists the status, rights and advantages, and
above all the legitimacy, of negotiating partners. We find governments according terrorist convicts the official and privileged status of
political prisoners, always and everywhere a blunder and a surrender
of the first magnitude. We find governments bowing to demands, an
invariable and well-organised part of terrorist strategy, for official
inquiries or international inquiries, into alleged ill-treatment of
terrorist suspects or convicts. We find newspapers and TV networks,
often indeed state TV networks, placing democratic governments and
the terrorists on a level of moral parity. We find governments failing,
time and again, in their duty to persuade the public – and this is the
heart of the matter – that terrorists are not misguided politicians:
they are, first, last and all the time, criminals; extraordinary
criminals indeed, in that they are exceptionally dangerous to us all
and pose a unique threat not merely to individuals they murder
without compunction but to the whole fabric of society, but
criminals all the same.

In short, the seventh and deadliest sin of terrorism is its attempt to
induce civilisation to commit suicide.

There are, then, seven distinct ways in which terrorism threatens
civilised society. And the point which needs to be stressed above all is
that terrorism is not a static threat: it is an increasing one. Not only is
the international infrastructure of terrorism becoming better organised and more efficient, but the terrorists' own sights have been
raised. By helping to destroy the legal government of Iran, they have
secured a new base and access to formidable sources of finance and
arms. They are now a factor in the struggle for control of the oil
supplies of the Middle East. Who can doubt, after their success in
Iran, that the terrorists will be emboldened to attempt the subversion
of the even wealthier state of Saudi Arabia? This state is already a
major contributor, perhaps the biggest, to terrorist funds; but that is
no guarantee of immunity to attack. On the contrary: we cannot rule
out the possibility that terrorists may one day secure direct access to
the Saudi wealth through a revolutionary government which, as in
Iran, they will help to install. Other oil states on the Persian Gulf are
even more vulnerable targets. We must, therefore, expect and
prepare for yet further improvements in the types of weapon
terrorists deploy. Indeed, without wishing to seem alarmist, we
cannot rule out the possibility that terrorists will obtain access to

nuclear devices or even to their productive process. If they get possession of such weapons, we may be absolutely certain that they will use them.

Terrorism, in conclusion, is no longer a marginal problem for the civilised world, something to be contained and lived with, a mere nuisance. It is a real, important and growing threat to the peace and legitimacy of all civilised states, that is all those states which live under the rule of law. It is an international threat: therein lies its power. That power can only be destroyed or emasculated when there is international recognition of its gravity, and international action, by the united forces of civilisation, to bring it under control.

CHAPTER 19

The Crisis of Leadership in the West

This article was written in 1979, when the weakness of the Carter presidency became overwhelmingly manifest, and published in Optima, *the magazine published by the Anglo-American Co-operation, De Beers and Charter Consolidated.*

No one can deny that the Western democracies are passing through a crisis of leadership. It is reflected in the division and disarray with which they face great common problems — problems which demand unified policies, resolutely pursued. The machinery designed to produce Western leadership, where it still exists, is in manifest decay. NATO is still functioning, but the notion of Western summits has lapsed; the Baghdad Pact and SEATO are no more; such devices as GATT have failed to develop into instruments for concerting democratic trading policies. The EEC has inevitably weakened transatlantic ties, but has failed to produce a compensatory alignment, among its members, of international aims and responses. At the UN and its agencies there is no co-ordinated democratic voice.

As a result, there is no Western leadership on central issues. A Western consensus on SALT-type negotiations does not exist. There is no common policy on human rights or on measures to combat international terrorism. The Soviet — Cuban penetration of central and southern Africa has been allowed to proceed unhindered by any united Western response. The overthrow of the Shah's liberal, pro-Western regime in Iran caught the West in what is now a characteristically supine and irresolute posture. The Vietnam refugee 'problem', created by the Hanoi and Moscow governments deliberately to advance their interests in South-East Asia, found the West confused and baffled. Most striking of all, repeated and unilateral decisions of the OPEC powers to increase the energy burdens of the Western industrial democracies — the most important single issue to emerge during the seventies — have met with no corresponding effort by the West to pool its resources and bargaining power.

Is this lack of leadership due to a failure of men — or a failure of institutions? History suggests that there is nothing in the democratic system of government which is intrinsically hostile to the idea of leadership. The career of Lincoln, and his conduct of the US government before and during the Civil War, show if anything the exact opposite. Here was a huge federal democracy, faced with a challenge to its existence, not only finding the right leader but promptly and generously investing him with all the powers and authority he deemed necessary to meet that challenge.

The Allied conduct of the Second World War was at no point inhibited by democratic restraints and weaknesses. Roosevelt conducted the US war effort in the most masterful fashion, and the mistakes that were made were his own; Congress and the nation always gave him the support and resources he requested. On the other side of the Atlantic, Churchill never failed to have his leadership overwhelmingly endorsed by Parliament, and at no point were his war policies frustrated by the democratic machinery. Nor did either of these two great leaders find it necessary to take into account the assumed reactions of the electorate before they arrived at decisions. Churchill specifically repudiated such a method. 'I see it said that leaders should keep their ears to the ground,' he told the House of Commons in September 1941. 'All I can say is that the British nation will find it very hard to look up to the leaders who are detected in that ungainly posture.'

Speed and secrecy have always been a vital ingredient in sucessful leadership. Francis Bacon, wisest of all observers on matters of state, wrote in his essay 'Of Delays': 'The helmet of Pluto, which maketh the politic man go invisible, is secrecy in the counsel and celerity in the execution.' Both were notable features of the Roosevelt and Churchill wartime administrations. Both leaders were committed not merely to democracy, but to the notion of democratic disclosure —

both, indeed, were outstanding communicators and educators of the public. But both knew when and how to wear the helmet of Pluto, and the American and British peoples were content to see them do it.

Nevertheless, the notions of democracy practised in the West during the last three decades have tended to discourage the notion of leading from the front. When electorates systematically punish governments for taking unpopular decisions – and constantly notify their intention to do so in opinion polls – survival-minded politicians tend to shift their place to the rear of the column. Thomas Carlyle, in his passionate plea for leadership, *Past and Present*, written in 1843, maintained that 'in the long run, every government is the exact symbol of its people, with their divisions and unwisdom'. Not always, I would argue; what is certainly true, however, is that irresolution and cowardice among the mass of the people tends to communicate itself upwards, with dire results. The point is well made in Joseph Conrad's perceptive novel, *Under Western Eyes* (1911), set in Russia on the eve of war and revolution: 'Nations it may be have fashioned their governments, but the governments have paid them back in the same coin.' Some Western leaders, especially from the liberal centre of the spectrum, tend to accept what I would term the defeatist view that leadership must be scaled down to the procrustean bed of the led. Seeking the presidency in September 1952, Adlai Stevenson told a great gathering at Chicago: 'Government cannot be stronger or more tough-minded than its people. It cannot be more inflexibly committed to the task than they are.' Some Western politicians, like Sir Harold Wilson, have stuck closely to this principle, and flourished mightily (unlike the countries they ruled). Others, like Sir Anthony Eden, have repudiated it to their cost.

Eden, indeed, was groomed to supreme office from an early age, but merely illustrated Tacitus's encapsulation of the Emperor Galba: *Omnium consensu capax imperii, nisi imperasset* – he would have rated as the perfect Prime Minister if he had not actually been one. Eden was a case of a man hustled into leadership by a supposed popular demand for strong action. In 1956, a rumbling storm of criticism at his ineffectual tenure of Ten Downing Street – headed by a famous article in *The Daily Telegraph* entitled 'Waiting for the Smack of Firm Government' – led him to aim that smack at Nasser's Egypt, with disastrous consequences, not least to himself. The lesson drawn from this lamentable episode, at any rate by most

British politicians, is that Adlai Stevenson was absolutely right, and that it is better to underestimate the popular resolve than to bank on it, and come a cropper. Hence, in foreign affairs especially, politicians as skilled and as dissimilar as Harold Macmillan and Henry Kissinger have systematically pursued policies based on appeasement and accommodation.

In this they have been in accord with what is, or was until very recently, the spirit of the times − a spirit based upon that formidable tripod of liberal (or pseudo-liberal) emotions: guilt among the strong, pity for the weak and hatred of elitism. In public affairs, guilt is a bad counsellor, especially if it is unsubstantiated or created by the ideological teaching of history. Pity is an even worse one − as Woodrow Wilson observed, the true and proper foundation of government is not pity, but justice.

The attack on elitism is still more absurd, launched as it has been chiefly by liberal pedagogues who by birth, education, preferment and disposition are elitist themselves. The truth is, elitism has been disastrously confused with privilege − quite a different matter. An elite is defined by the *Oxford English Dictionary* as 'The choice part or flower (of society)', etc. It comes from the Latin *elegere*, to choose or elect, via the French, meaning the pick, especially of an army − the bravest, those in the van. An elitist is one who believes the best should be chosen for a particular task. Hence, those who compose an Olympic Games selection committee are elitists; so, for that matter, are electors voting in a political contest − one can truthfully say that, in a democracy, 'we are all elitists now'. Elitism and its associated notions − the pursuit of excellence and of knowledge − form the very bedrock principle of a progressive civilisation; the history of human progress is essentially the history of elitism. The politics of pity, based on the notion of strengthening the weak by weakening the strong, must produce impoverishment; but the assault on elitism is still more socially destructive for it overthrows the principle of leadership itself and reduces human societies to herds of Gadarene swine.

Nevertheless, it is not surprising that post-war societies, in Europe at least, have held strong leadership in some suspicion. We tend to be the prisoners of our immediate past, and those who lived under Mussolini and Franco, Hitler and Stalin, were understandably determined that history should not repeat itself. The emotion is strong even in Soviet Russia, where since Stalin's death the ostensible stress has always been on 'collective leadership'. The Soviet dissident, Vladimir Bukovsky, told me that after Nikita Krushchev had exposed the evils of Stalinism at the XXII Party Congress, an anonymous written question was sent up to him on the podium, asking him what *he* had been doing while Stalin's crimes were committed. Krushchev flew, or affected to fly, into a rage, and demanded that the person who posed the question should instantly declare himself by standing up. Of course, all remained silent in their places. Krushchev's tirade continued for some minutes, until, abruptly changing mood, he said quietly: 'Now you know what I was doing – keeping silent in my place.'

Certainly, on this side of the Iron Curtain, one legacy of the Age of Dictators has been a profound distrust for those public men who have seemed too big for the constraints of the parliamentary system, and who have deliberately spoken to the nation over the heads of its elected representatives – Enoch Powell in Britain, Franz-Joseph Strauss in West Germany, General de Gaulle in France. Such men have not only been distrusted but widely and systematically misrepresented, having constantly attributed to them aims and methods which they specifically and publicly repudiated. If opinion-formers in the West have tended to confuse privilege and elites, they have also confounded strength and vehemence of conviction with dictatorial ambitions.

Yet despite this climate of opinion, leaders have emerged through the democratic machinery. In both the defeated Axis powers, men of stature came forward and were recognised as such by electorates. Konrad Adenauer in West Germany and Alcide de Gasperi in Italy both succeeded in bringing their nations out of the shadows by a display of determination and confidence, despite the handicaps of constitutions deliberately designed to provide checks and balances to counter personal rule. Both offered leadership when leadership was indispensable, and the voters were glad to provide them with the opportunity to exercise it. De Gasperi, it is true, has had no successor, but Adenauer's heirs have included only one man, Willy Brandt, who bent under the strain, and two, Erhard and Schmidt, of notable talent and force – exerted, to be sure, within the prudent and self-imposed limitations of West German policy.

In France, the case for strong leadership was brilliantly vindicated by the return to power of Charles de Gaulle in 1958. This was achieved, it is true, during a moment of grave constitutional crisis, when the Republic was in imminent danger of destruction at the hands of the military. But it was also achieved in the face of strong and widely based resistance, and despite the fact that De Gaulle made no secret of his sense of Messianic mission. It is worth recalling his words with which he re-entered French politics: 'Faced with problems too hard for the regime of parties to tackle, France has, for the past twelve years, followed a disastrous course. In the past, the country from its very depths entrusted me with the task of leading it to safety. Today, with new perils facing it, the country should know that I am ready to assume the powers of the Republic.' No one in post-war times — not even Churchill — has used the rhetoric of leadership more confidently. De Gaulle, indeed came close to resurrecting the sacramental theory of leadership, by which the nation is incorporated in the person of a king — an idea which goes back to the earliest Pharaonic dynasties of the early third millennium BC. Hence his ringing declaration 'I am a man who belongs to nobody, and who belongs to everybody,' and his own version of the 'royal plural', speaking of himself as an objective third person: 'If De Gaulle is given exceptional powers, for an exceptional task, at an exceptional moment, then — surely — De Gaulle must also be given powers by an exceptional procedure.'

That Western democratic electorates are capable of embracing strong leadership when they judge it necessary is demonstrated by the fact that the French, whose history has given them such good reason to fear 'the man on horseback', nevertheless endorsed the De Gaulle solution by a positive referendum verdict of nearly 80 per cent. And the Gaullist settlement has now given France more than 20 years of political stability, a span without precedent in modern French history, during which the country's standards of living have more than doubled and the French have recovered all their old self-confidence.

Nevertheless, it is important to note that this remarkable turn-about in France's fortunes is due not merely to the personality and leadership of De Gaulle but to the outstanding merits of the new constitution he persuaded the French to accept. The constitutions of the Third, and still more the Fourth, republics were deliberately framed to diffuse power and curb central authority; they succeeded in these aims all too well. The Fifth Republic severely redressed the balance — some claimed so severely as to make solitary leadership the central principle of government. In fact the constitution of the Fifth Republic is not an authoritarian document; it contains many and ingenious checks on any drift to Buonapartisme; and its workings have been repeatedly endorsed, in innumerable central and local elections and referenda, by the French voters, no mean judges of such things. The general election of 1978, which was in effect a verdict on a regime as well as on a government, suggests that the system De Gaulle designed has come to stay.

It is worth dwelling on the French experience because it shows that the availability of leadership cannot be separated from the process by which it is able to emerge. The personal and the constitutional elements are inextricably mixed. It is a paradox that strong leaders, if given the power, nearly always pick weak successors. It is as if they have an unconscious wish to terminate their mission with the grave and force their followers to wish their resurrection. Thus Churchill handed on Elijah's mantle to Eden, surely in the foreknowledge that it was too heavy for him. Dr Adenauer made strenuous (and happily unavailing) efforts to deny the succession to his natural heir, Erhard. It is no secret that De Gaulle's regime, in its moment of peril in 1968, was saved not so much by De Gaulle himself, as by the superior wisdom of his Prime Minister, Georges Pompidou. It is no secret, either, that De Gaulle never forgave Pompidou for the service, soon dismissed him, and did his best to deny him the succession to the presidency. He failed, by virtue of the constitutional system he himself had devised. It was De Gaulle who restored strong leadership to France, but it was the new constitutional system which consolidated the change by making it possible for Pompidou, and his very able successor Giscard d'Estaing, to take advantage of the machinery of election and to deploy the great powers the presidency confers.

But, it will be asked: if the presidential constitution of the Fifth Republic has enabled France to enjoy effective leadership for more than 20 years, why is it that the American constitution, which endows the presidency with even more extensive authority — since the President is head of state and head of government rolled into one — has on the whole failed to produce comparable leadership during the same period?

With this question, we reach the heart of the matter, for there can be little doubt that the crisis of leadership in the West is itself a global projection of what is in essence a crisis in the White House. Whether we like it or not, the well-being and cohesion of the Western industrial democracies depends very largely on the healthy functioning of the US governmental system. When that system is working well, as it did between 1941 and the early 1960s, and America is exercising the positive leadership inevitably conferred on her by her enormous economic predominance, any hesitation or cowardice or disarray, any self-destructive tendencies even, among the medium-sized Western powers, are only of marginal importance to the West as a whole. Thus, Britain's uninterrupted economic decline, France's agony over Algeria, the Suez fiasco, − to take only three examples − have inflicted surprisingly little permanent damage on the West's strength and confidence.

On the other hand, the moment American leadership errs or flags, the effects are immediate and fundamental, and they are felt throughout the democracies. To put it another way, any malfunction in the American system greatly outweighs any accretion of strength elsewhere in the democratic world. The enormous industrial power of West Germany, the resurgence of France, the astonishing performance of the Japanese economy − important and encouraging as all three are − do not and cannot compensate for the persistent and increasing failure of the American presidential system of government to give the West the leadership it had come to expect. It is to little avail to have the right man (or woman) in Paris or Westminster, in Bonn, Rome or Tokyo, if the wrong man sits in the Oval Office. At the periphery of the free world, poor leadership is a tactical handicap; in Washington it is a strategic catastrophe.

A brief résumé of post-war American history might read as follows. Under Harry S. Truman, the decisiveness and authority which marked the best years of Franklyn D. Roosevelt were abundantly and convincingly displayed. Then, for eight years, General Eisenhower ran a successful collegiate system, composed of formidable talents, over whom he exercised light-handed but unchallenged control. The watershed was crossed even before the first Kennedy assassination. For Kennedy, though able and energetic, and capable of learning from his errors, had not yet contrived to impose his will on Congress when he was killed. Thereafter it was downhill all the way. Lyndon Johnson could control Congress but he was overwhelmed by US foreign and military policy, and departed almost in despair. Richard Nixon had the will, understanding and capacity to resolve America's overseas problems, but he could not control his own fraudulent urges, or those of his subordinates, and departed in disgrace. Gerald Ford never contrived to efface the impression that he was selected as an amiable cypher, and, with all the resources of the presidency at his disposal, could not beat off a weak and inexperienced Democratic challenger. For Jimmy Carter the last point should be reversed: with America's majority party behind him — and the Republicans in almost total disarray — he barely contrived to beat one of the weakest presidents in US history.

It is a gruesome catalogue: three men of stature, each hopelessly flawed, followed by two lightweights. Few great nations have contrived to survive such repeated misfortunes at all; that the United States, if not exactly flourishing, has remained intact under such failures of leadership, is a testimony to the robustness of her people and constitution. Yet the damage has been enormous, and it is only during the sorry reign of Jimmy Carter that the free world has realised how dependent it is on the ability of the man in the White House to take the right decisions, or indeed to take decisions of any kind.

Jimmy Carter serves to remind us that leadership is in essence a combination of courage and judgment. Neither is much good without the other, and Mr Carter seems to lack both. He has taken Adlai Stevenson's defeatist maxim a stage further: his conduct of office seems to suggest a belief that government not only cannot be more resolute than the people it serves but has no access to a superior knowledge, let alone foresight. This peculiar view of democratic leadership — or anti-leadership — as the lowest common denominator of a nation's wit and wisdom is illuminated by Mr Carter's eccentric and sometimes desperate efforts to seek advice in America's highways and byways, as well as from the stream of cranks and busybodies who perambulate through his office. He calls irresistibly to mind Field Marshall Douglas Haig's caustic summation of his boss at the War Office, the Earl of Derby: 'He is like a feather cushion — he bears the impression of the last person who has sat on him.'

Mr Carter's apparent belief that political experience and

professionalism are not necessary — may indeed be a positive impediment — to successful government is linked of course to his profound contempt for the 'Washington system'. His view is both true and false. It is false in that his own dismal record makes it clear beyond peradventure not only that a president cannot govern against the system but that any radical alternative to the system is likely to be worse. It is also true, however, in that Mr Carter's mandate, in so far as he ever had one, was to improve the responsiveness of the system to national demands — a mandate which reflected a wide and deep-rooted view that the system can and must be improved.

The last proposition, it seems to me, is undeniable. If we look at the working of the system from the sole viewpoint of its ability to produce leadership, the record speaks for itself. Picking the President is not just a feature of the American constitution, it is the salient feature. If the President is the wrong man the system cannot work, for the Congress cannot provide an alternative centre of executive power and it cannot replace the President except for high crimes and misdemeanours. It is not a crime or even a misdemeanour to be stupid, or inept, or to lack leadership qualities. To be such a person is a disqualification for supreme office in the first place, which the electoral process is designed to enforce.

In theory, the presidential election is an exhaustive effort to discover the best available talent. It is open to any man or woman born in America. It progressively winnows out the unsuitable through the state primaries, through the party conventions, and finally through the universal election itself. It is designed to ensure the survival of the fittest. In fact it does nothing of the sort. How can it be said to do so when it eliminates, even at the stage of candidacy, such formidable contenders as Nelson Rockefeller or Henry Jackson, yet nominates lightweights like Goldwater or McGovern? When it re-elects, overwhelmingly, men of proven mendacity like Johnson and Nixon? When it confronts the elector with the hopeless alternative of Ford or Carter? Is it not true that four distinct and serious scandals — Watergate being only one — already overshadowed Nixon when he won every state in the Union except two? Were not the debilitating weaknesses of a Carter presidency foreseeable, indeed foreseen, when he carried the Democratic Convention, let alone the nation?

In his luminous essay, 'Of Great Place', Bacon asks himself why it is men should want supreme power in the first place:

It is a strange desire, to seek power and to lose liberty: or to seek power over others and to lose power over a man's self. The rising unto place is laborious; and by pains men come to greater pains; and it is sometimes base; and by indignities men come to dignities. The standing is slippery, and the regress is either a downfall, or at least an eclipse, which is a melancholy thing.

Such considerations are no less forceful today in discouraging able and upright leaders. And added to them are some formidable new disadvantages. These include the ever-present risk of assassination — not just to the leader but to his or her family — and the destructive and suffocating security precautions thereby made unavoidable; the relentless publicity, much of it malicious and cruel, which pursues the leader and his kin everywhere; and, not least, the ubiquitous spirit of criticism and indiscipline, which makes the exercise of any authority a constant effort, and which denies even to the President the traditional *magisterium* of office, the defence of *raison d'état* and the protection of executive privilege. America exacts a fearful price for the White House, even from those who never get there. All recent Presidents would endorse Bacon's warning: 'Great men had need to borrow other men's opinions, to think themselves happy.' In the light of this record, and in view of the daunting and in some ways increasing financial obstacles which American presidential candidates must overcome for any hope of nomination, there is no mystery about the decline in the quality of American leadership.

In the longer term, however, I am by no means despondent. The spirit of the age seems to be changing, and to be according a greater prominence — and respect — for the claims of leadership and the rights of authority. Throughout the democratic world, there is a profound revulsion against collectivism, the levelling process, the pursuit of equality for its own sake. The politics of pity are on the wane; the rights of the individual are being recognised afresh. The cry of 'Elitist!' no longer terminates rational discussion. The penalising and disparagement of merit is now seen for what it is: the legitimation of envy, the most corrosive of the deadly sins. Such destructive and irrational notions as 'positive discrimination' no longer command a reverential hearing. In this new intellectual climate, which is beginning to work its way into the political systems of the West, those who

aspire to lead and not to follow opinion will find more encouragement, wider scope and greater rewards.

The survival of the leadership principle in France, against all the
laws of the political pendulum, is one hopeful sign. Most striking of
all is the emergence of Margaret Thatcher as the dominant figure in
British politics. She does not believe in the irresistible power of collective forces, but in the salience of the individual and the virtues of
leadership. She repudiates the pursuit of equality, except (and the
exception is vital) equality before the law. She epitomises her
philosophy thus: 'Conservatism is about skilled people.' She believes
in contract not status, possessive individualism as opposed to class-
consciousness and collective morality, and she stresses duties rather
than rights. She is a leader in the old Churchillian mould who won an
election by repudiating the consensus and flaunting her convictions.
She is the first politician since 1945 to give a new direction to British
politics, and the impact of her personality will by no means be confined to the domestic scene.

These are no more than hopeful signs. I repeat: there is no
substitute for a rebirth of American leadership. But in America also
there are encouraging portents. It is of the very nature of politics that
egregious errors adumbrate their own correctives. The awesome experience of a Carter presidency – of being governed, as it were, by a
vacuum, or the political equivalent of a celestial Black Hole, has provoked a growing number of Americans to sigh for the lost virtues of
what was disparagingly termed 'the Imperial Presidency'. The overwhelming evidence of polls indicates that most Americans want their
country to reshoulder the burden of leading the free world, albeit
with greater circumspection and a keener awareness of the limitations
of power than in the past. And, though the American system has
many weaknesses, it has one outstanding merit: the comparative
speed with which a popular mood translates itself into political
realities. If Americans really want old-fashioned leadership, they will
get it. The only question is how soon. It cannot come too quickly for
the rest of us.

INDEX